Museum Thresholds

Museum Thresholds is a progressive, interdisciplinary volume and the first to explore the importance and potential of entrance spaces for visitor experience. Bringing together an international collection of writers from different disciplines, the chapters in this volume offer different theoretical perspectives on the nature of engagement, interaction and immersion in threshold spaces, and the factors that enable and inhibit those immersive possibilities.

Organised into themed sections, the book explores museum thresholds from three different perspectives. Considering them first as a problem space, the contributors then go on to explore thresholds through different media and, finally, draw upon other subjects and professions, including performance, gaming, retail and discourse studies, in order to examine them from an entirely new perspective. Drawing upon examples that span Asia, North America and Europe, the authors set the entrance space in its historical, social and architectural contexts. Together, the essays show how the challenges posed by the threshold can be rethought and reimagined from a variety of perspectives, each of which has much to bring to future thinking and design.

Combining both theory and practice, *Museum Thresholds* should be essential reading for academics, researchers and postgraduate students working in museum studies, digital heritage, architecture, design studies, retail studies and media studies. It will also be of great interest to museum practitioners working in a wide variety of institutions around the globe.

Ross Parry is Deputy Pro-Vice-Chancellor (Digital) at the University of Leicester (UK), and associate professor in its School of Museum Studies. For over twenty years, his interdisciplinary and highly collaborative research has considered the relationship between digital media and the cultural heritage sector. A former national chair of the UK's Museums Computer Group, and a Tate Research Fellow, he was one of the founding Trustees of the Jodi Mattes Trust – for accessible digital culture. He is the author of the book *Recoding the Museum* (the first major history of museum computing) and *Museums in a Digital Age* – a volume that helped define the subject area of 'digital heritage'.

Ruth Page spends her time teaching and writing about storytelling, especially focusing on the stories that people tell in social media contexts. She has written several books including *Stories and Social Media* (Routledge, 2012), *Narratives Online: Shared Stories and Social Media* (Cambridge University Press, 2018), and was the lead author of the student textbook, *Researching the Language of Social Media* (Routledge, 2014). Her publications in journals and edited collections have explored narratives in a wide range of contexts, from print literature and the mainstream media to conversational stories and stories published in online contexts such as blogs, social network sites and Wikipedia.

Alex Moseley is a National Teaching Fellow and Head of Curriculum Enhancement at the University of Leicester. He has had long experience as both practitioner and researcher of course design and development for higher education and also teaches innovative Digital Media courses in Museum Studies and Historical Studies. His principal research area is in games-based learning: he has written widely in this area including *Using Games to Enhance Teaching and Learning* (Routledge, 2012) and *New Traditional Games for Learning: A Case Book* (Routledge, 2013), has designed and consulted on a number of games for museum and education contexts, chairs the Association for Learning Technology special interest group on Playful Learning, and co-organises the Playful Learning conference.

Routledge Research in Museum Studies

Academics, Artists, and Museums: 21st-Century Partnerships ed. Irina Costache and Clare Kunny

Public Art and Museums in Cultural Districts J. Pedro Lorente

Museum Thresholds: The Design and Media of Arrival ed. Ross Parry, Ruth Page and Alex Moseley

Rodney: Personalization of the Museum Visit Seph Rodney

Collecting the Past: British Collectors and their Collections from the 18th to the 20th Centuries ed. Toby Burrows and Cynthia Johnston

Museum Communication and Social Media: The Connected Museum Kirsten Drotner, Kim Christian Schrøder

Climate Change and Museum Futures ed. Fiona Cameron and Brett Neilson

Introducing Peace Museums Joyce Apsel

Museums, Heritage and Indigenous Voice: Decolonizing Engagement Bryony Onciul

Exhibiting Madness in Museums: Remembering Psychiatry Through Collection and Display ed. Catharine Coleborne and Dolly MacKinnon

Belgian Museums of the Great War: Politics, Memory and Conference Karen Shelby

Museums, Immigrants, and Social Justice Sophia Labadi

Museum Storage and Meaning: Tales from the Crypt ed. Mirjam Brusius and Kavita Singh

Global and World Art in the Practice of the University Museum ed. Jane Chin Davidson and Sandra Esslinger

For more information on this series, please visit https://www.routledge.com/Routledge-Research-in-Museum-Studies/book-series/RRIMS

Museum Thresholds
The Design and Media of Arrival

Edited by Ross Parry, Ruth Page
and Alex Moseley

LONDON AND NEW YORK

First published 2018
by Routledge
2 Park Square, Milton Park, Abingdon, Oxon OX14 4RN

and by Routledge
711 Third Avenue, New York, NY 10017

Routledge is an imprint of the Taylor & Francis Group, an informa business

© 2018 selection and editorial matter, Ross Parry, Ruth Page and Alex Moseley; individual chapters, the contributors

The right of Ross Parry, Ruth Page and Alex Moseley to be identified as the authors of the editorial material, and of the authors for their individual chapters, has been asserted in accordance with sections 77 and 78 of the Copyright, Designs and Patents Act 1988.

All rights reserved. No part of this book may be reprinted or reproduced or utilised in any form or by any electronic, mechanical, or other means, now known or hereafter invented, including photocopying and recording, or in any information storage or retrieval system, without permission in writing from the publishers.

Trademark notice: Product or corporate names may be trademarks or registered trademarks, and are used only for identification and explanation without intent to infringe.

British Library Cataloguing-in-Publication Data
A catalogue record for this book is available from the British Library

Library of Congress Cataloging-in-Publication Data
A catalog record for this book has been requested

ISBN: 9781138646032 (hbk)
ISBN: 9781315627793 (ebk)

Typeset in Sabon
by Swales & Willis Ltd, Exeter, Devon, UK

Contents

List of figures   vii
List of tables   x
List of contributors   xi
Foreword   xv
Acknowledgements   xvii

1 On a new threshold   1
ROSS PARRY, RUTH PAGE AND ALEX MOSELEY

PART I
Locating and defining the threshold   11

2 Hysterical atria   13
KATHERINE SKELLON AND BEN TUNSTALL

3 The complexity of welcome: visitor experience at the museum threshold   33
COLIN MULBERG

   Conversation 1: The Royal Air Force Museum London   54

4 Design-driven innovation for museum entrances   58
MARCO MASON

PART II
Affordances and potential of the threshold   79

5 Suspended: art in the threshold   81
PETER RIDE

Contents

6 Curation at the threshold: making museum meanings through new interfaces   107
ANGELINA RUSSO AND PHILIP POND

Conversation 2: Birmingham Museum and Art Gallery   119

7 Using 3D visualisation technology to improve design and visitor orientation   124
DAVID BURDEN

8 Difficult thresholds: negotiating shared and embedded entrances   153
STEVEN KRUSE

PART III
The threshold rethought   173

9 Games in the lobby: a playful approach   175
ERIK KRISTIANSEN AND ALEX MOSELEY

Conversation 3: The British Postal Museum and Archive   189

10 Retail perspectives on the threshold   192
TRACY HARWOOD

11 Setting the tone for the visit: soundscape design   211
CHRISTIAN HVIID MORTENSEN AND ANGUS DEUCHARS

Conversation 4: The Royal Shakespeare Company   228

12 The visitor as evaluator: using appraisal theory to understand 'threshold fear'   231
RUTH PAGE

Index   254

Figures

2.1	V&A courtyard, visitors enjoying the sun	22
2.2	V&A Chihuly glass chandelier	23
2.3	Albert looks down on visitors	29
2.4	Walkway in new atrium	30
3.1	Typical visitor questions reflecting concerns about a visit	36
3.2	How museum visitors construct the visitor offer	39
3.3	The classic retail buying process gives insight into the stages of museum visitors' decision-making	41
3.4	How visitors structure their visit at the museum threshold	46
3.5	Portsmouth Historic Dockyard threshold before redevelopment: visitors were given little help in understanding the visitor offer, the various ticket options or working out what to see	50
3.6	PHD threshold after redevelopment: decision-making is supported by impressions of the experience of each attraction, purchase decisions are explained clearly and visitors are guided in structuring their visit	50
4.1	Conceptual map of the entire information system	60
4.2	Examples of pictures combined with short descriptions highlighting the essential insights to illustrate environments and activities	63
4.3	Customer experience journey map for the information system	64
4.4	Prototype of the multi-touch screen to test the interactions for the best combination(s) resulting from the user's choice	65
4.5	Paper prototype to try out interactions on the multi-touch screen	66
4.6	Mixed-fidelity prototype to try out interactions on the multi-touch screen	67
5.1	Bin Jelmood House, Msheireb Museum, Qatar, showing the projection of moving shadow figures in the threshold	84

viii List of figures

5.2	Dale Chihuly, V&A rotunda chandelier (2001) at the V&A, London	87
5.3	John Grade, *Wawona*. Seattle Museum of History and Industry (MOHAI), showing the positioning of the sculpture in the threshold	88
5.4	John Grade, *Wawona*. Seattle Museum of History and Industry (MOHAI), interior of sculpture, looking up	90
5.5	John Grade, *Wawona*. Seattle Museum of History and Industry (MOHAI), visitors interacting with sculpture	91
5.6	Aga Khan Museum, Toronto, exterior looking towards the main entrance	93
5.7	Aisha Khalid, *Your Way Begins on the Other Side* (2014). Aga Khan Museum, Toronto, interior	95
5.8	Artist Lee Mingwei, *The Moving Garden* (2009/2011). Brooklyn Museum	97
5.9	Brooklyn Museum visitor interacting with sculptures by Auguste Rodin, *Burghers of Calais* (1889), in the pavilion	98
5.10–5.13	Museum of London, following the visitors' entrance from the external rotunda, inside the rotunda to the foyer display	101
7.1	Developments in computer model rendering	125
7.2	Example Second Life builds	128
7.3	The Three Ring Model	132
7.4	The Virtual Library of Birmingham	133
7.5	Interaction systems in the Virtual Library of Birmingham	134
7.6	Virtual Library of Birmingham orientation	136
7.7	Virtual Library of Birmingham – Physical and Virtual comparisons	139
7.8	As-is and 'white room' models of the New Walk Museum threshold space	143
7.9	Virtual reality examples	149
8.1	Simplified plans of the museum within the university	157
8.2	Courtyard entrance of the museum and department	158
8.3	Simplified plans of the museum within the cathedral	160
8.4	West Entrance of Ely Cathedral	161
8.5	Simplified plans of the museum within the college	165
8.6	Front of the Royal College of Surgeons	166
9.1	The lobby design game	180
9.2	Chatsworth House front view, Derbyshire, England	184
9.3	Playful signage at Chatsworth House	185
10.1	Typical store layouts	197

10.2	Aspects of the store environment	198
10.3	Sight lines across store layouts	199
11.1	The mediating relationship between individual and environment through sound at the Petrie Museum	212
11.2	Positive vs negative ratings of how the stairwell prepared the visitor before the intervention	220
11.3	Positive vs negative ratings of how the stairwell prepared the visitor after the design intervention	222
12.1	New Walk Museum and Art Gallery approach to the entrance	237
12.2	New Walk Museum and Art Gallery view from the door into the foyer	238
12.3	Petrie Museum of Egyptian Archaeology approach to the entrance	239
12.4	Petrie Museum of Egyptian Archaeology view to the entrance door from the stairs	240

Tables

4.1	The design brief: design statement, the opportunity, and main goals	61
6.1	Top nine posts on Instagram on hashtag #Nicholson Museum	113
9.1	Museum visitors' transformative foyer practices	181
9.2	A typology of lobby games	182
11.1	Sample size and composition of participants in the pre- and post-intervention survey	217
11.2	Grouping of descriptors in the qualitative comments on the stairwell at the Petrie Museum before the intervention	221
11.3	Grouping of descriptors from the qualitative comments on the sound aspect of the design intervention	223
12.1	Appreciation of the threshold	244

Contributors

David Burden has been involved in virtual reality and immersive environments since the 1990s. David set up Daden Limited in 2004 to help organisations explore and exploit the social and commercial potential of using virtual environments for immersive learning and data visualisation. David and his team have delivered over 50 immersive learning and visualisation projects for clients in the UK, USA, Middle East and Far East. David has led collaborative research projects funded by InnovateUK and the MOD, and Daden projects have twice won Times Higher Education awards. David has authored over a dozen papers on virtual worlds and AI.

Angus Deuchars is an acoustic designer and works for the global engineering firm Arup. With a background in engineering and music, he brings a theoretical approach to acoustic design with an experienced ear for getting the sound right. Angus's project work touches a wide portfolio of sectors within the built environment advising artists, orchestras and architects on how to realise their acoustic ambitions. His particular passion is in the design of entertainment venues where the goal is to create great-sounding spaces that will bring lasting enjoyment to both concert-goers and performers.

Tracy Harwood is Reader in Digital Marketing and Consumer Culture within the Institute of Creative Technologies and Manager of the Usability Lab at De Montfort University, Leicester, UK. She is a National Teaching Fellow. Her transdisciplinary research interests are on application of creative technologies, focusing on use of emergent technologies such as Internet of Things, AI, robots and gamification. She has published in leading marketing and digital creativity journals.

Elaine Heumann Gurian is consultant/advisor/speaker/teacher to museums, universities, associations, and governments worldwide. She was deputy director of the US Holocaust Memorial Museum and National Museum of the American Indian following service as Deputy Assistant Secretary at the Smithsonian. She has received fellowships at the Georgia O'Keeffe Museum, the Exploratorium, Salzburg Seminar, and Fulbright Program.

Routledge published her book, *Civilizing the Museum*, in 2006. Most of her writings are now available at www.egurian.com. Elected to many offices in AAM and ICOM/CECA, Gurian was named to AAM's Centennial Honor Roll in 2006 and presented its Distinguished Service award in 2004. Gurian is a founder of the Museum Group.

Erik Kristiansen holds an MA in general linguistics and computer science from University of Copenhagen and a PhD in Performance Studies from Roskilde University. He is a former associate professor in Performance Design at Roskilde University, and currently holds a position as curator and head of interpretation at Museum Lolland-Falster, Denmark. He was a member of the board on the research project DREAM on digital installations in museums. He is currently conducting research in museum studies, design studies, and musical instruments.

Steven Kruse works at the Whipple Museum of the History of Science as Exhibition and Project Coordinator. His interest in shared and embedded entrances developed out of his experience at the Whipple, which is embedded in the University of Cambridge's Department of History and Philosophy of Science. His MA dissertation on this subject, completed in 2016 at the University of Leicester, was the subsequent basis of his contribution to this volume.

Marco Mason, with a PhD in Design Sciences (2012), is a Marie Curie fellow working at the intersection of Digital Heritage and Design Research for the study of digital media design and its practices in cultural heritage institutions. Marco is carrying on his second Marie Curie research project (H2020-MSCA-IF-2016-2018) with the University of Leicester, School of Museum Studies and the University of Cambridge, Fitzwilliam Museum. The study consists in a systematic analysis of Design Thinking in the domain of museums engaged in digital heritage projects. Marco's first Marie Curie fellowship (FP7-GF-2012-2015) investigated digital media design practice in museums in the USA. The project was conjunctly conducted with the Massachusetts Institute of Technology and the School of Museum Studies.

Christian Hviid Mortensen has been a curator at the Media Museum since 2007. Christian holds a PhD from the University of Southern Denmark with the thesis *Displaying Sound: Radio as Media Heritage in a Museological Perspective* (2014). He has curated exhibitions on diverse media-related subjects spanning video games, radio sound, comics and reality TV. Christian's research interests sit at the intersection of media studies with museology, popular culture and memory studies. Christian is a member of the editorial board for the peer-reviewed journal *MedieKultur: Journal for Media and Communication Research*.

Colin Mulberg trained as a designer, focusing on the interaction between people, products and spaces. For twelve years he was Interpretation Coordinator at the Victoria and Albert Museum, London, UK, playing a key part in developing high quality galleries and facilities. He applied a range of commercial research and design techniques to the deep understanding of different audiences and to analysing how visitors experience cultural spaces. He used this work to help shape many award-winning museum projects. Colin now uses his experience and skills to support a range of clients across the museum, arts, heritage and commercial sectors. He specialises in mapping audiences along with their characteristics and behaviour, analysing public spaces from the visitor's viewpoint and defining the visitor offer. He supports venues across the whole visitor journey – from websites, marketing, ticketing and entrances to large-scale projects, interpretation schemes and complete museums. Colin Mulberg is a Registered Engineering Designer (REngDes) and Member of the Institution of Engineering Designers (MIED). He is an Associate of the Museums Association (AMA) and a Mentor on the AMA scheme. He is also Lead Consultant for the Museums + Heritage Show, UK. Colin is co-founder of the Labelling Buildings scheme, that turns architecture into exhibits.

Philip Pond is a researcher in digital communication and software studies at RMIT University in Melbourne. He runs the Digital-Social Systems Lab, which designs research and builds software to study the impact of technology on society.

Peter Ride is the Course Leader for the Masters in Museums, Galleries and Contemporary Culture at the University of Westminster. His current academic research is into multi-sensory visitor engagement in museums and looking at the way in which digital media and interdisciplinary arts projects are presented within galleries and museums and similar spaces. As an independent curator he also develops projects with photography and digital media, commissioning artists and producing their work.

Angelina Russo is Co-director of Fabricate Studio. Her research explores the impact of design and technology on cultural practices. She is currently developing bespoke digital fabrication labs and training based on her cultural and design research.

Katherine Skellon is an interpretative designer with over 25 years of experience creating museums, exhibitions and visitor attractions in the UK and internationally. Having worked for a number of leading exhibition design companies, Katherine formed Skellon Studio with Ben Tunstall in 2014. Alongside her practice, Katherine has been active in exploring the thinking behind museum design: teaching exhibition design at both undergraduate and postgraduate level, presenting at conferences and leading workshops aimed at investigating and progressing questions of how museums effectively design the experiences visitors gain.

Ben Tunstall has a background in Fine Art and an MSc in Modernity, Space and Place from UCL. He has worked in a range of communication-design contexts and is the author of *Play Slum: All you need to build your own mega slum* (Superfold, 2016). In 2014, with Katherine Skellon, Ben formed Skellon Studio, where he brings these various strands of thinking to bear on exhibition design projects, including Fire! Fire! for the Museum of London and the refurbishment of the Pagoda in Kew Gardens.

Foreword
The space in front of the door

Elaine Heumann Gurian

Museums need, and will always need, perspectives on themselves that are not unitary. We thrive as an area of practice and as a scholarly subject because of the multiple ideas and epistemologies we collect, and respect, from so many different disciplines. This variety, this openness, is a characteristic of writing and activity of those of us in this area, as perfectly signalled by this book. By assembling architects and digital designers, linguists and acoustic engineers, game theorists and visitor studies specialists, its strength is in this multiplicity of viewpoints and disciplinary takes. It tells us about other hopeful ways of thinking about the museum, but it also reminds us of how we need to re-examine museums, through a multidisciplinary approach. These authors present us ways of intellectually framing the same raw data, the same object – the foyer. In this way, bringing us these different methodologies, their words and ways of looking at the museum make us stretch.

Anyone who has been involved in major planning in museums will know that the foyer is endlessly complex. Architecturally, there is more demand on the lobby than any other space in the museum. Indeed, the 'volumes and adjacencies' identified in those initial architectural programme planning exercises will always expose the multi-use of the entrance. As we start to identify the size and proximity of things that will form our visitor offer, and when, as an institution, we begin to think clearly and deeply about how we operate (and how we want to operate), we need to decide how we will move our audiences through the building. It is then that we see, as this book sees, the complexity of this transition space. It is then that we see the museum threshold not as a throwaway space, but rather an intricate place for both real and metaphoric distribution.

What surfaces in planning processes such as this, and what needs to be considered much more now that we have this book, is that the foyer is more than a foyer. I would argue that when we design our museums and when we think about museum visitation, we have an opportunity to dissolve the idea of the gallery visit as the primary activity. A huge percentage of visitors are, of course, passing through to the exhibition spaces. And yet, we can still design the museum entrance in such a way that the route to the galleries is just part of the panoply from which people are free to choose. This means recognising that whilst the museum entrance might be a hub and foyer to something else, it can also work independently in itself. It could be the 'welcome' of many different, and wider, things.

This is in part about acknowledging the processes that need to work in that space – the placement and use of the cloakroom, the location for the bus-parking of school groups. But it is also about embracing the other autonomous uses of that space – the evening reception, the cinema event, the high-end restaurant, the café for daily carry-out. When these narratives are allowed to be part of our space planning, they not only heighten the design challenge, but they also expand the usage and the demographics.

By exposing the complexity of the threshold, by equipping us with the perspectives from multiple disciplines, and by alerting us to the wider organisational and societal significances of the museum entrance, I would suggest that this book is about much more than just the membrane between the museum and the outside world. These are discussions, at their heart, about the functions of the institution itself, its philosophy and mission. Without these types of discussions, and openings, we design for the status quo.

And this is the key point about this book, and about museum entrances generally. The authors collected here call out the space, and in doing so demand that we look at the institution holistically. To design a museum entrance is to decide upon what your institution is for. To plan the content of the foyer, and the placement of its services, is to identify and understand a variety of visits, visitors and visitor experiences. In other words, turning outwardly, to shape a museum threshold requires an understanding of the museum in the wider context of public space. Museums in the civic society belong to a public organisation, and collectively have a responsibility to civil peace. This is manifest in having public space where strangers can safely pass and see each other. It is this public thoroughfare to which museums have a responsibility.

Consequently, what becomes important is the space before the threshold, where people will actually and metaphorically begin their visit, and how the museum actions this transition from civic public to its private space. It is to that space, and this action, that this volume helpfully leads us. After all, the audiences considered in the various chapters here are those who have already decided to go through the door of the museum. What we need to think about next is the space in front of the door.

Acknowledgements

Like a foyer, a book like this is a confluence of many different people.

The chapters shared here (and the initial research project that inspired them) represent the expertise and generous contribution of a wide variety of practitioners and academics working from an international array of universities, companies and museums. As editors, we remain moved by the depth of their creativity, energy and intellectual challenge that they showed throughout this work, and the focus they sustained on our central question – of what, today, happens at a museum threshold.

We are grateful to the UK's Arts and Humanities Research Council (AHRC) for their support of the 'Transforming Thresholds' research workshop project (2012–2014), from which this book grows. Led by the University of Leicester, the project was a collaboration between: the ERDF-funded Digital Humanities Demonstrator at the University of Birmingham; the University of Westminster; University College London; De Montfort University; the University of Northampton; Birmingham Museums and Art Galleries; The British Museum; Chatsworth House Trust; Leicester Arts and Museums Service; The Petrie Museum, London; Citizen 598; Blip Creative; Daden; Forth Digital Consultancy; Star-dot-star; Studio Bonito; and Arup. With respect to this foundation research, we express our thanks, in particular, to Maja Rudloff, Geuntae Park, Jennifer Walklate, Amy Hetherington and Sarah Allard for their roles as research assistants at crucial stages in the project's literature review, fieldwork and data analysis. Further financial support came from the Research Development Fund of the University of Leicester's College of Social Sciences, Arts and Humanities. This support allowed for the visits, fieldwork and film-making that have materialised as the case study 'Conversations' interleaved across the volume, and for which we also extend thanks to our generous interviewees at The Postal Museum, The Royal Shakespeare Company, Birmingham Museum and Art Gallery, and the Royal Air Force Museum.

At key stages in the development of the book we have had the opportunity as editors to share and reflect upon this project with peers, at a number of high-profile events. Two events were highly instructive for us, for the feedback and guidance we received from our extended research community. We offer our gratitude first, therefore, to the AHRC-funded 'Creative

Exchange' at Lancaster University, as part of the work of its knowledge exchange hub, which between 2012 and 2016 created innovative partnerships between universities, businesses and communities, exploring creative applications of digital media and technology within society. This provided us with a platform to share the workings and findings of our 'creative charette' methodology – the means by which we have been able to support and structure the collaborations between our diverse partners. Second, we thank the organising committee of the international 'Museums and the Web 2014' conference in Baltimore (US) for providing us with an opportunity to interrogate our ideas around the threshold (particularly some of our practical threshold 'experiments' in real museums) with the world's pre-eminent cultural technology and digital heritage community.

The contribution of everyone on an extended, multi-dimensional piece of research such as this, is valued. The support of one partner in particular, however, has been especially valuable to us – both in terms of the endurance of the partnership and the influence it had on out thinking. We are indebted to DREAM (Danish Research Centre on Education and Advanced Media Materials) at the University of Southern Denmark, particularly for their openness in working alongside us at key stages in this work, and in connecting their parallel investigation into museum entrances with us. Working from a communication studies perspective, their work has helped to identify not only a typology and nomenclature for articulating and differentiating visitor activities in museum entrances, but also, importantly, a robust empirical basis on which to assume the multifunctional use that visitors make of these spaces. Just as we were able to share our findings with them, so DREAM opened to us their qualitative studies at the Arken Museum of Modern Art, the National Gallery in Copenhagen, Moesgård Museum, the Media Museum in Odense, and the Experimentarium in Copenhagen. DREAM's research in this area helped us to see the museum foyer as a multi-layered space of communication, characterised by a series of transformative practices and interactions by both staff and visitors. Their typology of entry ('arrival', 'orientation', 'service' and 'preparation'), and 'exit' ('preparation', 'service', 'evaluation' and 'departure') has informed our work throughout.

To the work of DREAM, we would also add the personal contributions made by museum curator Laura Hadland and film-maker and creative producer Nathan Human, whose vision helped us to see what this project could become if followed with courage and flair.

At the heart of our creative methods for this collaborative research was our idea of the 'charette', bringing a diverse group of people together to imagine and then to physically build new types of museum thresholds. The key, we found, for that method was to build trust, empathy and respect between participants. 'Trust, empathy and respect' seems not just a good lesson for those following practice-led, interdisciplinary academic research, but also a mantra for what's ultimately important at the museum threshold.

Ross, Ruth and Alex

1 On a new threshold

Ross Parry, Ruth Page and Alex Moseley

Museums have never really had one threshold. There have always been many ways to find the museum, to start a museum experience, to build a relationship with it. Indeed, theirs is a story of multiplying entry points. From the publication of catalogues and books to the sponsoring of specialist interest groups and societies, to the choreographing of travelling exhibitions and the loaning of objects, up to the programming of outreach services and the atomisation of online provision, watching the museum through its recent history is to see an organisation in motion – continuing to increase the connections, interventions and approaches that it can make with its society. And, as it does so, these varied methods through which collections and expertise have escaped into the world have always been matched by the ever more creative routes that audiences have found into the museum. It means that for many institutions the idea of a single point of entry (one threshold to the museum) is, largely, unrecognisable. Instead, through mobile content, open data, and social media, the museum continues to develop modes through which visitors might (re-)encounter and (re-)enter the museum. Today, rather than time-constrained and event-bound, the museum is always on, and on-demand. Rather than being encompassing and immersive, the museum experience might be fleeting and fragmentary – one of many headlines from a news feed, a single contribution to a page of image search results, one 'friend' or 'tweet' among many, another pin on an information-rich map. Therefore, with in-transit audiences pulling on museums amidst the everyday, and museums pushing content to the places where users go, institution and visitor have together continued to challenge the idea of a single entry point into the museum.

And yet, despite this multidimensional and distributive threshold, it is the entry into the physical museum that remains as a highly visible and symbolic space. Amidst a revolution of museology and digitality (where the shape, location and capabilities of the museum have been appraised and reappraised), the iconic physical entrance persists. Even when the postdigital museum (Parry, 2013) and 'museum as platform' reaches out across multichannels to its connected and networked audience, the physical entrance endures.

In fact, what endures in these entrances is a cultural trope, belonging to the birth of the museum. It is a trope that we see recurring within, and echoing across, the literature, pageantry and theatre of the early modern European condition from which the museum concept emerged (Von Naredi-Rainer, 2004). The façade of the early museum entrances paralleled the 'frontispieces' (specifically the antique architectural forms of emblematic title-pages) used in books of the time (Corbett & Lightbown, 1979, pp. 4–5). The entry point for many Renaissance readers into these literary works was through fantastical representations of portals, archways and gateways. To turn these opening pages – to step into these works – was to notice and acknowledge that the architectural conceit of the front page was more than just a metaphor, but was a metonym of the ordering and harmonising principles of the Renaissance imagination that assumed direct analogues between architectures of thought and built architectures. Similarly, drawing again upon the classical pattern of columns, capitals, pediments and pilasters, it was the same threshold device behind the grand triumphant archways, which marked entry points on days of civic ceremony (Strong, 1984). Europe's pageantry archways (some permanent features of the cityscape, others the temporary exhibitry and stagecraft of carnival and festival) reflected this similar culture of threshold-making, drawing upon equivalent architectural elements. Likewise, it was this same framing and threshold trope that we see forming the first proscenium arches in European theatre history (Wickham, 1972), demarcating the stage performance as a separate representational space. The formal museum entrance has origins in all of these traditions. The physical museum threshold (like the trope of the literary frontispiece, the triumphal arch, and the theatrical proscenium) is the formal architectural entry to the staging of a cultural act.

Today, museums continue to leverage the power of this threshold tradition. When the British Museum opened its Great Court in 2000, the reshaping of its principal threshold space was conveyed as a signature statement for the future of the institution as a whole. The museum had not just created (in its own words) a new 'accessible nucleus', but also 'a new kind of museum-going experience [. . .] another new beginning, both symbolic and practical' (Anderson, 2000, pp. 97–100). In the same year, the opening of the new Turbine Hall at Tate Modern became a defining act for the museum, at once both iconic and iconoclastic in its audacity and splendour as the entry space for visitors (Leahy, 2010). Both museums used the making and remodelling of their thresholds as an agent for their organisational reinvention.

However, what these two relatively new iconic thresholds also remind us is that spaces such as these do more than provide symbolic and physical gateways. In terms of the visitor experience, the museum entrance space simultaneously performs multiple complex functions, from way-finding and informational exchange, to rule-setting and ambience-setting. For the visitor, museum thresholds are places where trust and expectations are built, protocols established and affordances noted. The threshold's function may be ritualistic (Duncan & Wallach, 1978); or it may be the start of a holistically conceived interpretive programme (Lord & Lord, 2002); or it may be a critical opening 'component' (Falk & Dierking, 1992) of the visitor's narrative within the museum (Psarra, 2009; Skolnick, 2005). We might see – as James Clifford (1997) does – the entrance as part of the institution's 'contact zone', or as an example of Viv Golding's (2009) 'frontier space' within the museum. Whether in their physical properties (Royal Ontario Museum, 1999; Peponis & Hedin, 1982), or the modes of thought they represent (Watson, 2010; Bonet, 2006; Bullen, 2006; Dernie, 2006; Gregory, 2004; Liebchen, 2001; Lampugnani & Sachs, 1999), or indeed the sociological behaviour they frame (Tsybulskaya & Camhi, 2009; Macdonald, 1998; Duncan, 1995), it is evident that the entrance to the on-site museum – the physical threshold – remains historically resonant, sociologically complex, interpretatively meaningful, and pivotal to the visit event.

It seems reasonable to ask, therefore, whether the idea and function of the museum's physical threshold warrants reconsideration. What, in other words, do museum entrances do today, and what could they be for? Moreover – and perhaps more challengingly – we might also ask if visitors' experiences of playing, buying, discovering and learning in other parts of their lives, point to alternative means of scaffolding the museum threshold event. Are, for instance, the perennial informational metaphors that museums present to visitors on arrival (such as the classic architectural plan) sensitive to the modern media literacies of today's visitors? Does a labelled plan of the building still warrant being the most prominent first device to present to a visitor to help frame a museum experience? Might instead contemporary media and digital life actually offer other visual grammars and systems through which a visitor might usefully (perhaps more usefully) imagine their visit? Certainly, we know orientation and thresholds in museums are not always successful. We need only look towards the observational analysis of visitor behaviour by Christina Goulding (2000), to evidence an example of what happens when orientation fails. Likewise, reflecting on the politics of entering the museum, Elaine Heumann Gurian (2005) presents us with the intellectual equipment to question militantly our museum threshold spaces. Perhaps amongst all of the literature on museum entrances and foyers, it is Gurian's concept of 'threshold fear' that resonates most, capturing as it does the profoundly political dimension of entry, just how much is at stake in the design and use of space within the museum foyer, and what a fundamental barrier unsuccessful (unsympathetic) design can be.

This book, therefore, represents a coordinated and collaborative attempt to explore some of these questions around museum entrance design and experience. We have brought together a multidisciplinary network of practitioners, academics as well as commercial and cultural experts, with the shared aim of investigating progressive ways of reconceiving the museum entrance in a postdigital world. All of the authors worked from the principle that museum thresholds could be influenced usefully by other disciplines and sectors that might be seen to offer alternative or more evolved concepts and practices around 'threshold', 'orientation' and 'initiation'. And in turn, we feel that this interdisciplinary approach – sharing and learning from other sectors – provides a valuable learning experience, and offers a way forward for rethinking the threshold for the twenty-first century.

The chapters of this book are organised in three parts. The first part, 'Locating and Defining the Threshold', sets out to define and locate the threshold as a rich, varied and multifaceted 'problem space'. Its three chapters help to articulate the puzzle of the threshold, each from a different intellectual and professional perspective. The first chapter, 'Hysterical Atria' by designers Katherine Skellon and Ben Tunstall, situates the museum threshold in an architectural, historical and theoretical context. Skellon and Tunstall paint a bold picture which illustrates the diverse, liminal potential of the threshold. Drawing on an international range of museum thresholds, they question the cultural politics that might govern the design and use of the threshold. In so doing, they explore how thresholds might be used for a variety of purposes, from taking a yoga class to making a purchase before or after a museum visit. Thresholds are not just an entrance space that prepares visitors to enter the gallery spaces. Their interrogation of the design and use of these spaces critically questions how far and in what ways this diversity liberates, authorises, reworks and revises earlier assumptions about the museum and its status within the cultural economy. The transformation of the threshold becomes emblematic of much wider political and social shifts. The second chapter, 'The Complexity of Welcome: Visitor Experience at the Museum Threshold', shifts our attention to the visitor experience of the threshold. As a visitor experience consultant, Colin Mulberg draws on a series of illustrative examples, including the National Museum of the Royal Navy in Portsmouth and the World Rugby Museum in Twickenham, both in the United Kingdom, to explore the complex work visitors engage in as they move towards and through the threshold on their visit to a museum. Mulberg sets out the progressive stages of the 'visitor offer' as they commit and prepare for their entrance. He argues that museums can reduce the work for visitors through the resources that they provide in this threshold experience, both before and during the visit itself. The chapter has implications for museum marketing, signage and ticketing procedures, and more generally for better understanding of visitor motivation. The last chapter in this part, 'Design-driven Innovation for Museum Entrances' by Marco Mason, focuses on the complex challenges that thresholds pose for designers. As a digital designer, Mason draws on the innovations that have been applied to the threshold experience in the hotel industry. Whilst there are clear differences between a visit to a hotel and a visit to a museum, the need for welcome and orientation is central in both. Mason's chapter explores the threshold design as a collaborative process. He shows how the transformation of a threshold experience needs to incorporate the aspirations of the institution (whether hotel or museum) and be grounded in the observations of the visitors and their 'journey' through the threshold. In this case, the design solution was an interactive multitouch screen. The chapter shows the value of interdisciplinarity, collaboration and the importance of thinking strategically about design of the threshold.

The second part of the book, 'Affordances and Potential of the Threshold', examines a series of specific thresholds and the connections that are made in, through and between the threshold and other aspects of the visitors' experiences. In the first chapter in Part II, 'Suspended: Art in the Threshold', Peter Ride uses the metaphor of the threshold as a window to create insight into the museum. Drawing on an international range of museums, including the Msheireb Museum in Qatar, the Seattle Museum of Industry and History, and the Aga Khan Museum in Toronto, Ride shows how artworks of different kinds can be used to preface, restate and extend the narratives of the museum's identity, collections and cultural context. The second chapter in this part, by Angelina Russo and Philip Pond, 'Curation at the Threshold: Making Museum Meanings through New Interfaces', considers the ways in which the threshold is experienced as part of the 'connected museum'. Rather than focusing on the artwork that is curated within the threshold, Russo and Pond show how visitors collect and curate their experiences by taking photographic images of particular thresholds and uploading them to the photo-sharing site, Instagram. Their work shows how the threshold can be extended beyond the visitor's physical, on-site engagement to incorporate their virtual, online interactions, such as posting, tagging and browsing images within Instagram. The third chapter in Part II, by David Burden, similarly focuses on the ways in which virtual technology can be used to extend the threshold experience. He focuses on the use of 3D game engines and virtual world environments in the design of thresholds for large, architectural projects. Drawing on his experience of working with the staff, consultants and architects who designed the library of Birmingham, Burden documents the place of 3D visualisation in supporting the staff and visitor experience of the new library, even before the doors of the physical library opened to the public. The fourth and final chapter in this part, 'Difficult Thresholds: Negotiating Shared and Embedded Entrances' by Steve Kruse, examines a distinctive context, the thresholds that are embedded in entrances that are shared by a museum and another institution. Kruse's chapter examines three contrasting shared entrances, one in the Museum of Archaeology and Anthropology in the University of Cambridge, the Stained Glass Museum in Ely Cathedral and the Hunterian Museum in the Royal College of Surgeons. These examples illustrate the complex ways in which the design and use of the threshold space can become embedded not only in physical locations, but in the historical development of a building as it has changed over time. The multiple socio-historical, institutional and physical aspects of these embedded thresholds pose particular challenges for the visitors who pass through them and for the practitioners who manage these spaces.

The final part of the book, 'The Threshold Rethought', shifts its focus to practical and experimental examples of changes that have been made to particular thresholds. Each chapter takes a different discipline or area of professional practice as its start point, specifically gaming design, retail studies and applied linguistics. These different approaches focus on the visitor experience and the transformation that takes place at the museum threshold. The first chapter in this part, 'Games in the Lobby: A Playful Approach' by Erik Kristiansen and Alex Moseley, shows how a gaming perspective provides a new way of thinking about and working with entrance spaces like the museum lobby. Drawing on classical understanding of games and play, they show how the lobby can be analysed as a boundary through which visitors pass to enter the 'magic circle' of the museum. Practically, the chapter shows how playful approaches can support the design of thresholds, using a metagame to help museum practitioners think through the challenges and rewards that visitors might encounter as they pass through threshold spaces such as the lobby, and through a playful installation at Chatsworth House in Derbyshire, UK. More specifically, Kristiansen and Moseley set out a typology of games that might support the different communicative functions of the threshold and use playfulness to transform visitor experience in these spaces.

The second chapter in this part, by Tracy Harwood, uses retail perspectives to draw comparisons and contrasts between the thresholds found in shop design and those found in museums. Harwood shows how the use of light, sound, colour and layout are used to construct the 'servicescape' in the retail sector. These sensory design cues have much to offer as the means by which the visitor's attention can also be engaged in the entrances to museums. Examples include visual (images, signs and light), auditory (music and auditory branding), tactile (texture), olfactory and social stimuli, each of which can deepen the immersive potential of the threshold environment.

The third chapter in this part, 'Setting the Tone for the Visit: Soundscape Design' by Christian Hviid Mortensen and Angus Deuchars, explores one form of sensory cue in depth: sound. In their chapter, Mortensen and Deuchars describe the process of designing a soundscape as a form of action research for the Petrie Museum of Egyptian Archaeology in London. The soundscape was designed as part of a multimodal installation in a challenging threshold: essentially a stairwell via which visitors access and exit the museum galleries. The visitors' responses to the soundscape gathered through a semi-structured survey suggested that sound could be a useful way to demarcate a point of contrast between the outer world and the world evoked by the collections within the gallery. This included perceptions of a change in atmosphere and the potential to imagine a time and space related to the music and sound effects.

The visitor's affective response to their experience of the threshold is at the heart of the final chapter in the collection, 'The Visitor as Evaluator: Using Appraisal Theory to Understand "Threshold Fear"'. In this chapter,

Ruth Page returns to Elaine Heumann Gurian's (2005) provocative metaphor of 'threshold anxiety'. Using an emerging framework from applied linguistics, she analyses the responses from visitors at two museums in the United Kingdom (the Petrie Museum of Egyptian Archeology in London, and New Walk Museum and Art Gallery in Leicester). The analysis of the language that these visitors used allows her to give empirical substance to the notion of threshold fear and teases out the multifaceted forms in which this affective response might be expressed. The appraisal analysis suggests that threshold fear consists of the need for physical, cognitive and emotional orientation, which can be alleviated when the threshold space is 'scaffolded' effectively (Wood et al., 1976).

At the start of our thinking around the threshold, and our ideas for this book, we were keen to ground our work in existing and future practice within museums, both local and (inter)national. To this end, we visited four very different museums, and invited them to talk to us about their own thresholds. In some cases, we found spaces that were already going through a change; in others plans to develop or redesign the thresholds were afoot. We present these *conversations* throughout the book, as authentic insights into real issues and approaches to the threshold from a range of museums.

This book itself is intended as a threshold, of sorts. As the first volume to attempt a systematic analysis of museum entrances, the aim has been to begin – rather than end – a discourse. Rather than assuming to be comprehensive, and so closing a discussion down, this book instead looks to open up what it sees as a new seam of grounded scholarship and a new facet of reflective museum practice around the museum threshold. The contributions here represent the beginnings, therefore, of lines of enquiry, of debates, of suggested practice for others to add to, to challenge and to take forward. And yet, in its overt multidisciplinary approach, the book is also intentionally signalling that this future research will benefit from being inclusive and open in the expertise it welcomes (Moseley, Page & Parry, 2013). To the acoustic engineers, sociolinguists, game designers, retail experts, museologists, cultural technologists, visual culture scholars, visitor studies consultants and museum practitioners involved here, there are (and, indeed, need to be) many more contributors and thought leaders in this space from both within and without the academy.

Collectively, the contributions in this volume vividly challenge the perception of the museum entrance as a passive perfunctory space. What emerges instead is the threshold – demanding our attention – as a complex multidimensional concept open for consideration in architectural, technical, ethnographic, marketing, engineering and philosophical terms. Viewed from one angle it is a design challenge: open to reimagining by tools from gaming, retail and service design. Looked at again, it is a cultural piece to be read: a lesson in identity politics, a lens through which to see the museum and its society. But then from another perspective it stands as a business object: a key operational touchpoint, the capabilities of which need to be determined and managed. However, recurring through all of these perspectives is the sense of an entity that carries with it all of the traits we would expect from a boundary object. The museum threshold is both a space (a place to traverse) and time (a condition to progress within). It is betwixt and between the everyday and the imaginary, carrying the characteristics and affordances of both. It is liminal and transitory (full of transformations and suspension), and yet distinctive and fixed (a place and time for transaction, decision and resolution). It is both shared and owned: where the public negotiates its place with the museum and the museum reaches out to the everyday. And it is typically a place and moment of both beginnings and endings.

At its origins, the museum entrance's traditional gateways and framing devices were symbolic and iconic in setting it apart for its world. Today, its modern qualities (at once space and time, inside and out, public and private, shared and owned, fixed and fluid) speak to a new iconicity. This is the museum threshold as engagement, encounter, openness, transparency, access and affordance. It shows us everything the museum is, and wants to be.

References

Anderson, R. (2000). *The Great Court and the British Museum*. London: British Museum Press.
Bonet, L. (2006). *Exhibition Design*. Gloucester, MA: Rockport Publishers.
Bullen, J. B. (2006). 'Alfred Waterhouse's Romanesque "Temple of Nature": The Natural History Museum, London', *Architectural History* 49, pp. 257–285.
Clifford, J. (1997). 'Museums as Contact Zones'. In J. Clifford (Ed.) *Routes: Travel and Translation in the Later Twentieth Century*. Cambridge, MA: Harvard University Press, pp. 188–219.
Corbett, M. & R. Lightbown. (1979). *The Comely Frontispiece: The Emblematic Title-page in England 1550–1660*. London, Henley and Boston: Routledge & Kegan Paul.
Dernie, D. (2006). *Exhibition Design*. London: Laurence King Publishing.
Duncan, C. (1995). *Civilizing Rituals: Inside Public Art Museums*. London: Routledge.
Duncan, C. & A. Wallach. (1978). 'The Museum of Modern Art as Late Capitalist Ritual: An Iconographic Analysis', *Marxist Perspectives* 4, pp. 28–51.
Falk, J. H. & L. D. Dierking. (1992). *The Museum Experience*. Ann Arbor, MI: Edwards Brothers.
Golding, V. (2009). *Learning at the Museum Frontiers: Identity, Race and Power*. Farnham, UK: Ashgate.
Goulding, C. (2000). 'The Museum Environment and the Visitor Experience', *European Journal of Marketing* 34:3/4, pp. 261–278.
Gregory, R. (2004). 'Bankside Revisited', *The Architectural Review* 215:1288, pp. 82–87.
Gurian, E. H. (2005). 'Threshold Fear'. In S. MacLeod (Ed.) *Reshaping Museum Space: Architecture, Design, Exhibitions*. Abingdon, UK: Routledge, pp. 203–214.
Lampugnani, V. M. & A. Sachs (Eds). (1999). *Museums for a New Millennium: Concepts, Projects, Buildings*. London: Prestel.

Leahy, H. R. (2010). 'Watch Your Step: Embodiment and Encounter at Tate Modern'. In S. Dudley (Ed.) *Museum Materialities*. Abingdon, UK: Routledge, pp. 162–174.

Liebchen, J. (spring 2001). 'Power Station for Art vs. Art for Power Station', trans. Patricia Belkin, *Art Journal* 60:1, pp. 12–19.

Lord, B. & G. D. Lord. (2002). *The Manual of Museum Exhibitions*. New York and Oxford: Alta Mira.

Macdonald, S. (Ed.). (1998). *The Politics of Museum Display: Museums, Science, Culture*. London: Routledge.

Moseley, A., R. Page & R. Parry. (2013). 'The Creative Charette: Enabling Collaboration in the AHRC Research Network, Transforming Thresholds'. *The Knowledge Exchange, an Interactive Conference*, Lancaster University. Accessed 5 January 2014. Available http://thecreativeexchange.org/sites/default/files/ke_conf_papers/paper_2.pdf.

Parry, R. (2013). 'The End of the Beginning: Normativity in the Postdigital Museum', *Museum Worlds* 1, pp. 24–39.

Peponis J. & J. Hedin. (1982). 'The Layout of Theories in the Natural History Museum', *9H* 3, pp. 12–25.

Psarra, S. (2009). *Architecture and Narrative: The Formation of Space and Cultural Meaning*. Abingdon, UK: Routledge.

Royal Ontario Museum, Communications Design Team. (1999). 'Spatial Considerations'. In E. Hooper-Greenhill. *The Educational Role of the Museum*. London: Routledge, pp. 178–190.

Skolnick, L. H. (2005). 'Towards a New Museum Architecture: Narrative and Representation'. In S. MacLeod (Ed.) *Reshaping Museum Space: Architecture, Design, Exhibitions*. London: Routledge, pp. 118–130.

Strong, R. (1984). *Art and Power: Renaissance Festivals, 1450–1650*. Woodbridge, UK: Boydell Press.

Tsybulskaya, D. & J. Camhi. (January 2009). 'Accessing and Incorporating Visitors' Entrance Narratives in Guided Museum Tours', *Curator* 51:1, pp. 81–100.

Von Naredi-Rainer, P. (2004). *Museum Buildings: A Design Manual*. Basel: Birkhauser.

Watson, H. (2010). 'Ashmolean Museum, Oxford', *Architectural Design* 80:3, pp. 102–105.

Wickham, G. (1972). *Early English Stages 1300 to 1660*, 2 vols. London and New York: Routledge and Kegan Paul and Columbia University Press.

Wood, D., J. S. Bruner & G. Ross. (1976). 'The Role of Tutoring in Problem Solving', *Journal of Child Psychology and Psychiatry* 17:2, pp. 89–100.

Part I
Locating and defining the threshold

2 Hysterical atria

Katherine Skellon and Ben Tunstall

Museum atria are spaces of arrival and practicality. But they are also spaces of symbolism and aspiration, where the museum gives expression to its institutional being, addressing visitors directly about the museum's values, expectations and history. In their grandeur atria can awe and inspire visitors, or in their intimacy they can welcome and comfort. But they can also produce other effects. Contemporary atria can contain blurring zones and vague spaces. They are places in which playful forms can appear. Consequently, they are spaces that speak to the historical moment of our social relations in particular ways. We might say that museum atria are spaces where visitors place themselves most clearly under the gaze of the institution. Unlike the main body of the museum, atria can be devoid of artefacts, thus making visitors themselves the objects. But we might also say that instead of 'objects', the museum makes them into 'subjects'. For example, in Bennett's (1995) classic Foucauldian analysis of the development of museums through the Victorian period, the museum was a site of 'disciplinary power', placing the masses under a disciplinary gaze, in which values of civilisation and civics were brought to bear on the visitor, creating museum visitors as museum subjects, subjects of the museum. As the entrance to the museum where the visitor must first be subjugated and subjectivised, the atrium would perhaps be the foremost arena of this panoptic institutional gaze.

Today, these earlier forms of disciplinary power seem to be subverted in museum atria and new forms of atrium culture have emerged. Inclusive or progressive museum cultures seek to create a space of welcome instead of intimidation for visitors, of diversity instead of homogeneity, and atria are often playful liberatory spaces, sites of complementary activities, educational workshops, self-improvement practices, and consumer attractions. If we follow the developments in Foucault's own thinking, we might say that today the atrium is more an ethical space of the 'technologies of the self', a space in which visitors may attempt to 'operate' upon the self, and thereby transform themselves – their bodies, minds and souls – towards the achievement of self-fulfilment. As we hope to demonstrate, there are numerous examples of atrium practice and aesthetic forms that pertain to this Foucauldian view.

However, we will also argue that the Foucauldian stance does not account for a number of aspects of the contemporary museum atrium. While his analysis may speak to a liberatory culture and politics, the kinds of liberation at play in the contemporary atrium might speak to other forces at work. We will propose that instead of understanding the atrium solely through a Foucauldian lens, Lacanian psychoanalysis can provide an alternative – or complementary – tool to explore a variety of aspects of atrium culture. Whereas Foucault takes 'subjectivation' as a matter of the historical effects of power, psychoanalysis sees the process of becoming a subject as a matter that takes places in all times and in all contexts – it is the process of our becoming subject to the 'symbolic', the abstract social realm of language and law that entwines itself with our pre-linguistic bodily being. Regardless of historical period, the question of humanity's relation to the symbolic is core to what it is to be a subject. Atria, as symbolically charged social spaces filled with images, bodies and meanings, stage our position in relation to the symbolic order, and confront the questions, pleasures and vicissitudes inherent to it. Looking at atria through this lens allows us to explore atrium culture from a point of view less to do with assumed struggles of liberation between selves and power, and more to do with a breadth of possible response informed by how individuals negotiate their particular positions in relation to a broader set of interlinked phenomena – language, law, fantasy, the body, other people. Indeed, it allows us to suggest that the very notion of the liberatory atrium is a particular stance towards the symbolic itself, one which has its own historical moment, but which is in many ways a staging of a particular stance of subjectivity. Lacan (2007) suggested that there are four 'discourses' by which subjects deal with their position within the symbolic, four kinds of 'social link'. We will argue that where the museum atrium – seen through the lens of Foucault's disciplinary power – placed visitors as subjects of the 'university discourse' – a discourse of bureaucratic knowledge, behind which a 'master' is hidden, the contemporary atrium is often a space of the 'hysteric's discourse' – that seeks to find a master, question and undermine the master, evade or subvert the notion of the symbolic per se. We will suggest how contemporary atria attempt to avoid, mould or play with this hystericisation, and the manner in which this may provoke enjoyments and anxieties within visitors. Our aim is thereby to nuance our thinking about visitor responses to atria and atrium culture.

The hyper-crowd's atrium is not the disciplinary atrium

Writing in 1991, Fredric Jameson identified the atria of the Bonaventure Hotel in LA, the Eaton Centre Shopping Mall in Toronto, and the Pompidou Centre in Paris as the definition of postmodern space. Buildings like these 'do not wish to be a part of the city, but rather its equivalent and its replacement or substitute'. Entrances of this kind of building do not assert themselves, they minimise themselves and allow the city beyond to simply get on by themselves. Instead, this kind of building:

> aspires to being a total space, a complete world, a kind of miniature city (and I would want to add that to this new total space corresponds a new collective practice, a new mode in which individuals move and congregate, something like the practice of a new and historically original kind of hyper-crowd).
>
> (Jameson, 1991, p. 40)

Core to this total space of congregation, beyond the non-entrance, is the atrium. Since Jameson wrote this, the number of buildings where hyper-crowds congregate in 'complete worlds' has surely grown. In London, the Great Court at the British Museum seems like a Renaissance town; Tate Modern engulfs visitors in its Turbine Hall and disorienting lobbies of its Switchhouse extension. In Paris, we might include the Palais de Tokyo as well as the Pompidou, in Bilbao the Guggenheim, and we might argue each has its own hyper-crowd. In some way, the hyper-crowd is dependent on the social totality of the space, is contained within it. However, given that crowds of visitors have been going to large contained atrium spaces since museums and shopping arcades were open to the public, what is the historical originality of this situation? Why is the crowd 'hyper', and why does the atrium space seem to pose itself as a totality?

Zukin (1993) questioned whether Jameson's hyper-crowd was in fact so original. She claimed that Henry James identified a similar crowd in his *The American Scene*, 'the great collective, plastic public':

> No less than Jameson in the atrium, James sees 'the whole housed populace move as in mild consenting suspicion of its captured and governed state, its having to consent in inordinate fusion as the price of what it seemed pleased to regard as inordinate luxury'. There is a direct line of visual consumption from Henry James at the Waldorf Astoria in New York in 1905 to Fredric Jameson at the Los Angeles Bonaventure. But the public use of private space *inside* the hotel only symbolises change in the surrounding city.
>
> (Zukin, 1993, p. 53)

Zukin went on to define the interiorisation of the public as the basis of the hyper-crowd, on the basis of the loss of public space outside. Within museums in particular, she also saw it as a product of the blurring of the private and public, between that which is for-the-market and that which is not. Within a web of relations based on brand-patronage and museum marketing, the hyper-crowd of the museum is, for Zukin, the commercial crowd of the mall brought into the museum. Zukin's analysis seems partly right, partly wrong. Undoubtedly, the blurring of the commercial and the museum informs atrium culture in many contexts today where it can be argued that neoliberal cultural policy requires museums to compete within a marketplace of possible activities (see for example Stallabrass, 2014). Hence spectacular atria, cafes, shops. We might suggest the museum competes with the city beyond, has no relationship with it and seeks to replace it, as Jameson observes, because it aims to make visitors stay in it, use the museum cafe, spend their money in its shop. However, is the 'great collective, plastic public' that Zukin takes from Henry James in the late nineteenth and early twentieth centuries really the same as the hyper-crowd? Does the postmodern hyper-crowd really 'move as in mild consenting suspicion of its captured and governed state, its having to consent in inordinate fusion' as Zukin suggests? Is it really 'collective' or 'plastic'?

If we look to James's *American Scene* itself, for further signs of similarity or difference between the museum crowd of now and of 1905, we find another passage (which Zukin doesn't quote), in which James describes how the:

> British Museum, the Louvre, the Bibliotheque Nationale, the treasures of South Kensington, are assuredly, under forms, at the disposal of the people; but it is to be observed, I think, that the people walk there more or less under the shadow of the right waited for and conceded.
> (James, 1907, pp. 249–250)

Such a description of the position of the visitor in the nineteenth- and early twentieth-century museum echoes other influential descriptions of the museum culture of the time. For example, Duncan (1995) analyses the museum in relation to rituals of state and citizenship, giving theoretical flesh to James's notion of 'the right waited for and conceded', the movement from museums as 'princely collections' in the sixteenth and seventeenth century to become public institutions of the nation states of the eighteenth and nineteenth centuries. In this period, the modern state made use of the symbolism of the museum as a progressive institution, including citizens into a sacred space predicated on, and symbolically infused with, the values of civilisation and civic virtue. Thus the museum implicated the crowd of visitors both into a new relationship with the nation state 'as benefactor' (Duncan, 1995, p. 94) and into a new identity as a homogeneous public of citizens, with rights and responsibilities, based within the ideal of civilisation as the climax of a universal history.

Preeminent amongst theorists of the 'capture and governance' of the nineteenth-century museum visitor must be Tony Bennett, who (alongside Hooper-Greenhill) stands as founder of the use of the theory of Michel Foucault within museum studies. Indeed, as a result of Bennett's work, Conn (2010) refers to Foucault as 'the patron saint of the new museum studies' (Conn, 2010, p. 3). In his classic studies of the 'disciplinary power' of the prison and other state institutions, Foucault (1977) described a model of power that he based on Jeremy Bentham's design for a 'Panopticon' prison, wherein all are subject to the unseen gaze of a central eye of power. The subject of this unseen power internalises the sense of its gaze, and is made docile. Foucault analysed many state institutions – the prison, the hospital, the asylum – through the lens of power and how it created subjects through its gaze. In later adaptations to his theory, Foucault modified his concept of power to decentralise it into civil society, into a mentality of government or a 'governmentality' that moderated the behaviour of all by all, and governing the 'conduct of conducts' (Foucault, 2002, p. 341).

Bennett shows that the Victorian museum, or 'exhibitionary complex', was a space in which this disciplinary gaze also functioned. Drawing on accounts from the time, he shows how Victorian bourgeois concern to civilise the masses was effected within the museum.

> As micro-worlds rendered constantly visible to themselves, expositions realized some of the ideals of panopticism in transforming the crowd into a constantly surveyed, self-watching, self-regulating, and as the historical record suggests, consistently orderly public – a society watching over itself.
> (Bennett, 1995, p. 69)

Bennett was himself at pains to make clear that he did not view the museum as a carceral institution as such, but one, more like Duncan's analysis above, where the state brings the citizen into a hegemonic relationship to the citizen's benefit. Nonetheless, the sense of the disciplinary gaze pervades Bennett's work, and certainly within other influential Foucault-inspired works of the 'new museology', the sense of the museum's disciplinary power is less moderated. For example, Crimp (1993) states:

> Foucault analyzed modern institutions of confinement – the asylum, the clinic, and the prison – and their respective discursive formations – madness, illness, and criminality. There is another such institution of confinement awaiting archeological analysis – the museum – and another discipline – art history.
> (Crimp, 1993, p. 48)

Thus, we can see from a range of theoretical and historical perspectives that the nineteenth-century museum crowd was very much 'governed and captured', made from individuals subjectivated under the eye of power, emulating a model of civility within a relationship of grateful, obedient subject to beneficent state. By the same token, however, things are clearly somewhat different today. In all areas of social analysis, theorists have sought to define the new, more amorphous, horizontal forms of social organisation that exist within postmodern society. We live within 'weak social ties' (Granovetter, 1973), the 'network society' (Castells, 1996), we are 'expressive individuals' (Bellah, 1985). Within this context a variety of crowd-like phenomena seem to give definitive expression to our time. Theorists such as Žižek (2005) and Kluitenberg (2006) help us to reflect upon forms such as the 'flash-mob' of strangers or the 'silent disco' in which everyone dances together yet listens on headphones to the music they individually choose.

For museum curatorial approaches, the postmodern has brought a valuing of diversity, of difference to the institution. Writers have found other forms of diversity than those of the market at work in the museum. For instance, seeking to extend his earlier terms, Bennett's (2015) describes some of the ways post-disciplinary museums have been 'retooled [. . .] as instruments for a critical cosmopolitanism, as "differencing machines" promoting new forms of cultural hybridity, or, in James Clifford's terms, as contact zones'. In the atrium itself, such diversity is expressed not only in relation to curatorial practices, but also in the way different activities are made available to visitors. Writing in 1991, for example, Duncan described the change in the atrium in terms of the shifting value given to civilisation within the new configuration of wings and atria in the Boston Museum of Fine Art:

> The concept of the public and the reverence for the classical Western past that informed the older museum do not operate in the modern one, just as the new, more alienated kind of individualism celebrated there is very different from the idealised citizen–state relationship implicit in the older museum [. . .] Because the new wing has in practice become the museum's main entrance, the classical galleries, the old museum's opening statement, now occupy the most remote reaches of the building – remote, that is, in relation to the new entrance. The museum's opening statement now consists of a large gallery of modern art, three new restaurants, a space for special exhibitions, and a large gift-and-book store. It is now possible to visit the museum, see a show, go shopping, and eat, and never once be reminded of the heritage of Civilisation.
> (Duncan, 1991, pp. 100–101)

Duncan situates the nineteenth-century museum within the transition from the Princely State to the Nation State. If we were to extend this analysis with reference to the distinction Bobbitt (2002) draws between the Princely State and the Nation State, and then between the Nation State and today's Market State, this might go some way to giving a state-theorist basis to the blurring of the market and non-market Zukin describes. The market is brought in not only as a blurring of these spheres of life, but also because the market has been brought into the state as a logic of government itself, and a reconfiguration of the state–citizen relationship. Within this relationship, the value of citizenship is no longer brought to bear on the visitors of the museum – instead, the hyper-crowd is able to share in the marketised options of the atrium without going anywhere near the heritage of civilisation; its 'alienated kind of individualism' is both perhaps less bound into expected convention, and rather than disciplined, 'celebrated'.

Within this theoretical context, Foucault's own foundational analysis of power has not simply been descriptive but a normative project of challenging disciplinary power, the 'top-down' institutions of the state. As a part of postmodern or poststructuralist theory in general, Foucault's work has been part of the project to undermine hierarchies and recourses to origins, positing instead a culture of open creative play. Indeed the Pompidou Centre, whose hyper-crowd Jameson noticed, was created by President Pompidou in reaction to the spirit of 1960s radicalism and the 'bottom-up' approach to social power Foucault advocated. Designed by Renzo Piano and Richard Rogers in 1976, the Pompidou Centre was a manifestation of the radical paper-architectural ideas of Archigram and Cedric Price's Fun Palace. Thus, to return to the contemporary museum atrium, it seems hard to agree with Zukin that there is a direct lineage between James's 'housed populace' of 1905 and Jameson's 'hyper-crowd' of 1995. The hyper-crowd of the 1990s – and up to today – is surely a different entity, less monolithic, less collective, and perhaps also less 'governed' by the institution.

In later work, Foucault went on to propose an alternative model of the development of the self, which opened a space away from the operations of disciplinary power, in which the self could operate on itself. In place of the panoptic diagram he had described, Foucault proposed another model of subjectivity – the 'technologies of the self' (Foucault, 1988) and of 'practices of freedom' (Foucault, 1997) that the individual might use to develop the self. This model might itself provide a basis for thinking about subjectivity in the contemporary atria that Zukin and Duncan describe above, where a range of subsidiary, often commercial, activities are available to visitors in contemporary atria.

For example, the American online magazine mu[see]um.net, which says it 'goes beyond the main purpose of a traditional art venue', asserts: 'We encourage our readers to visit museums for the sake of mind-blowing architecture, amazing food, unconventional shopping, breathtaking gardens and stimulating learning activities – everything that makes modern museums stand out and become important creative and communication centers' (Filippenko, 2016). It presents museum visits as a quest for ethical connectedness and aesthetic self-exploration.

In the contemporary atrium, a 'practice of the self' mu[see]um.net reports on is yoga. At the Brooklyn Museum, a yoga class for 300–400 people takes place in the central atrium. The participants do the yoga on coloured mats that fill the entire floor space of the atrium. They are given instructions by a yogi flanked by speakers, and classical musicians accompany the yoga. Speaking to mu[see]um.net, the leader of the yoga class sees the atrium space as adding to the practice: 'because in a museum the space is held sacred, there is a really special atmosphere that very much compliments the practice'. They go on to say:

> Space can be seen as a sort of artwork, feng shui is important because the energy of the space will have an effect on the body and the practice. While we don't necessarily reference artwork in the practice, it's nice to relate to the artistic nature of the practice.

The Adult Programs Manager says of the yoga class: 'By joining us at the Museum for this restorative program, you can connect back to yourself and your spirit in a beautiful, non-traditional space. Those are the memories that can leave an imprint that can last a lifetime.' Here we can see, instead of a panoptic power, Foucault's aesthetic 'care of the self' imbuing the visitor's use of the atrium.

Aside from yoga, we might also say that shopping – the bringing of the mall into the atrium, as Zukin critiqued it – is another prominent 'practice of the self' of the contemporary atrium. The shop in the British Museum's Great Court, for example, adds to the Great Court's sense of being a contained world – all town squares need a shop. Likewise, the shop at the V&A (London) is an almost seamless extension of the atrium, forming a gateway to the rest of the museum – which seems to be an extension of the shop, which is not inappropriate given that it is a museum of the design of commodities over the ages. This attitude has been present within the V&A for some time. Its embrace of the new commercialism caused outrage when its advertising campaign of 1988 advertised its 'ace café' with 'quite a nice museum attached' as a cheeky afterthought. Its 2016 exhibition about the social, political and cultural revolutions of the 1960s contains an Andy Warhol quote that speaks to this sense of the museum: 'When you think about it, department stores are kind of like museums.'

Consumerism's place in the contemporary museum atrium is, as we have already noted, itself a source of some comment. Aside from Zukin's and Duncan's comments cited above, numerous theorists and social critics have, since the 1990s, and partly influenced by the work of theorists such as Jean Baudrillard, engaged in a critique of the 'Disneyfication' of the museum. Architect Rem Koolhaas's essay 'Junkspace', for example, makes a veiled critique of the commercialism of Tate Modern, wherein the terms are reversed – rather than critiquing the commercialisation of the museum, he views Tate Modern as the museumification of the commercial:

> Monasteries inflated to the scale of department stores [. . .] curators plot hangings and unexpected encounters in a donor-plate labyrinth with the finesse of the retailer: lingerie becomes 'Nude, Action, Body' cosmetics 'History, Memory, Society'. All paintings based on black grids are herded together in a single white room. Large spiders in the humongous conversion offer delirium for the masses.
>
> (Koolhaas, 2016, p. 34)

As well as Koolhaas's rage at this Warholian conflation of department store with curatorial conceit, Koolhaas's satire is also directed at the faux sanctimony of the museum, which we imagine he might well direct at the use of the 'sacred' within the Brooklyn Museum's yoga practice.

We might say that museum atria are now spaces where, in a wide variety of ways, a panoply of different activities and forms celebrate liberated expression, difference, social relations and self-development, away from the subjectivating disciplinary gaze of yesteryear. As consumer theory would attest (for example Miller, 1998), visitors can engage in constructing the self through shopping – and here in particular through the acquisition of culturally validated artefacts; and they can take part in self-developmental workshops and other activities. Thus, if we take a Foucauldian stance to the atrium, we might say that the post-disciplinary atrium has given way to the self-developmental atrium where visitors can enjoy a wide range of possibilities. To use Foucault's (1998) own term, the museum has become doubly 'heterotopic' – where before the museum was a morgue-like storehouse of different objects and time periods, today it also contains the flamboyant differences of a festival. The 'hyper' aspect of the hyper-crowd is in its not being a homogeneous mass, but rather an assemblage of individuals in eurphoric pursuit of their own self-directed enjoyments and developments in a looser form of individual diversity.

The hyper-crowd's atrium is a denial of the disciplinary atrium

However, we take the view that this historical trajectory from the atrium of disciplinary subjectivation to the atrium of self-development is not the whole story. In what follows, we will draw attention to some aspects of the contemporary atrium that do not quite fit with this account, and from there we will suggest a different approach to Foucault's disciplinary power – one informed by Lacanian psychoanalysis – that allows us to draw some different conclusions about the contemporary atrium and the place of the visitor within it. What are these aspects? First, it is striking to us that these various liberated, self-developmental atrium activities seem to take place precisely in contradistinction to the expected function, or presumed disciplinary stance of the museum. Notice how mu[see]um.net is about the extras, it 'goes beyond the main purpose of a traditional art venue', or how for Duncan 'It is now possible to visit the museum, see a show, go shopping, and eat, and never once be reminded of the heritage of Civilisation.' Notice how the V&A itself infamously played on this very distinction by the cheekiness of its privileging the cafe over the museum. In the Great Court of the British Museum, we come to the shop round the side of the great central building, which, rather like the Ducal palace of a pastiche Renaissance town, acts like the representative of Panoptic power – as though some unseen eye observes the visitors from behind its narrow windows up high. Indeed, it is hard not to see the central cylinder of the Great Court as almost modelled on Bentham's

22 *Katherine Skellon and Ben Tunstall*

panopticon. But, it is a panopticon that we are able to evade. Confronted by it when we first arrive in the court, when we walk round it and pass out of its view, we find beneath its side, in its lea, a space of affordance, where we can relax a little – a space in which we can indulge in the 'practice of the self' through shopping. There is a liberation – an allowance given to the self – made precisely by the distinction of the activity as one for the self rather than for the expected function of the museum. Part of the pleasure of the contemporary atrium is precisely in its giving visitors the option to not do what they are meant to be doing. This sense of liberation as distinct from the disciplinary is evident in other aspects of contemporary museum atria. Creative and artistic interventions within the atrium subvert the old disciplinary power or stage some kind of liberation through the opposition between the old disciplinary power and the new decentralised forms.

To take one of numerous examples, the central courtyard of the V&A museum, which functions in many ways like one of the grand atria of other major museums, has recently featured temporary installations of biomorphic forms of architectural design (developed by the University of Stuttgart) being built by robots.

A simple logic of juxtaposition may be seen to be at work here. The background of neoclassicism is put in opposition to emergent biomorphic forms, which challenge the harmony and proportion of the traditional institution

Figure 2.1 V&A courtyard, visitors enjoying the sun
Source: Ben Tunstall

Figure 2.2 V&A Chihuly glass chandelier
Source: Ben Tunstall

and its disciplinary power. Visitors amassed in the courtyard, having lunch from the cafe, enjoying the sun (Figure 2.1), can also feel themselves lightly set free from the sober requirements of the old institution by the example set by the sculptures. In the atrium proper, above the ticket desk, hangs a Dale Chihuly glass chandelier (Figure 2.2) whose intricate multicoloured extravagance both reasserts the museum's traditional valuing of craft and updates it to an exuberant, pop contemporary mannerism.

On a more enormous scale, at London's Tate Modern the industrial statist functionalism of the power station is juxtaposed, challenged and run through internally with functionless artworks. Its atrium, the great Turbine Hall, hosts temporary projects that are prime draws for visitors. The artworks blur the bounds between visitor and artwork: artworks as playgrounds (Holler's helter-skelters, Morris's timber playgrounds); a Segal performance where the performers appear to be ordinary visitors, until they rush through the space and collectively engage in inexplicable huddles. And artworks that play with the architecture of the atrium: a Kapoor biomorphic sculpture similar in spirit to those in the V&A courtyard whose form is unresolvable, whose inside and outside are interchangeable, filling the space in a mock display of freedom that renders the architecture dour; a crack running the length of the atrium's floor, destabilising the dependable, masculine solidity of the building.

Even the roof of the British Museum's Great Court has something of this, the Ove Arup super high-tech roof giving a sense of a hyper-real intervention into the old building. The shape of the roof, built from a self-supporting mesh of triangles, makes use of engineering that is self-ordering, and sits in opposition to the stable, transcendental values of classical architecture. Like a built diagram of the two forms of subjectivation in Foucault, self-creating form is juxtaposed with form constrained according to the external, timeless principles of classicism.

Henry James's sense of atria as spaces that 'capture and govern' the crowd or that 'concede rights' lives on in within the atrium, at the very least as a reminder of that which the liberated culture of the atrium has escaped. Indeed, we might suggest that the exuberance that informs postmodern culture exists in part simply because it posits a freedom away from disciplinary powers. Such juxtapositional practices and forms in some sense do not seek to simply get rid of the disciplinary form because they, in fact, arguably rely on the old disciplinary form of the museum, at the very least as a foil against which to stage their liberation. Within museum studies too, it has been commented by a number of writers that there is a dependence on the Foucauldian disciplinary power to posit a bugbear against which theorists may rail. Conn (2010) suggests that, in some studies, 'museums resemble penitentiaries, but with better interior decorating'.

A second feature of the accounts above is that they frequently feature not only liberation, but a degree of disorientation. For example, for Zukin the blurring of the commercial and the museum creates 'disorienting liminality'. For Koolhaas, Jameson's 'hyper-crowd' is the 'delirious masses'. Duncan suggests that the positioning of the new primitive art galleries in the Metropolitan Museum of Art nearest the atrium, which necessitated moving the Greek civilisation gallery further away, constructs 'the modern soul' as yearning 'not for the light of classical antiquity but for the presumably dark and incomprehensible creations of supposedly precivilized, ahistorical cultures' (Duncan, 1991, p. 101). Foucauldian museum studies has itself come in for attacks that it is itself based within a kind of anxiety. For example, Gaskell (1995) terms much of the Foucault-inspired anti-museum writing of the time as 'museophobic', a pathological stance which he takes as being based within a fear of looking at art objects in their undefinable complexity.

This continued – yet somehow disavowed – dependence on disciplinary power within the atrium, combined with this pervasive sense of disorientation and anxiety alongside liberation, suggest that there may be another side to the Foucauldian historical trajectory of the museum atrium. The movement beyond the panoptic may appear to produce not only liberations but anxieties – or in fact anxiety-provoking liberations. And beyond this, as we will see, we might even sense a slight kink within the cosmopolitan networked sense of the hyper-crowd, an anxiety that is less one of being governed, than an anxiety of not being governed. To explore these questions further, we turn to psychoanalysis.

The hysterical atrium

Instead of understanding the space of the atrium through a Foucauldian lens as a space where power acts on individuals and turns them into subjects, psychoanalysis allows us to think about the atrium as a space in which the pre-existing problems of subjectivity are dealt with in particular ways. For Lacanian psychoanalysis, the subject comes into being through the complex interaction of inherent, ahistorical factors within human existence and the particular social conditions through which these are expressed. For psychoanalysis, the equivalent of Foucault's power is the big Other (Dolar, 1998) – a locus that embodies the symbolic order – the abstract realm of law, kinship structures and linguistic logic that structures human relations. Human subjectivity is made up from the interaction between the way we enter into the symbolic order – through the acquisition of language, our being subject to social law and so on.

But in entering the symbolic, other aspects of human existence are left behind – the primal relation to the body and its biological drives, for example. Left behind within what Lacan calls the 'real', they are un-representable but continue to 'insist' beneath the symbolic. Entry into the symbolic order occurs through interrelations with the others who interact with us. For, Lacan there are two kinds of big Other – a symbolic Other and a real Other. The real Other is originally the child's mother, an obscure presence that is both a source of love and of deep anxiety as to what it wants (what it seems to lack) of the infant. To free the infant of the demands of the real Other, comes the symbolic Other, which in Lacan is the 'paternal functional' – not necessarily a father as such, but something that takes the maternal Other away from the infant (perhaps her work) and thereby opens a space of symbolisation for the infant and makes the infant realise they are not that thing that can fill the lack in the Other's desire. Following Hook (2010), we might argue that in fact there is a compatibility between the Foucauldian and psychoanalytic theories. In different historical periods, different historically specific symbolic orders come into existence, and though they may have oppressive forms of power within them, they also serve as collective means of managing anxiety in our proximity with the real Other. In the atrium then, we can replace the sense of panoptic power with the figment of the big Other. What this would mean is that within the disciplinary museum, while it may have been oppressive, it also functioned to organise the symbolic within the space – to create symbolic space that could prevent the anxieties of proximous other bodies, of our own drives, or perhaps of the institution as a whole, engulfing the visitor. It is a force of sublimation.

The psychoanalytic sense of the atrium as symbolic order allows us to think about further aspects of the contemporary atrium. Whereas for Foucault we are subjects of power, for Lacan, subjectivity is an ahistorical question of our being subject to language. Our 'subjectivation' is a matter of how we enter (or do not) into the symbolic. People who enter into the symbolic are neurotic (those for whom – for whatever reason – the symbolic is 'foreclosed' are psychotic, and are unseparated from the engulfments of the real). The basic position of neurosis is hysteria – a position of being a divided subject. This is a problem for the hysteric – they are within the symbolic and yet something still insists beyond the symbolic – the real. The real – the drives of the body – wander through their bodies (as the Ancient Greek's womb wandered through the hysteric's body). Where they cannot speak, their bodies do, in symptoms. In order to deal with the impossibilities within their being, hysterics seek out big Others. The first of these is the father, but he is only the first in a long line of big Others such as religion and ideology. Of the big Other, the hysteric asks the questions 'What am I?', 'Am I a man or a woman?' and the big Other is to answer what they are. However, the hysteric senses the lack within the big Other, provokes the desire of the big Other, but then cannot bear being the object of that desire. Thus while they search for the desire of the Other, seek for a master, once it is found, they undermine it. It is this that accounts for the simultaneous locating and evading of the image of the big Other within the contemporary atrium.

For the Lacanian divided subject, dealing with the impossibility of attaining the real object they lost when they entered the symbolic order, and which generates their desire, is via one of four discourses – that of the master, the university, the hysteric or the analyst. Each of these deals with the impossibility of their subjective position in a different way. These we can regard as having different salience in different historic periods. If we recall Duncan's historic movement of the museum from that of the prince to that of the nation state (and then arguably today to Bobbitt's 'market state'), we can also see this movement in relation to the historicity of the discourses. Žižek explains:

> The master's discourse stands not for the premodern master, but for the absolute monarchy, the first figure of modernity that effectively undermined the articulate network of feudal relations and interdependencies

[. . .] it is the 'Sun-King' Louis XIV with his *l'etat, c'est moi* who is the master par excellence. Hysterical discourse and university discourse then deploy two outcomes of the vacillation of the direct reign of the master: the expert-rule of bureaucracy that culminates in the biopolitics of reducing the population to a collection of *homo sacer* (what [. . .] Foucault [called] the society of 'discipline and punish'); the explosion of the hysterical capitalist subject that reproduces itself through permanent self-revolutionizing, the integration of the excess into the 'normal' functioning of the social link.

(Žižek, 2006, pp. 109–110)

Thus, the disciplinary museum sits within the university discourse, the dominant discourse of modernity. But the contemporary atrium introduces into that space the discourse of the hysteric. In so doing, it might be said to continue in its subjectivating role – but one in which the hystericisation – rather than the disciplining as such – of the subject is foregrounded towards the ends of the creation of the creative, entrepreneurial, flexibilised neoliberal subject.[1]

Contrasting the disciplinary and hysterical atrium

To conclude, we would like to contrast two atrium spaces which are perhaps more able to demonstrate the question of the historical shift that we have been exploring in this discussion. One space is from the Victorian period and the other is from the twenty-first century, but poignantly both are present today in the same building. The Royal Albert Memorial Museum in Exeter (RAMM) provides an interesting case showing both the disciplinary and hysterical atria. RAMM underwent a refurbishment project from 2005 to 2011. Led by Allies and Morrison Architects, it involved opening clearer routes through the old Victorian galleries, the creation of a central courtyard for a cafe and workshops, and the creation of a new entrance, which was at the back of the museum. At the time of the refurbishment, this new entrance was intended to become the new main entrance, giving visitors better wheelchair access and connecting to the park at the back of the museum. The atrium is a double height white cube. As well as a reception desk and shop display, it contains, at high level, a walkway that passes out of the atrium, allowing visitors to see the Roman wall that runs alongside the back of the museum. Leading from this new atrium are a temporary exhibition gallery and an initial gallery displaying icons from the collection including the museum favourite, a taxidermied giraffe known locally as Gerald. This space then leads onto the new routes that have been carved through the old labyrinthine spaces of the Victorian museum.

However, the museum also retained its old entrance, which leads directly from bustling Queen Street at the front of the building. An arched Victorian gothic entrance, it leads into a fairly small, although grand, entrance hall that confronts visitors with a flight of stairs directly ahead of them. On the balcony stands a statue of Albert, the Prince Consort. In the years after opening the refurbished museum, the majority of visitors continued to use the old entrance. The notion that the new entrance might become the main entrance became something of a quandary for the museum. By 2016, the shop was being moved from the new entrance to the old entrance. The museum had come to see the two entrances as being equal in status, and expressive of the multiple dimensions of the museum's character and programme. Traditional exhibitions – for example about the Tudor period or about Victorian Gothic architecture – are shown in galleries nearer to the old entrance. New exhibitions, such as a Gilbert and George exhibition, are shown in the temporary exhibition space at the back of the museum, and visitors interested in the museum's more contemporary programme enter the museum through the new entrance. The old entrance clearly continues to be popular because it is more convenient. However, there is also a sense that while visitors might be expected to find the traditional Victorian setting of the front entrance intimidating, they may in fact find the new entrance to be the intimidating way in. The atrium is not a piece of radical biomorphic architecture, it is a clean minimalist block. We might say it is somewhat austere in its minimalist whiteness, but we might also say that the space is a little vague. It is not quite clear where a visitor's attention should be focused, there is no central feature to the space, the symbolic representative of the institution is the initials RAMM in a somewhat anonymous-corporate logo.

We can, therefore, try to think about the entrances through our two lenses of Foucault and Lacan – and to what extent they represent a disciplinary and a hysterical atrium. In fact the intuition that the Victorian entrance might be more intimidating – and yet surprisingly is less so – might speak directly to the opposition between the two theoretical positions we have delineated. For a Foucauldian reading, we might suggest the Victorian entrance may seem like the embodiment of the panoptic disciplinary institution. Visitors enter and are expected to behave correctly, Albert looks down on the visitor with the stern stare of a patriarch (Figure 2.3). But on the other hand it is hard not to feel that perhaps it is the walkway overhead in the new atrium that might be more reminiscent of the panopticon (Figure 2.4). Underused by visitors, it appears to the newly arrived visitor to the atrium as a walkway from which someone high up – a representative of the institution presumably – might look down. Does an image of the unseen gaze of institutional power loom there?

For a Lacanian reading, Prince Albert's statue might be seen as an embodiment of the big Other. It secures the symbolic order by means of an architectural code that speaks to the sacred, and a master signifier of nationhood – Albert – and thereby places a visitor's relation to the institution and a wider web of symbolic institutional relations of the state. If we recall the transition from princely collection to that of the nation, Albert may here sit as lynchpin between the discourse of the sovereign master and the disciplinary power of the discourse of the university.

Figure 2.3 Albert looks down on visitors
Source: Ben Tunstall

The new entrance, on the other hand, both spatially and materially more diffuse and without a symbolic point of focus, leaves visitors less clear about their place within it, or about the kinds of symbolic structures of the state in which it might be implicated. Visitors with a more metropolitan outlook are thought to be more drawn to the new atrium, no doubt in part because of the more avant-garde temporary exhibitions, but perhaps in some way

Figure 2.4 Walkway in new atrium
Source: Ben Tunstall

also because the new entrance is itself expressive of their stance – of the way their relation to the symbolic order is organised, indeed because the new atrium allows them the hysteric's sense of both entering the museum, and yet evading the gaze of the 'master' figure of the big Other, Albert, which they know to be located at the old entrance. However, visitors whose cultural outlook is focused on more local and traditional values are apparently less likely to enter via the new space,. They seem happy to place themselves under Albert's gaze, and have their initial relation to the museum organised around him.

Such a reading may seem to advocate a conservative organisation of the museum, a return to deference before a sovereign to keep visitor anxiety at bay. But do more tangible signifiers of the big Other have to be conservative? Maybe the presence of a hysterical figure in the new atrium might make it equally appealing for both audiences. Perhaps part of the appeal of the pink walls in the old entrance is that they present a kind of hysterical counterpoint to Albert's master. Perhaps the new atrium could feature a statue of a son of Exeter, Fred Karno, born five years after Albert's death and three years before the founding of RAMM, who was a music hall impresario in the early twentieth century, who popularised custard-pie-in-the-face routines and gave Charlie Chaplin his first break. Or perhaps it is simply a shame that Gerald the Giraffe is positioned just around the corner from the atrium. Maybe Gerald's lofty yet benign animal gaze, entirely unknowably other, outside history, could best hold at bay the anxieties of the atrium.

Note

1 Perhaps the clearest example of the hysteria of the contemporary atrium is shown within the 2016 advertisement for Kenzo perfume in which a young woman rampages through a set of concert hall foyers and atria, her body writhing with roving libidinal energy as she confronts the patriarchal effigies of the institution and mirrors of her own image.

References

Bellah, R. (1985) *Habits of the Heart*, Berkeley, CA: University of California Press.
Bennett, T. (1995) *The Birth of the Museum*, London: Routledge.
Bennett, T. (2015) 'Thinking (with) Museums: From Exhibitionary Complex to Governmental Assemblage', in Macdonald, S. and Rees Leahy, H. (eds) *The International Handbooks of Museum Studies*, Chichester: Wiley.
Bobbitt, P. (2002) *The Shield of Achilles*, London: Penguin.
Castells, M. (1996) *The Rise of the Network Society, The Information Age: Economy, Society and Culture* Vol. I, Oxford: Blackwell.
Conn, S. (2010) *Do Museums Still Need Objects?* Philadelphia, PA: University of Pennsylvania Press.
Crimp, D. (1993) *On the Museum's Ruins*, Cambridge, MA: MIT Press.
Dolar, M. (1998) 'Where Does Power Come From?', *New Formations* 35.
Duncan, C. (1991) 'Art Museums and the Ritual of Citizenship', in Karp, I. and Lavine, S. (eds) *Exhibiting Cultures: The Poetics and Politics of Museum Display*, Washington: Smithsonian Institution Press.
Filippenko, A. (2016) Yoga in Museums around the World. Part I, *mu[see]um.net*, www.museeum.com/these-us-museums-invite-you-to-do-yoga-next-to-their-artworks/ Accessed February 2018.
Foucault, M. (1977) *Discipline and Punish*, London: Allen Lane.
Foucault, M. (1988) *Technologies of the Self: A Seminar with Michel Foucault*, Amherst, MA: University of Massachusetts Press.

Foucault, M. (1997) 'The Ethics of the Concern of the Self as a Practice of Freedom', in Rabinow, P. (ed.) *Essential Works of Foucault 1954–1984* Vol. 1, *Ethics*, London: Penguin.

Foucault, M. (1998) 'Different Spaces', in Faubion, J. (ed.) *Essential Works of Foucault 1954–1984* Vol. 2, *Aesthetics*, London: Penguin.

Foucault, M. (2002) 'The Subject and Power', in Faubion, J. (ed.) *Essential Works of Foucault 1954–1984* Vol. 3, *Power*, London: Penguin.

Gaskell, I. (1995) 'Review of "On the Museum's Ruins" by Douglas Crimp', *The Art Bulletin*, 77, 4.

Granovetter, M. (1973) 'The Strength of Weak Ties', *American Journal of Sociology*, 78:6.

Hook, D. (2010) 'The Powers of Emptiness', *Theory and Psychology*, 20:6, 855–870.

James, W. (1907) *The American Scene*, London: Chapman and Hall.

Jameson, F. (1991) *Postmodernism or the Cultural Logic of Late Capitalism*, London: Verso.

Kluitenberg, E. (2006) 'The Network of Waves: Living and Acting in a Hybrid Space', *Open*, 11, 6–16.

Koolhaas, R. and Foster, H. (2016) *Junkspace with Running Room*, New York: New York Review Books.

Lacan, J. (2007) *The Other Side of Psychoanalysis: Seminar XVII*, trans. Grigg, R., New York: W. W. Norton.

Miller, D. (1998) *A Theory of Shopping*, London: Polity.

Stallabrass, J. (2014) 'The Branding of the Museum', *Art History*, 37:1, 4–199.

Žižek, S. (2005) *Iraq: The Borrowed Kettle*, London: Verso.

Žižek, S. (2006) '*Objet a* in Social Links', in Clemens, J. and Grigg, R. (eds) *Jacques Lacan and the Other Side of Psychoanalysis*, Durham, NC: Duke University Press.

Zukin, S. (1993) *Landscapes of Power: From Detroit to Disney World*, Berkeley, CA: University of California Press.

3 The complexity of welcome
Visitor experience at the museum threshold

Colin Mulberg

Typically, when museums present images of visitors at their entrance and foyer, they tend to pick one type of scene. Many promotional films, photos and pictorials of design proposals have a tendency to show interested visitors in the midst of social activity – people are meeting and greeting family and friends, standing or sometimes sitting and chatting, waiting for others, using their mobile phones or tablets, or engaging with the venue and its contents. Visitors are often smiling, booked groups or school classes are paying rapt attention to whoever is addressing them and families already look full of wonder and enjoyment. Spend a day observing museum thresholds and, indeed, in many cases you will see much of this actually happen. For visitors, their visit starts well before they see the first display. A popular museum at peak time is quite a whirl of activity, making the threshold spaces busy, lively, noisy places. It is understandable, therefore, that museums want to present all of this as part of the experience of visiting.

But this is not the whole story of the visitor experience. There are other activities that take place at museum thresholds that are not so easy to see. Observe for an extended period of time and you might see people enter and look around anxiously, stand and study notices and price lists intently, glare at posters and temporary boards, read leaflets and digital information screens, re-read guidebooks in digital or print form and seek out direction signs. In many cases they are certainly not smiling, but looking confused or anxious. For these activities, social interaction with others is often directed and perfunctory. Sometimes, visitors are frowning and clearly far from enjoying themselves.

Visitor tracking studies in museum threshold spaces can reveal a surprising, complex picture. For example, a large tracking study of over 700 visitors to New Walk Museum and Art Gallery, Leicester (UK) observed and tracked individual visitors and groups as they negotiated the museum foyer. Though there were preferred routes through the space, visitors often engaged in a range of activites, taking different amounts of time, and moved around in varied ways. Many visitors engaged with the foyer in a very individual fashion. Even though the foyer is a visually simple square, the study suggests that the threshold can be a complicated space in terms of visitor experience.

Even though we may observe visitors, the signs for some activities at thresholds are subtle and only hint at what visitors are experiencing. Dig deeper and we uncover a whole, extended process that visitors have to go through before they start their visit, a process that involves time, effort, energy, emotional engagement and thought. To understand what happens to visitors at museum thresholds we therefore need to examine these activities and the process of visiting in more detail. For this stage not only holds the key to whether visitors decide to visit and what visitors think their visit will be, but it has the potential also to colour their subsequent experience. In many instances, visitors have to work quite hard before they start their visit and this work comes before they can enjoy their leisure time. A crucial element in understanding the visitor experience is to analyse the nature of this work as well as when and where it occurs.

How visitors 'work' at the threshold

For visitors, museums are rarely the centre of their world. To get to a visitor's perspective, we need to understand that visits do not just happen; visitors decide to make them happen. There are many other things that visitors could choose to do and indeed do choose (Black, 2012, p. 28). Museums that are mentioned on social media or rated on travel websites and mobile apps are seen alongside a wealth of alternative activities. As a visit is not inevitable, visitors somehow have to find out about a museum, think about a visit and come to a decision before they arrive, step inside and start their visit. This is rarely instantaneous and nearly always involves a process of different types of physical and cognitive effort.

The idea of visitors having to apply effort as part of the museum experience is well established. Back in 1994, Eilean Hooper-Greenhill (2011) flagged up how visitors are actively engaged in the process of communication, have to apply effort when they visit and that a range of work is needed on arrival. More recent examples include Falk and Dierking's (2013) exploration of decision-making and judgement as part of the visitor experience and the analysis by Bitgood (2013) into the work that visitors do when experiencing museum displays. Though models of the visitor experience by these authors and others focus mostly on what happens once a visit has already started, they are useful for highlighting that when visitors work, they go through a process of decision-making involving several stages. For example, in Bitgood's Attention-Value model, visitor attention is dependent on detection plus value; engaged attention leads to a range of desirable outcomes. In this model visitors go through a process of searching for and detecting exhibits while avoiding distractions. They then follow a decision-making process to make a value judgement on whether to engage with what they have found or seek alternative actions. Visitors must combine physical factors with a whole raft of other issues including satisfaction, interest and available alternatives into value judgements as part of their decision-making. Bitgood calls the amount of time and effort the 'workload' (Bitgood, 2013, pp. 68–9; 95), whereas another description is 'energisation of behaviour (the amount of energy or effort expended)' (Packer and Ballantyne, 2002, p. 185).

For a deeper understanding of the nature of this decision-making, it is useful to borrow from research outside the museum, heritage and cultural sectors. The first helpful discipline is that of designing online user experiences (UX design). Instead of focusing on the content of a website from the owner's viewpoint, UX design develops the approach of understanding the process from the user's point of view, including methods to research what users are thinking and feeling, the decisions that they make and the effort they put in as they progress through a site.

Though digital websites are a different environment from physical museum thresholds, there are specific similarities and parallels that are useful. Pioneers such as Krug (2000) and Cohen (2003) emphasised that websites were not central to the world of the user, who makes choices on whether to visit a site, stay on it or leave. Moreover, putting in effort and making decisions is a form of work 'and once they arrive, their work's only just begun. They have to figure out what your site does, how it works, and where to find what they need' (Cohen, 2003, p. 45). Krug's main premise is that for users, 'work' is where they have to ask questions and find the answers. Sometimes, these questions could be about what to do or how to do something, but they could equally be about how the users can get what they want or as part of making a decision. If the answer is obvious, the question is answered and the question mark disappears. For Krug, the aim is for the user to look at each screen and understand 'what it is about and how to use it – without expending any effort thinking about it' (Krug, 2000, p. 11). The aim for good web design is therefore to eliminate question marks (Krug, 2000, p. 17).

In museums, and heritage and cultural venues, visitors could go through a similar process. Hennes (2002, p. 115) notes that 'the visitor is the one who initiates the experience itself, becoming an active explorer, a problem solver seeking an answer to his or her own question'. Kolb (2013, p. 127) suggests that there are three types of question relating to features, benefits and values that people ask before deciding to attend: 'What is it? What does it do for me? What does it mean to me?' Black (2012, pp. 70–1) gives a longer list of questions that visitors to museums ask on arrival or when working out the conceptual orientation of a venue:

> What is there to see and do? What options are there? How long will it take? Where can I have coffee? Who is there to help? What activities are on today? What is this museum/exhibition/activity about? What has it got to do with me, the visitor? How is it organised, thematically and physically? What can I, the visitor, expect to gain from it?

Visitors clearly need answers to a range of questions about a potential visit, as part of their decision-making process. A typical list of questions highlighting concerns about the nature of the visit could look something like Figure 3.1.

This list is by no means exhaustive, as studies into visitor experience and visitor motivations in museums and heritage venues suggest other possibilities. For example, visitors can be looking for a social experience as they often come in pairs or small groups (Coffee, 2007; Black, 2012, p. 66). They can also be motivated by personal reasons for visiting, opportunities for cognitive activity, opportunities for learning/discovery and perceptions of an interest-arousing environment as well as enjoyment, restoration/relaxation and self-fulfilment (Packer and Ballantyne, 2002, pp. 187–9). The exact mix of questions and their relative importance might well be down to personal preference as well as the nature of a particular venue (Packer and Ballantyne, 2002, p. 185). Equally, for some visitors, key questions will arise before others, or questions will be linked; for example, 'How special is this?' could relate to 'How cool is this?' and to posting something on social media.

When considering a museum threshold, though questions and concerns are individual, there may be some that are common to a number of visitors. For example, working with the Project Team for the redevelopment of the Royal Marines Museum at Southsea, Hampshire (UK) we undertook a complete knowledge audit to review everything we knew about the museum's audiences and then conducted extensive targeted visitor research to

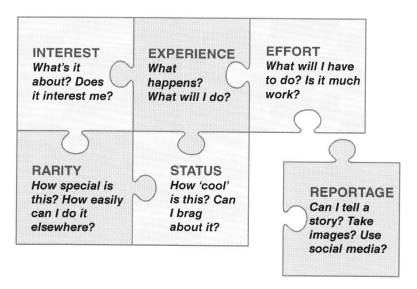

Figure 3.1 Typical visitor questions reflecting concerns about a visit
Source: Colin Mulberg

plug the gaps in visitor knowledge. The research included visitor interviews, observation, focus groups, questionnaires, visitor tracking and visitor journey modelling. A key concern that surfaced many times was the logistics of planning and reaching the museum and what else was nearby, to make the journey into more of an occasion (Royal Marines Museum, 2014). Yet, during visitor research for the redevelopment of the World Rugby Museum at Twickenham Stadium, Twickenham, Middlesex (UK) travel did not seem a worry, especially for fans going to a match there anyway. A different concern was revealed: that if visitors entered the museum built into the stadium, they would be pitch-side and not able to leave again to meet friends in the stadium precincts before the game. For these rugby fans, the museum could come between them and enjoying food, drink and sharing a great sporting occasion at one of the best and most famous rugby stadiums in the world (World Rugby Museum, 2011).

Understanding the 'visitor offer'

The questions and concerns of visitors can also relate to their audience type. A Europe-wide research project into senior visitors (over 55) identified a range of characteristics, covering physical factors (e.g. greater requirement for rest), intellectual (e.g. increased interest in researching information), emotional (e.g. preference to reflect on personal experiences), social (e.g. desire for personal engagement with staff/volunteers) and cultural (e.g. desire for sites to be placed in context) (Seccombe and Lehnes, 2015). These visitor concerns and questions tally with another widely shared view, that museum visitors have their own agendas. Hooper-Greenhill (2011, p. 47) notes that personal agenda is one of the factors that affect how audiences interpret their experiences of museums. Falk and Dierking (2013, p. 98) suggest that the visitor agenda is a key part in shaping the visitor experience. The visitor agenda includes identity-related motivations, expectations, prior interest and knowledge. In the Attention-Value model, 'previsit agendas are an important aspect of the satisfaction and benefits derived from a museum visit' (Bitgood, 2013, p. 69). Again, there are lessons from UX design, where users approach the site for their own purposes and priorities and use each screen in their own way, which may differ from that envisioned by the owners and designers. Users are in control of their own web experience (Cohen, 2003, p. 45). Likewise, for museums, visitors 'pursue personal interests' so 'the visitor drives the experience' (Hennes, 2002, pp. 106; 113). More than this, 'not all visitors seek the same experience from museums. In fact, the opposite is the case – museum users increasingly seek to customise their visits to meet their own specific needs' (Black, 2012, p. 52). Museum visitors have their own agendas when approaching the museum, and these are reflected in the questions they ask. They use these questions and subsequent answers to form ideas about whether to visit, how to visit, what a visit will be like and how worthwhile it will be.

Though visitors' agendas are ultimately individual, they have substantial elements that can be determined with patient research. For example, during the redevelopment of the National Football Museum, Manchester (UK), the project looked at the agendas of various football fans. At first it seemed that their agendas were so diverse that one museum could not hope to give these visitors what they wanted. Detailed, qualitative visitor research revealed some themes that were central to fans, including: the team they supported; their national team; national and international competitions; football heritage; football heroes; the modern game; playing football; the role of fans; popular culture around football; doing something practical in the museum; and how dedicated and knowledgeable a supporter they were. The majority of each fan's agenda was made up of varying combinations from understandable themes (National Football Museum, 2010a; 2010b; 2011).

There are parallels between visitor agendas and another area outside the museum, heritage and cultural sectors: retail. In the retail sector it is understood that a key focus is on how well the retailer matches the customer's needs and wishes. However, there is no objective measure of this. What is important is the customer's perception of how well their needs and wishes are being met. This perception is a combination of physical factors (retail environment, product and service selection) and relationships (engagement). When combined with price, this becomes the Value Proposition (Murray, 2013). Applied to museum visitors, this is useful in that it suggests a number of things are happening during the decision-making process. First, it is clear that visitor's questions, concerns and agendas are varied; they are multi-dimensional as they relate to more than one aspect of their visit. They combine a variety of concerns, including physical, social, emotional and economic, all packaged together. Second, visitors are matching the answers against their own agenda. How well they match determines judgements about value and how worthwhile a visit will be. As part of the matching process, visitors construct a view and understanding of what the visit will be like for them. This contains perceptions, judgements and values. As in UX design, visitors are in control. Like the stages of asking questions and seeking answers, this matching stage of the process takes time and effort.

Exploring the concept of how value propositions could relate to the museum visitor experience a little further, we could call the outcome of this matching process the 'visitor offer'. This shares similarities with 'the cultural package' in the cultural sector, which 'is the complete package of the performance/object along with everything else the experience has to offer' (Kolb, 2013, pp. 133–4). In the case of museums, the visitor offer would be the visitor's idea of what the museum is going to offer them. If the visitor offer closely matches their agenda, then the offer will seem strong, with great potential. If the visitor offer does not really match a visitor's agenda then the visitor offer will seem weak and only of limited interest.

Figure 3.2 How museum visitors construct the visitor offer
Source: Colin Mulberg

The key point here is that, seen through the assumptions of the 'Value Proposition' model, the visitor offer is the visitor's impression of what is on offer. It is their perception of everything about the visit that is worth thinking about. For visitors at this stage, before they have started their visit or even decided to visit, the visitor offer *is* the visit; even if this differs from what the museum thinks it offers. The process of formulating their concerns into questions, working to find answers, and comparing the answers against their own agendas to construct the visitor offer creates their own 'visit universe'. We can think of this as the whole visit as perceived by the visitor and captured in their imagination; it is a mental picture of the visit that visitors create. The visit universe is formed by each visitor as they go through the process of understanding the visitor offer. The picture will be complete for some visitors and hazy for others, depending on how thoroughly they have tackled the formation process.

Visitor 'investment' and the value of a visit

It is misleading to think of the cost of a visit to a museum as only the price that visitors pay for things such as tickets, transport and refreshments. In terms of the museum and cultural visitor experience, the cost to visitors is more than monetary, as 'even if there is no charge for attendance or other monetary cost, there is still the cost to the customer in time and effort to attend' (Kolb, 2013, p. 73). Borrowing another financial term, visitors could be said to be 'investing' in their visit. They invest time, effort and sometimes money in the experience of visiting. They do this in the hope of getting something back from their visit that is rewarding to them – a 'return'. Falk and Dierking (2013, p. 44) call this return visitor 'benefits' and list a variety of forms that these could take, such as social, recreational, learning and personal enrichment, hobby and professional interest, and reverential. Other researchers also see the visitor return in terms of benefits and/or satisfaction (Harrison and Shaw, 2004; Packer, 2008; Chen and Chen, 2010; Bitgood, 2014). In retail terms, the price that consumers pay is linked to the perceived value of the services on offer. It is important to note that prices do not create value, they only capture it; they encompass the value consumers perceive in the retailer's goods and services (Murray, 2013, p. 10). This is also true for museum, heritage and cultural visiting, as:

> when making purchase decisions, consumers will consider the benefits they will receive versus the cost. *Value* is the term used to describe this relationship between the satisfaction the benefits provide and the cost the consumer must pay . . . While it is true that price is important to most consumers, financial costs are not the only factor when assessing value. Consumers also consider the entire package of benefits they will receive from attending.
>
> (Kolb, 2013, p. 73, original emphasis)

Again, as in retail, this is very much a personal judgement and based on individual perception: 'What's important is that all of these "benefits" are self-referential – it's not whether someone else would consider them valuable or not, it's whether I find them valuable' (Falk and Dierking, 2013, p. 43).

Yet the returns from a museum visit are not guaranteed. More than this, they are largely unknown for visitors before a visit has started and especially so before visitors have either reached or crossed the museum threshold. However, visitors have to estimate both the likely investment that a visit will require and the returns of matching their own agendas when they work through the process of constructing their own visitor offer and assessing its value. It could be argued, however, that what many visitors might well add up is the amount of work that they have put in so far – their investment to date. This could have a considerable bearing on their estimate of what their total investment will have to be. Again, looking at the experience of web users is helpful. The amount of work is crucial in UX design as 'if something requires a large investment of time – or looks like it will – it's less likely to be used' (Krug, 2000, p. 6).

As with visitors in museums, website users are constantly making value judgements and the amount of work they have to do is part of this judgement. Krug (2000, p. 15) argues, that:

> As a rule, people don't *like* to puzzle over how to do things. The fact that the people who built the site didn't care enough to make things obvious – and easy – can erode our confidence in the site and its publishers.
>
> (original emphasis)

For museum visitors, higher costs decrease value (Bitgood, 2014). In simple terms, if visitors have to work hard finding answers to their questions to match against their own agendas, then they could well view a visit as needing a high investment of their time and effort. This means that the return will also have to be high for the visit to be valued. This, in turn, will colour the perception of how worthwhile a visit will be. So visitors' perception of a visit includes their investment of time and effort so far.

Building visitor 'commitment' towards a visit

To understand what happens to visitors as they work through the different stages of constructing the visitor offer before they decide to visit, we can turn to another aspect of retailing. The retail buying process describes the process that consumers follow when making buying decisions. A classic buying process looks something like that shown in Figure 3.3.

This has useful similarities to the decision-making process of museum visitors. The first stage is for a visitor to feel a need or want that can be considered a problem. The natural response to this problem state is to seek a solution. A visit will only occur if the solution to the problem could involve visiting a museum. The 'problem' state may be expressed in a vague way, for example, 'I am bored', or in a specific way, 'I want to go to Alton Towers' (Cox and Brittain, 2004, p. 79). The Pre-Purchase Activity is a problem-solving stage and will involve the visitor becoming aware of a particular museum, working out the visitor offer, perceiving the visitor offer favourably when compared to alternatives, deciding the visitor offer is compelling enough to visit, then finally deciding to visit (Kolb, 2013, pp. 75–7). The Purchase Decision occurs when the visitor takes active steps to visit and turns this into action, by arriving at the museum, crossing

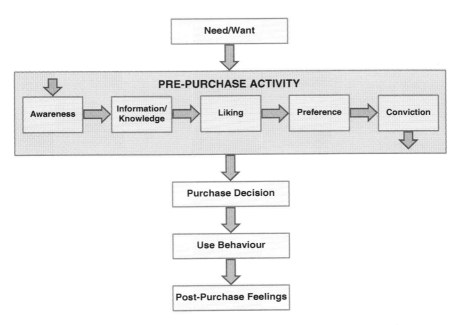

Figure 3.3 The classic retail buying process gives insight into the stages of museum visitors' decision-making

Source: Colin Mulberg, adapted from Cox and Brittain (2004); Kolb (2013)

the threshold, making any necessary purchases and starting a visit. Even starting this stage does not guarantee a purchase, as 'the purchase decision is not a single decision but a bundle of decisions, any one of which can result in a change of mind and an alternative route being followed' (Cox and Brittain, 2004, p. 80).

The retail buying process does not stop once a purchase has been made. Sometimes customers are disappointed by the performance of their purchase or experience 'post-cognitive dissonance', which is dissatisfaction with their purchase and the purchase process, even if their purchase is performing well. Dissatisfaction can be caused by a range of factors, 'such as the tension created by wondering if the right choice has been made – particularly if the alternatives were also attractive' (Cox and Brittain, 2004, p. 80). In a similar fashion, in the retail Value Proposition customer satisfaction is based on a comparison with customer expectations. Customers are satisfied when their experience exceeds their expectations and dissatisfied when their experience is below their expectations (Murray, 2013, pp. 123–4).

Retail viewpoints are useful in understanding what happens to visitors in museums. Museums could be described as selling an experience, rather than the delivery of a service or a product you can hold in your hand, and the quality of this experience is key to visitor expectations and perceived value (Goulding, 2000; Chen and Chen, 2010). Museum visitors' experience of working through the retail buying process has similarities with users' experience of working through websites in that both take work in terms of time and effort. The cost of this work contributes directly to the success of the purchase and satisfaction during use and afterwards. In retail, successful retailers focus on making the problem-solving stage of Pre-Purchase Activity easy for consumers (Cox and Brittain, 2004, pp. 79–80).

The retail buying process also highlights how each stage needs to be completed successfully before consumers/visitors will progress to the next. At any stage, they can select alternatives or stop working and abandon the purchase. More than this, each stage is dependent on the previous stages and builds on what went before. Furthermore, completing one stage successfully merely builds commitment to explore the next stage. As the consumer/visitor progresses through the stages, the commitment to the purchase accumulates. In the early stages, commitment might well be weak. Only as the case for making a purchase takes shape does commitment strengthen through stage after stage, until it is strong enough to lead to a decision to purchase.

In this model, consumers/visitors do not abandon their commitment once they have reached the purchase stage. In the retail buying process their commitment also affects the stages further on. Continuing with this approach to visitor expectations, having worked through many stages and developed commitment, this then becomes the benchmark against which performance and post-purchase feelings are measured. In terms of museum visitors, they could well be comparing how satisfying their visit was with their expectations developed in the decision-making process (Sheng and Cheng, 2012). High visitor satisfaction levels are also related to post-purchase perceptions, intentions and behaviour, such as a return visit or recommending to others (Harrison and Shaw, 2004).

For museums, visitors will need to develop and build commitment as they work through the stages of Pre-Purchase Activity. Ideally this will build a commitment strong enough to rouse them to take action, plan a visit and arrive at the museum threshold. At this point visitors' commitment must stay strong or strengthen, so that they follow through their purchase decision by starting their visit. What visitors do and feel during their visit and afterwards is also directly related to the judgements and commitment they have made leading up to their visit. It determines their perception of the visit and how enjoyable it was in comparison.

Where visitor 'work' happens

Before a visit

The different approaches to understanding what happens to visitors when they visit (Visitor Experience models; Digital UX Design; retail Value Proposition; Visitor Offer; Visitor Investment and Value; Retail Buying Process) all point to the same thing: visitors have to follow a decision-making process, and work, before they start their visit.

Though some visitors may only encounter a museum as they are passing by, for most visitors some of their work happens before they arrive at the threshold. To consider a museum as the destination for a possible visit, at the very least visitors need to know something about it – the Awareness stage in the Retail Buying Process:

> Before consumers can make a decision to consume a product, they need to first be aware of its availability. Their product awareness or knowledge level can vary from the superficial, knowing the product exists, to comprehensive familiarity with all the types and levels of the product.
> (Kolb, 2013, p. 125)

As museum visitors progress through the stages of the decision-making process, they will need to find sources that will help them answer their questions, make judgements and build commitment to visit. Typically, different visitors use a variety of sources for their pre-arrival activity. To take the example of the Camera Obscura and World of Illusions, Edinburgh (UK), this includes: the museum website; leaflets; adverts; social media; museum listed on other websites; other brochures/leaflets; tourist information centre; independent tourist guidebooks (Visitrac, 2015). Other sources of information for museum venues include emails from museum, posters, museum featured in media and word-of-mouth.

However, the picture is probably more complicated than merely finding out how many visitors use each information source – a standard marketing question. It is highly likely that no-one uses all these sources to work through their pre-visit decisions and no single source is used by everyone. Visitors could well be using multiple sources with differing weighting/levels of influence. Though it may be possible to identify trends with particular types of audience (e.g. how visitors aged 16–24 use social media), it is probable that the total mix of sources used by visitors is an individual choice, similar to the way that a visitor's concerns and questions are individual. It could also be that particular sources have differing impacts depending on when visitors encounter them in the decision-making process.

The list of sources is also a mix of those where the museum has direct control (e.g. museum website, leaflets, posters, adverts, direct emails, generated social media), sources where the museum has partial control (e.g. features in media, tourist information) and those where the museum has little control (e.g. most social media, other websites, independent tourist guidebooks). Sources will therefore vary in clarity, accuracy, quality and usefulness.

Outside the museum

Putting all this together suggests that visitors do not arrive at the museum threshold with a uniform view of the museum. Depending on what sources they found, how they used them, at what stage in the decision-making process they accessed them, how useful they were and how much work was involved, visitors could arrive at a museum with anything ranging from a fully formed view of what their visit will be like, to only a hazy notion of what awaits them. They will have differing perceptions of their visit, differing judgements as to its value and differing levels of commitment. This is especially true of different members of a party, who may not have been involved equally in every step of the decision-making process.

The result is that when visitors reach the threshold of a museum, they will most likely still have work to do. Data from visitor research suggests that some of this work starts outside, at the approach to the museum entrance. For example, 17 per cent of visitors to the Camera Obscura and World of Illusions, Edinburgh (UK), stated that they did not look at a source of information before they visited (Visitrac, 2015), so presumably these visitors will therefore start forming much of their judgement about their visit as they reach the museum. At other venues, visitors say that on-street promotion (e.g. banners/posters) outside the museum were influential. Falk and Dierking (2013, p. 180) note that the architecture of museums, including the façade, conveys messages and contributes to first impressions.

For museums that have significant passing trade, visitors have to go through the decision-making process on the spot, to arrive at a judgement about whether to investigate further. In terms of the retail buying process, the outside of the museum should build visitor commitment to move on to the next stage of the process. In retailing, the entrance should be designed to encourage the customer into the store (Cox and Brittain, 2004, p. 186) and to be the retail experience gateway as 'the first few steps that the customer takes into a store set the stage for the shopping experience' (Murray, 2013, p. 50).

Inside the museum

Once visitors are inside, the aim is to continue building commitment through the remaining buying process stages: 'The actual time of purchase is important since it can help or hinder the decision process [. . .] Finally, the purchase transaction is important as it is the last impression the customer has of the purchase situation' (Cox and Brittain, 2004, p. 80). For museum visitors, entering the museum is therefore not the end of their work. The first step is one of transformation. Visitors have to change modes from being a traveller to being a visitor. This often involves time and space to adjust clothing, bags, umbrellas, travel maps, baby buggies, and to prepare for the tasks ahead.

A main activity for visitors at the threshold is to complete their understanding of the visitor offer, based on what they see and experience around them. If visitors come with a fully formed view of their offer, then the threshold can fill in any gaps and reinforce their judgement. If a visitor's understanding of the offer is only partial, then they may look for clues, impressions, information and anything else that will help them grasp what their visit will be like and how closely it will match their agenda. Even though visitors have travelled to the museum and are not likely to withdraw from visiting, a positive commitment is important. It will be used to guide their decisions while visiting and help form their expectations, against which the success of their visit will later be judged. It could also influence their commitment to undertake or purchase various extra activities, such as tours or events.

The influence of the museum environment or setting on visitor experience, enjoyment and expectations is well recognised, though mainly in relation to exhibits and interpretation (e.g. Goulding, 2000; Packer, 2008). More than this, the museum experience itself can be seen as the interrelationship between visitors and the museum environment (Roppola, 2012). The threshold could well be a physical area of the museum where this is also true. Visitors seeking to add to their understanding of the visitor offer could use the opportunity of their physical surrounds just as they arrive to seek further information, clues and impressions. Visitors could draw on information panels, slogans, images, small displays, posters, leaflets, 'What's on' boards, digital screens and anything else that will help them to form an idea of the likely visitor offer that awaits them. They may well visit the information desk, ask questions of staff and look at ticket categories and prices

46 Colin Mulberg

and the names of different options, attractions, galleries, exhibitions and museum spaces.

Once visitors commit to visit, they might have to make further decisions, such as which type of ticket to give the best value – single ticket/s versus bundled package; individual ticket versus group or family ticket; one-off entry versus ticket that gives free entry for a year; pay extra for additional attractions or booked tours, etc. In some cases, visitors also need to book a time slot to visit popular attractions or exhibitions, decide whether to hire an audio guide and/or buy a printed museum guide now and carry it around, or perhaps decide later.

Even with a ticket, museum map and leaflets in hand, there is still more work to be done. Visitors need to decide their plan of action and where to start. For a small museum or single exhibition, visitors can successfully adopt the default strategy of starting at the first thing and seeing everything from that point on. For larger venues, the default approach can feel unsatisfactory, as there is no guarantee that time spent on early experiences will give visitors what they want. In these cases, visitors may have to interpret the visitor offer in terms of how much they want to see, where it is (e.g. how far, how many floors), how easy/difficult it is to get there, how long seeing it will take, how much time they want to spend, when the venue closes and how to get value and a return on their investment.

Structuring a visit is a combination of the visitor's ideals for their visit combined with making sense of the practicalities in front of them. Visitors need to map the visitor offer onto the physical museum. This includes understanding a range of factors, such as the building they are in, the cognitive structure or framework that governs the museum and how its displays are organised, the nature of the institution itself, where various visitor facilities are and how to find them (Hooper-Greenhill, 2011, pp. 91–3; Falk and Dierking, 2013, pp. 183–8; 266–7).

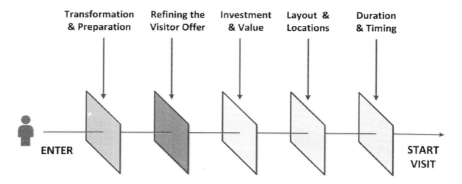

Figure 3.4 How visitors structure their visit at the museum threshold
Source: Colin Mulberg

For some museums, a successful experience may only be possible with a structured visit. For example, when visitors enter the main entrance to a number of venues, they may not be completely aware of the sheer size of the museum and the number of floors, galleries and displays. It is sometimes possible to look at the information in the foyer, enter and approach the information desk without addressing the scale of what awaits inside.

Experience of working with many museums on this challenge suggests that visitors seem to deal with this situation in different ways. Some visitors plan their visit near the information desk, standing with their museum map and discussing where to go. Others start planning their visit once they focus on the main exhibition hall, or the point at which they are confronted with the sight of a vast atrium with many floors or a large gallery extending as far as their eye can see. Some visitors start at the nearest exhibit and progress along the first gallery and then change to planning the rest of their time by studying an information panel, consulting their map or seeking help. Whichever approach visitors take, it is another situation where they work by putting in time and effort. Structuring a visit is yet more investment in a visit before the return of enjoying the displays.

The challenge for museums

A major task for any museum is to understand the amount of work that visitors do pre-visit and at their threshold so as to reduce this work as much as possible. Further, museums can play a supporting role to help visitors answer their own questions by providing guidance, resources, information and tools or other means that visitors require (Hennes, 2002, p. 115). Doing this will increase the likelihood of people visiting and improve their experience when they do. However, to reduce visitor work requires museums facing up to a series of challenges, some of which require a long, hard look at how much museums understand their visitors and what exactly they offer them.

Developing visitor insight

If museums are to reduce the amount of work that visitors do, then they need to help them to answer their questions and construct visitor offers. To do this, they need to understand what questions visitors might ask, what their agendas are likely to be and how visitors work through the decision-making process. This has similarities to the ways that businesses strive to understand their customers. This is a challenge for museums, as this level of visitor insight has not previously been a strength of the sector. Museums will need to develop ways of learning about their visitors across a wide range of activities, to build up an extensive picture of visitor motivations, interests, concerns and values. Each museum will need to look at where opportunities arise to gain visitor insight within the organisation while using available resources. Reducing visitor work will require museums to develop a variety of ways of thinking about their visitors. Sometimes, it will be helpful to aggregate visitors into distinct audience groups with shared characteristics, to better understand commonalities. At other times, it will be necessary to recognise that visitors are making decisions as individuals, so that their experience on the ground is what matters to them. In this way, museums can support visitors to customise their experience and tailor it to their individual requirements (Black, 2012, p. 68). On a strategic level, gaining visitor insight is part of developing a widespread focus on visitors and becoming a learning organisation – every interaction with visitors is an opportunity to learn. In many cases this will be require a change of organisational culture, away from a focus on simply delivering content and programmes.

Refining museum marketing

A key role of museum marketing is to communicate with visitors. Venues are adapting to a changing marketing landscape, including a fragmentation of the market over multiple communication channels and the growing importance of digital and social media. However, museums will need to move away from the aim of merely raising awareness, as this is only the first stage in the retail buying process. They will need to consider layered marketing that supports different stages in the decision-making process that meets the needs of visitors at each stage – 'making the intangible tangible' (Black, 2012, p. 50). This more sophisticated approach is highly dependent on gaining deep visitor insight and aligns the marketing needs of museums with the development of a visitor-centred focus.

Shaping pre-purchase activity

Using the retail decision-making model to understand visitors' pre-purchase activity, it is highly likely that overall, visitors draw on a range of sources when building a picture of the visitor offer, prior to committing to visit. Though museums do not have total control over all these sources, they can make the most of the sources they do control and can influence. For example, museums can 'make anticipation of the visit part of the experience through the image projected beyond the museum' (Black, 2012, p. 68). A change in approach would involve museums moving away from the notion of merely supplying information and slogans, to a more detailed approach to addressing visitors' concerns and promoting a visit as matching visitors' agendas. To do this, museums will need to reassess and refocus their publicity and social media, to work harder on supporting pre-purchase activity. This could include the messages that are put across in the media, what advertising and promotional literature promises potential visitors and how it influences expectations as well as the look and branding, including the website (Black, 2012, p. 50). If the museum can provide visitors directly with much of what they want through these stages of the process, then there will be less need for them to look elsewhere for other sources.

Using the museum threshold effectively

Museums mostly control what happens at their thresholds, both outside the museum, at the museum entrance and inside. This gives great scope for them to reduce the work that visitors have to do before starting a visit. A key first step is for museums to understand and acknowledge that visitors will be answering questions, building a picture of the visitor offer, working through a purchase process and structuring a visit, all at their threshold. If this is combined with deep insight into what their visitors want and value, then the threshold can be used to build up commitment, reinforce positive aspects of the visitor offer, help with decision-making and reduce time and effort. To do this, museums will need to move away from thinking of their thresholds as neutral spaces, to viewing threshold areas as spaces that have much to deliver and that require at least as much planning as exhibitions and displays. Part of this change of approach will require museums to examine ways of communicating the visitor offer in easily understood packages that match the agendas of different audiences and help visitors to structure a visit. Possibilities include reviewing the effectiveness of signage that leads first-time visitors to the venue, how the first impression compares to the expectations and perceptions raised in the media and in promotional literature and the appearance and motivational appeal of the entrance (Black, 2012, p. 50). Museums will benefit from planning in depth how to deal with visitors on arrival. The museum entrance and inside-threshold can be developed as a series of 'scene setters' that enhance understanding of the visitor offer and serve to locate the visitor in time and space, as well as providing detailed orientation to the venue. If this is done effectively, visitors start their visit feeling comfortable and are more likely to have an enjoyable and satisfying experience. If this provision is absent at the start, visitors could well begin their visit feeling negative and their experience starts with frustration, anxiety and disorientation (Goulding, 2000, pp. 271–4). Reworking museum thresholds may also result in reordering interior spaces into different zones that fulfil specific functions, what we might call transformation and orientation zones. Physical activities can also be developed in detail, from orientation through to ticketing, spatial layout and structuring a visit (Goulding, 2000, pp. 273–4; Black, 2012, p. 50).

Developing an integrated approach

The redevelopment of Portsmouth Historic Dockyard (PHD) (UK), is a useful example of meeting these challenges. Visitor research on perceptions of the Dockyard showed that many visitors did not understand the visitor

Figure 3.5 Portsmouth Historic Dockyard threshold before redevelopment: visitors were given little help in understanding the visitor offer, the various ticket options or working out what to see

Source: National Museum of the Royal Navy

Figure 3.6 PHD threshold after redevelopment: decision-making is supported by impressions of the experience of each attraction, purchase decisions are explained clearly and visitors are guided in structuring their visit

Source: National Museum of the Royal Navy

offer and arrived at the threshold and started their visit in confusion. Visitor interviews and observation on site revealed that visitors found almost every step of the decision-making process hard work. Even buying a ticket seemed complex, with different categories and options, but little help or visual support. In some cases, the work was too much for visitors, who simply gave up and left. The National Museum of the Royal Navy focused on improving the visitor experience by taking an integrated approach to redeveloping the PHD threshold. The first step was to reinterpret existing visitor research and audience profiling to develop packaged visitor offers that these audiences would find compelling. This required a move away from explaining the features of different attractions to promoting the benefits of a whole visit, including explaining unique opportunities and the nature of the different types of experience available to visitors around the whole Dockyard. The Dockyard entrance and threshold were then redesigned with the visitor decision-making process in mind. Guidance on ticketing and queueing started right at the front gate, with staff working the queues during busy periods to help build commitment. The visitor centre was redesigned to communicate the experience of visiting each attraction, including a range of images, line drawings, digital screens, summary of the offer and reasons to buy. Buying a ticket was simplified, with a clearer explanation of the value of packaged deals. Visitors can see all this while they are queueing, so that when they reach a ticket desk they have already decided what they want or have specific questions. Ticketing became easier and faster, with noticeable gains during peak times.

Once visitors have bought their ticket, they have space and time in a separate zone to structure their visit. Dedicated displays show how to get to the attractions, times of waterbuses to reach the attractions across the bay, locations of visitor facilities, closing times, etc. The zone has a café, so that visitors can sit and plan their day in comfort. Clear signing shows visitors where to start when they leave the ticket office. The focus on visitor decision-making is supported by changes to pre-purchase activity, through refocused website, leaflets, etc.

Before the changes to the visitor centre, the understanding and perception was that visitors were motivated by the individual elements of the site. This influenced how the site was marketed. In contrast, after the new centre was opened, visitor research and benchmarking indicated that 69 per cent of visitors to the site were motivated by the complete story (BDRC, 2015; National Museum of the Royal Navy, 2016).

Conclusions

Museum thresholds are far more complex places than they first appear. Using a range of diverse approaches (many from outside the museum sector) helps us to reveal the work that museum visitors undertake as they move through the decision-making process related to their visit. In common with the experience of website users, museum visitors ask questions related to their own agendas and concerns and then seek answers to build a picture of what the visit will offer them. Applying models from the retail sector suggests that visitors then use the perceptions they have created to make judgements about how much time and effort they must invest in a visit and therefore how much value they will get in return. The amount of work they put into the process could well be part of their value judgement. As visitors work through the process building up their perceptions of the visitor offer they probably also build commitment towards making a visit and more positive feelings about how good a visit will be. Adapting the retail buying process model indicates that once at the museum, visitors do not abandon all this work, as their perception of the visitor offer is used to help assess the quality, value and satisfaction of their museum experience, while they are at the museum and after their visit has finished. Using these models, we can see how some of this process happens before visitors arrive at the museum, some at the entrance, and then perceptions get completed at the museum threshold inside the venue. Where this is the case, the museum threshold could be far more important than it is often given credit for. For many visitors, it could be the place where they have to work to understand the value of the visitor offer and in some instances, visitors may have to work quite hard. In the sense that the museum threshold contributes to visitors' perceptions of the visitor offer, the threshold directly contributes to both the start of the visitor experience and how the value of the whole experience will be judged.

References

BDRC (2015), *Understanding Brand Penetration: Secondary Analysis of PHD Audience Segmentation*, unpublished.

Bitgood, Stephen (2013), *Attention and Value: Keys to Understanding Museum Visitors*, Walnut Creek, California, USA: Left Coast Press.

Bitgood, Stephen (2014), 'Too Much Temptation, Not Enough Value: Why Visitors Lack Commitment', *InterpNEWS*, Nov.–Dec., pp. 1–4.

Black, Graham (2012), *Transforming Museums in the Twenty-First Century*, Abingdon, Oxfordshire, UK: Routledge.

Chen, Ching-Fu and Chen, Fu-Shian (2010), 'Experience Quality, Perceived Value, Satisfaction and Behavioural Intentions for Heritage Tourists', *Tourism Management*, 31, pp. 29–35.

Coffee, Kevin (2007), 'Audience Research and the Museum Experience as Social Practice', *Museum Management and Curatorship*, 22:4, pp. 377–89.

Cohen, June (2003), *The Unusually Useful Web Book*, Indianapolis, Indiana, USA: New Riders.

Cox, Roger and Brittain, Paul (2004), *Retailing: An Introduction* (5th Edition), London: FT Prentice Hall.

Falk, John and Dierking, Lynn (2013), *The Museum Experience Revisited*, Walnut Creek, California, USA: Left Coast Press.

Goulding, Christina (2000), 'The Museum Environment and the Visitor Experience', *European Journal of Marketing* 34:3/4, pp. 261–78.

Harrison, Paul and Shaw, Robin (2004), 'Consumer Satisfaction and Post-purchase Intentions: An Exploratory Study of Museum Visitors', *International Journal of Arts Management*, 6:2, pp. 23–31.

Hennes, Tom (2002), 'Rethinking the Visitor Experience: Transforming Obstacle into Purpose', *Curator* 45:2, pp. 105–17.

Hooper-Greenhill, Eilean ([1994] 2011), *Museums and Their Visitors*, London: Routledge.

Kolb, Bonita M. (2013), *Marketing for Cultural Organizations* (3rd Edition), Abingdon, Oxfordshire, UK: Routledge.

Krug, Steve (2000), *Don't Make Me Think: A Common Sense Approach to Web Usability*, Indianapolis, Indiana, USA: New Riders.

Murray, Kyle (2013), *The Retail Value Proposition*, Toronto: University of Toronto Press.

National Football Museum (2010a), *National Football Museum Visitor and Non Visitor Research Detailed Findings*, unpublished.

National Football Museum (2010b), *National Football Museum Concept Testing 1*, unpublished.

National Football Museum (2011), *National Football Museum Visitor Experience Concept Testing*, unpublished.

National Museum of the Royal Navy (2016), *Marketing Communications Strategy and Plan*, unpublished.

Packer, Jan (2008), 'Beyond Learning: Exploring Visitors' Perceptions of the Value and Benefits of Museum Experiences', *Curator*, 51:1, pp. 33–54.

Packer, Jan and Ballantyne, Roy (2002), 'Motivational Factors and the Visitor Experience: A Comparison of Three Sites', *Curator*, 43:3, pp. 183–98.

Roppola, Tiina (2012), *Designing for the Museum Visitor Experience*, Abingdon, Oxfordshire, UK: Routledge.

Royal Marines Museum (2014), *Audience Research Supporting HLF Bid*, unpublished reports.

Seccombe, Peter and Lehnes, Patrick (editors) (2015), *Heritage Interpretation for Senior Audiences*, Interpret Europe/European Association for Heritage Interpretation, published online July 2015. Available: www.interpret-europe.net/fileadmin/Documents/projects/HISA/HISA_handbook.pdf Accessed: 20 November 2015.

Sheng, Chieh-Wen and Chen, Ming-Chia (2012), 'A Study of Experience Expectations of Museum Visitors', *Tourism Management*, 33, pp. 53–60.

Visitrac (2015), *Camera Obscura and World of Illusions Visitor Feedback: Survey Response Analysis*, unpublished.

World Rugby Museum (2011), *World Rugby Museum Redevelopment Project: Audience Insight Research*, unpublished.

Conversation 1
The Royal Air Force Museum London

In this first of four conversations presented throughout the book, Ross Parry [RP] interviews Rebecca Dalley [RD], Centenary Project Manager with The Royal Air Force Museum, London.

RP: *Could you tell us a little bit about where we are? Tell us about the museum, the institution.*
RD: Well, the Royal Air Force Museum is younger than most people usually think. It's just over 40 years old, although the Royal Air Force is nearly 100 years old. So it was set up in the 1960s as a legacy of the 50th birthday of the Royal Air Force. And it was set up here at Hendon, where there was an old, old airfield right from the earliest days of aviation.
   The RAF has sponsored the RAF Museum since its inception, and that continues to this day. So about 70 per cent of our core funding comes from the Royal Air Force. And then we make up the rest through our own commercial activities. It is a charity, though, so it's completely separate from the RAF. One of the RAF's senior commanders sits on our board. But other than that, it's constituted very similarly to most of the other museums, although we don't sit with the DCMS: we sit with the Ministry of Defence.
RP: *Could you tell us a little bit about the estate here at the museum?*
RD: The museum is situated in a number of hangars, some of which date back to the First World War. So we're sitting today in a hangar that was in fact moved from a development site, because we're now swallowed up by the London borough of Barnet. So this whole building was moved brick-by-brick by the developers. But it was an original 1917 World War I aircraft factory. So we've got great opportunities to display our collections in some very historic buildings, and to keep alive some of the heritage of the area.
RP: *Can you tell us about the mission of the museum?*
RD: The museum's been very clear about its mission over the last couple of years, and that's about telling the story of the Royal Air Force. We're here to tell the story not just of the aeroplanes, which is what

people generally think of when they think about the RAF Museum; they think about planes, because that's in general what we've displayed over the years. And there's a huge reason for us being much clearer about the story that we have to tell around those planes. And that's to do with the very changing nature of our audience.

RP: *Can you tell us a little bit more about your visitors? Who comes to the museum?*

RD: About 70 per cent of our audience are just families on a good day out. And about a third of those come from a half an hour journey from us. So we have the opportunities of the fact that we're a free museum, thanks to the Ministry of Defence, and we have a nice, big car park.

We also have quite a big imbalance between male and female. But that is balanced out by those family groups. And so what we find is we get a lot of intergenerational all-male groups. So Dad will bring Grandpa and the kids for the day out, when Mum might be doing something else. So there is a gender imbalance there that we are looking to address. But that's quite a nice thing to have. It's a nice problem to have, to have those kind of intergenerational, special times.

RP: *Do you know where those visitors come from? Are they from London? Are they from the UK? Are they international visitors?*

RD: Well, about a third of our visitors come from London. London's a big place, so it's a nice big catchment area. About a third of our visitors are coming from the rest of the UK. And then, up to a third of our visitors are now coming from overseas. And that's a real change for us.

The game changer has actually been TripAdvisor, because we had a very, very low profile. We've never had a big marketing budget at the museum. So people coming and finding us for themselves, and rating us very highly on TripAdvisor, has really allowed us to get a profile with the international visitors that we never had before.

RP: *Tell us about the threshold of the museum. What's it for? What should it do? And what are the complexities of the threshold at this particular institution?*

RD: Right at the middle of the site is a really nice, big car park. And around it are a number of different buildings which contain different exhibitions with lots of big aeroplanes, and tell the story of the RAF. One of our issues is that we don't have one single point of entry, so people cross the edge of our site, and then are faced with a barrage of different building entrances to go into.

The site was never master-planned, but it has undergone a lot of development over the last 30 years. So we moved this current building onto one part of the site. We built another building onto the back of the site. Other parts of the buildings were built over time without any coherence. So although we have a relatively small circle of buildings with a car park in the middle, we have a very confusing site with a number of different entrances. And that becomes a real challenge for us in terms of orientating our visitors.

RP: *What changed the institution's thinking around thresholds, both in terms of concepts, but also practically?*

RD: A workshop that we ran with all the key stakeholders in our organisations (some from the local council, because we are in a regeneration area so we work extremely closely with Barnet Council), and with some external people who were looking at the same issues that we did, started looking at audience issues. Who are our audiences? Were people really clear about who was coming to the museum?

We also got them thinking about how welcoming different thresholds were. So having run around the South Bank snapping snaps of lots of people's thresholds, it actually made us feel slightly better that there's a lot of people with quite bad thresholds. Getting people to critique lots of big institutions' thresholds, and how they made them feel as a potential audience member (we put people into characters to do that) was really helpful.

And that led up to an afternoon of fun and games following the model of the 'playing the lobby' work (see Chapter 9) that Erik Kristiansen took us through. And we used a little artistic licence with quite a lot of Lego and some household objects, just to go through that exercise of putting yourself into a different person's shoes, and finding out how they would feel about different lobby areas.

It was really helping people to think through the practical issues, as well as stepping back into those shoes at every turn to say: how does this work for the visitor? Not the visitor who has already made a mental decision to come here, but the visitor who is just that little bit curious, but maybe was just passing in the car, maybe walks past to take the kids to school, but who just needs that little nudge over the threshold to say, ooh, well maybe this is for me.

And then there's the second stage of that lobby: how do you then welcome them properly, orientate them properly, make them feel at home, do all the things that we want to do in our lobby spaces that give them an environment in which they're feeling really, really comfortable, to then bring them on into possibly seeing themselves as a museum visitor?

RP: *So what are your future plans for thresholds here at the museum?*

RD: Well, we think they're very exciting. And they're tied into the RAF Centenary programme that we're currently fundraising for. They've become, I think I mentioned already, a real metaphor for the way that the museum is expanding out into its local community, the way that it's trying to engage visitors who've never engaged with it before. We are working with some fantastic designers, who have come up with some wonderful ideas to give us that sense of the airfield back, that sense of not being a barrier, but being an open space that the community can be a real and proud part of.

So we found that the hero image for our whole project has become that of the threshold, because it says everything about what we want to do. When you take a picture of a fence with a missile behind it – which is essentially what you get at the moment at the RAF Museum – and turn it into a beautiful green space with no barriers: that's the metaphor that we want to stand strong for our future visitor experience.

4 Design-driven innovation for museum entrances

Marco Mason

The museum threshold presents a fascinating design challenge. Can we (or do we) overtly design a space that is *liminal*? In today's condition, one suggested as a 'postdigital' space (Parry, 2013), should media play a crucial role in redefining how visitors encounter information and experience? And, in such a transitional space, how can digital media and physical space be interwoven, to accommodate and lead visitor flow, and to create a new type of 'information space'?

The contributing authors of this book have carefully investigated the various implications arising from these questions in proposing their interesting perspectives. The museum entrance is a space of 'arrival and practicality' yet also 'symbolism and aspiration' (see Skellon and Tunstall, Chapter 2 of this volume) that facilitates the transition from the external experience (pre-visit) to the learning experience of the museum visit. These spaces require the creation of an adequate information space to promote the experiential transition 'from being a traveller to a being a visitor' (see Mulberg, Chapter 3 of this volume). They might offer services that not only guide the visitor but are also themselves exhibition spaces that introduce visitors to the museum experience through 'artworks in the museum threshold' (see Ride, Chapter 5 of this volume). This information space can be further enhanced with audiovisual aspects that form or arise from an immersive environment (see Mortensen and Deuchars, Chapter 11 of this volume) and the visitor experience of the physical space can be expanded through virtual presence such as social media (see Russo and Pond, Chapter 6 of this volume). From the contributions of the different authors emerges an interesting view that depicts the complexity and richness of these spaces. The intensification of interactions, relationships and experiences fostered by new thresholds (Parry et al., 2014) increases awareness of the challenges that designers have to face when reshaping museum thresholds.

With these considerations in mind, this chapter reflects upon the ways in which the museum threshold may be understood from a 'design thinking' perspective – an approach defined by its human-centred mindset, integrative process and cross-collaborative methodology. This chapter is mindful of the approaches deployed in other sectors and draws on the direct experience gained on the occasion of a design exploration for a hotel information system aiming to enhance the customer experience. It will reflect upon how design thinking offers a crucial approach both to conceptualise the problem of the threshold, and also as a means to improve the visitor experience in these spaces.

The 'Future Hotel Experience' project: an illustrative example

While at the Massachusetts Institute of Technology during the two-year outgoing phase of my Marie Curie fellowship,[1] I had the opportunity to be involved in a design exploration conducted by the Mobile Experience Lab at the MIT Program in Comparative Media Studies.[2] The context was furnished by the Designing Interactions: Media and Mobile Technologies[3] laboratory through which the MIT worked in partnership with Marriott International to explore how digital media could be integrated into the physical space of the hotel lobby in order to transform the hotel experience. Although this project took place within an academic setting, working closely with Marriott International on practical problems offered a real design context. For this reason, this case is presented as an illustrative example for a more theoretical argument on the contribution design thinking might offer to museum thresholds.

The two design contexts, the Marriott hotel lobby and the museum threshold, present several analogies as they are both 'transition spaces' that also provide 'orientation'; they integrate physical and digital worlds; include social media; present environments characterised by dynamic flows, rich interactions and experiences; and constitute multimedia environments that consider sound together with other media.

The laboratory brought together students and researchers from many different disciplines (social science, media studies, mechanical and electrical engineering, computer science, architecture and design) who worked in close collaboration with professionals from Marriott International (creative strategy insight and strategy, plus innovation, interactive strategy, and eCommerce specialists). In particular, I collaborated within a multidisciplinary team of four individuals;[4] in addition to myself, the team was composed of two MIT students, interested in computer science and mechanical engineering respectively, and an experience designer from the Massachusetts College of Art and Design. Like the other groups, we closely collaborated with the Marriott team. We developed a design concept that explored both the physical architecture as well as digital media. We realised a prototype for a service integrating a mobile app, a website and a tangible interface to engage customers with the socio-cultural environment of the city of Boston through a visual-based information system (Figure 4.1). The underlying idea of our design was to transform the lobby space into an epicentre of social energy that integrated the hotel within the surrounding cultural community of the city.

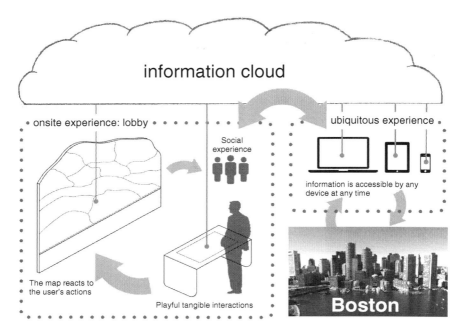

Figure 4.1 Conceptual map of the entire information system
Source: Kaitlyn Bailey, Kiranmayi Bhattaram, Sky Tien-Yun Huang, and Marco Mason; MIT Mobile Experience Lab

For the purposes of this chapter I am more interested in the design thinking process (designing) rather than the elements that constitute the final design system resulting from the process (the design). For this reason, the focus is on the design activities. In this section I present design activities conducted and methods employed in an illustrative example before turning to the more theoretical question (see 'Discussion' below) of whether and how a design thinking culture might offer an effective means to improve the visitor experience of the threshold.

The design process essentially consisted of the following five phases: defining the design brief and finding opportunities; understanding (contextual inquiry); defining the experience (shaping the concept); shaping interactions and refining the design; and implementing the final prototype.

Finding the design opportunity: the design brief[5]

The purpose of this initial phase was to clearly define the design statements in order to identify the design opportunity and state the main design goals, to guide the whole process (Table 4.1). The collaboration with the

Table 4.1 The design brief: design statement, the opportunity, and main goals

Reinventing the hotel lobby experience – the design brief		
Design statement	The contemporary business traveller is looking for a familiar environment and a comfortable balance between life and work.	They want to be able to authentically experience the local cultural offering and connect socially at the hotel as well as with the social network they left back at home.
The opportunity	How can the lobby be designed as a social hub for the contemporary business traveller, weaving work with social interactions and immersive localised and customised experiences?	
Design goals	Design and prototype the future lobby – an epicentre of social energy that integrates the hotel with the surrounding local community.	By exploring the intersection between digital media and physical architecture, students will be asked to radically reinvent the hospitality experience.

stakeholders from Marriott International was particularly intense during this initial phase. The initial customer research in combination with visual documents representing the company's vision and branding culminated in a design brief, which was the starting point for framing the design problem. It was also a fruitful way to converge the project objectives with the company's strategy (e.g. marketing and branding). Design was a strategic asset as it contributed, from the very beginning, to the early framing of the problem of the hotel lobby. The design thinking approach provided a holistic point of view that fostered a deep understanding of the complex network of relationships between customers, company and lobby space in order to delineate key opportunities.

Understanding: the exploratory phase of the design process

Following the initial brief came the understanding phase.[6] This phase consisted of two interwoven sub-phases: the understanding of the design context and empathising with Marriott hotel customers. The former provided knowledge about the environment, context and circumstances that surrounded the use of the lobby space. The outcome of this research was extremely helpful for our team as it identified: the culture of the company; the main drivers that would shape the future of travel experiences; how the hotel space is changing; and how emerging technologies could touch upon every aspect of the guest experience. The latter furnished a deeper understanding of customer needs, and was an activity that we conducted in the field through an ethnographic research methodology. In this phase we literally moved *in the field* to observe and conduct contextual interviews. We applied Design Ethnography (Crabtree et al., 2012, pp. 1–4; Schneider and Stickdorn, 2011, p. 108) to better understand the people for whom we were going to design. This activity was crucial to build up an empathetic understanding of the users. It involves different methods of data collection and, subsequently, techniques to interpret and visually communicate the information gathered. We started observing people in the research context (e.g. the hotel lobby, and surrounding external areas). The *observation* required attentive looking and systematic recording of phenomena that did not only include customer behaviours and interactions, but also those of employers, services and the internal and external environments. We conducted a systematic observation at different times and on different days by using some ethnographic techniques such as *fly-on-the-wall* (Saffer, 2009, p. 86; Hanington and Martin, 2012, p. 90), *behavioural mapping* using annotated maps (Curedale, 2013, p. 205; Hanington and Martin, 2012, p. 90), *picture* and *video recording* (Hanington and Martin, 2012, p. 120) and extensive field notes. Also, I personally used a *day-in-the-life* technique (Curedale, 2013, p. 230); by which, for two days, I studied the context and captured data from the customer point of view (i.e. I booked a room in the Marriott hotel to become a real customer). Finally, we conducted some informal interviews with guests and hotel practitioners to clarify some aspects and collect other useful data.

All the data collected would have been of little use if it had not been properly analysed and clearly represented and communicated amongst team members. We wrote a brief report in which we synthesised the main insights. We made extensive use of pictures – combined with short descriptions highlighting the essential insights – to illustrate environments and activities (Figure 4.2). From the ethnographic exploration we understood that the users for whom we had to design our service were discerning, busy and energetic, and always connected; they liked to explore the city, discover new things and meet new people. In order to describe the user we created an archetypical character called a *persona* (Pruitt and Adlin, 2010). This was a page-length description of an individual with a name, picture and a narrative story describing the individual's key aspects, goals and behaviours relevant to the design. We considered this *persona* as a great exercise in empathy; we constantly referred to it during the entire design process whenever a question or concern arose about how aspects of the system should be designed.

Finally, we created an *experience journey map*[7] that was the visualisation of the experiences that customers had as they used the lobby; it essentially pinpointed the interacting factors that formed the existing guests' experiences. These visual deliverables (where the textual information was minimal and was subservient to visual communication) turned out to be very useful for discussing and sharing insights with other teams and stakeholders and, in turn, informed the entire design process.

Design-driven innovation for museum entrances 63

Figure 4.2 Examples of pictures combined with short descriptions highlighting the essential insights to illustrate environments and activities
Source: Kaitlyn Bailey, Kiranmayi Bhattaram, Sky Tien-Yun Huang, and Marco Mason; MIT Mobile Experience Lab

The understanding gained was pivotal to work on the next phase: the definition of the *user experience framework*.

Identifying the experience: the user experience framework

In this phase, we conceptualised the guest experience by first characterising and then framing the customer experience. Based on what we learnt in the exploration phase, our team started a series of brainstorming sessions in which we elaborated general concepts to conceptualise different experiences. We generated many ideas supported by thinking tools such as sketches and then we quickly tested them through representations such as *scenarios* (Carroll, 2000). This iterative process helped us to (re)define the experience concept defined by the *experience statement* previously identified:

> create an experience for guests to 'enter in contact' with the city in order to explore and find out about the city, 'putting guests in contact' with the local cultural offering and enabling them to connect socially at the hotel. The experience should be accessible and provide a fun way to access information. It should also happen through an authentic exploration by introducing guests to the city as locals.

The experience statement worked as a guide for framing the *user experience framework* through which we envisioned the customer experiences. In particular, we used a *customer experience journey map* (Figure 4.3), which is essentially a way to express the experience framework visually. This visual representation of the customer experience was particularly useful when combined with the persona, as we could experiment how our user (or, as we

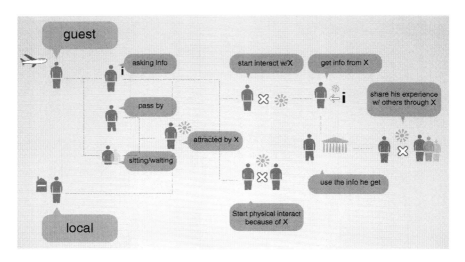

Figure 4.3 Customer experience journey map for the information system
Source: Kaitlyn Bailey, Kiranmayi Bhattaram, Sky Tien-Yun Huang, and Marco Mason; MIT Mobile Experience Lab

called him, 'Steve') could move in his 'journey'; the map facilitated empathic engagement with Steve and allowed us to think and then identify which interactions best suited the different experiences we identified in the experience journey map.

We then used this map to move forward with the design. It was, for us, a tool for thinking about and generating ideas for possible interactions users could perform. The journey map was useful in framing not only the customer experience, but also the beginning of the interaction design phase, which is the definition of essential touchpoints[8] through which customers interact with the service. In other words, once the visitor experience framework was defined, the *experience journey map* helped us to explore high-level interactions that 'Steve' could perform during his experience in the hotel lobby and in the city of Boston.

Shaping interactions and refining the design

Once we had defined the touchpoints and high-level interactions, we took those interactions to a further level of definition by using a *storyboard* to provide a visual narrative that helped us understand how the context, experiences and interactions could come together with technical factors. The storyboard worked as a visual tool to foster discussion amongst different team members with heterogeneous expertise. This storytelling technique was particularly helpful for defining *where, how* and *why* our user engaged with

Design-driven innovation for museum entrances 65

the elements of the system we were designing (the *what*). In our collaborative workshops the storyboards were able to clearly point out the key elements of the service we were developing, encouraging discussion on which interactions might or might not work. The storyboard worked as a low-fidelity prototype for quickly testing ideas and adopting the most promising one, and then moving forward with the design of each element of the system (mobile app, website, multi-touch screen, the tangible wall).

The storyboard provided a common interaction framework that gave our team the opportunity to focus on single parts of the system independently, without losing the coherence of the overall design. For example, we could focus on the design of the multi-touch table, which was a particularly challenging element of the system. In order to give hotel guests the opportunity to experience a tangible interaction for manipulating digital data, the user could choose to put objects on the screen that were equipped with sensors and located in the proximity of a multi-touch table. Each object represented a specific and significant sociocultural aspect of the city of Boston (e.g. the lobster represented the 'local food'). If the user put an object (e.g. the lobster) on the multi-touch table, the interface reacted by suggesting the neighbourhoods with a high concentration of restaurants serving local food (Figure 4.4). If the user decided to put another object on the same screen (e.g. the shopping bag, which represented 'shopping') the interface automatically suggested the neighbourhood(s) resulting from the combination of restaurants and shops. Basically, a dynamic infographic – supported by a database – showed the best combination(s) resulting from the user's choice. Simultaneously, the screen right in front of the user displayed the neighbourhood(s) on a large tangible map and showed pictures that evoked the atmosphere of those neighbourhoods.

The information simultaneously displayed on both the multi-touch table and the tangible wall was uploaded in real time on the web mobile app, as the database was stored on the Internet, and each element of the system – the multi-touch screen, the tangible wall and the web mobile app – was part of the network.

Figure 4.4 Prototype of the multi-touch screen to test the interactions for the best combination(s) resulting from the user's choice

Source: Kaitlyn Bailey, Kiranmayi Bhattaram, Sky Tien-Yun Huang, and Marco Mason; MIT Mobile Experience Lab

66 *Marco Mason*

In order to design and develop each element we made great use of different prototypes. We started with 'quick and dirty' paper prototypes (Figure 4.5), then used mixed-fidelity prototypes (Figure 4.6) and Wizard-of-Oz simulation (Hanington and Martin, 2012, p. 204), and finally high-fidelity prototypes. Following a series of successive prototype iterations, we moved from an abstract framework to more tangible interactions, then to concrete graphic and tangible interfaces.

The iterative design process towards the final design solution

We adopted a successive cycle of iterations as our process, each constituting an understanding of the specific problem (analysis), followed by idea generation and identification of possible solutions (synthesis) and concluding with testing the solution with prototypes (testing). At the end of each iteration, we verified our solution against the whole design framework defined in the previous phases. As our design process was strongly iterative, the solutions we found at the end of each iteration required us to revisit the whole experience framework and eventually make small refinements.

We moved forward through several layers of design, from abstract concepts to experience to interactions and finally the granular details. In order to accomplish this process, we performed design activities on more than one

Figure 4.5 Paper prototype to try out interactions on the multi-touch screen

Source: Kaitlyn Bailey, Kiranmayi Bhattaram, Sky Tien-Yun Huang, and Marco Mason; MIT Mobile Experience Lab

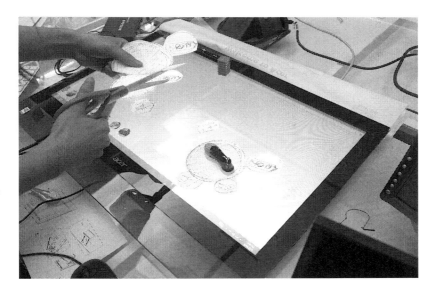

Figure 4.6 Mixed-fidelity prototype to try out interactions on the multi-touch screen
Source: Kaitlyn Bailey, Kiranmayi Bhattaram, Sky Tien-Yun Huang, and Marco Mason; MIT Mobile Experience Lab

level throughout the project. We have to think of our process as a system of design decisions we made whilst the activities were taking place, at different levels of design: experience, interaction and interface. At the more abstract level we defined the high-level *experience framework* of the comprehensive structure of the visitor's experience, which is the conceptual foundation for further design on the interaction level. On the *level of interaction* we defined the functional structure constituted by: a) the information architecture that structured the content; and b) the interaction framework that defined the interactions with the information system. At this level it is about structuring content and designing interactions. Finally, at the *level of interface* we developed the granular and detailed components of the digital interfaces constituting the information system. At this level it is about designing the layout, navigation and graphic elements of the digital artefact, considering these as part of the overall context of experience and interactions.

The 'future lobby experience' offers an example of design practice that, starting from *empathy* with users, followed a *collaborative* and cross-disciplinary approach that made significant use of *visual tools* and *prototypes* of all sorts throughout the entire *iterative design process*, which culminated in an innovative solution for the problem of lobby space in the hotel.

How can this design thinking practice be harnessed to rethink the idea of the museum threshold? In the following sections I will answer this question by framing the discussion around these underlying principles – empathy, collaboration, iterative process, prototypes, and visual tools – with the purpose of articulating them around a suitable theoretical argument for stimulating readers' reflections and offering the basis to support practical approaches.

Discussion

Design thinking as strategic asset

In the Marriott project the expertise and way of thinking designers employ to solve complex problems were brought in at the start of the process in order to frame the problems properly, identify design opportunities, and generate ideas – rather than focusing right away on a specific technology and what it can do. Brown (2008, p. 84) stresses how, in the past, the development process has considered *design* as a conclusive step in which designers emerged late in the process to 'put a beautiful wrapper around the idea'. In his seminal article on design thinking, the author goes on to describe how, during the last two decades, this tendency has been inverted and nowadays, the contribution of designers has increasingly become a strategic asset. This should also be the case for museums that are facing new challenges, including revisiting threshold spaces and the experiences they foster. Verganti, one of the first scholars to promote 'design-driven innovation', stressed the value of design thinking culture for industry and organisations such as museums to innovate, as it goes beyond the aesthetic and technical aspects of design (Verganti, 2013). Also, Macdonald (2007, pp. 149–162) confirms a similar tendency when she writes that, in the recent past, exhibition designers were only required to supply 'a more or less attractive medium for presenting content', whereas now design is (or should be) an integral part of the visitor experience with 'far-reaching implications for structuring the very nature of that experience'.

The challenges posed by the new museum threshold – such as the use of media that promotes new types of encounters and the demand for the integration of the experiences of playing, learning, discovering and buying – requires radically rethinking the visitor experience. Design, therefore, becomes a strategic innovative asset by promoting the early exploration of opportunities; and the building-up of new ideas leading to innovation is strongly encouraged in the very early stages of the project (Baeck and Gremett, 2011, pp. 229–250).

This shift entails a deep understanding of the visitors' needs, motivations, and emotions, and a different way of thinking and doing that is based on a cross-disciplinary approach supported by suitable design methods and techniques.

Empathic understanding of user experience

The main challenge posed by the Marriot hotel threshold design was envisioning a new way of engaging the customer and offering them a new type of service. We adopted a design thinking approach that employed empathic user research methods – such as observations and contextual interviews – to identify unrealised needs and expectations in order to design an innovative product, system, or service that has yet to be thought of. Moggridge (2008, pp. 1–12) says that in innovative designs the goal is to create something new that is difficult to explain even to research participants. This scenario reveals a similar purpose to the research and experimental projects presented in this book, which aim at reframing museum thresholds in a way that actual visitors might not envisage yet. For this reason, reinventing these spaces requires discovering latent needs and desires and responds with innovative solutions that should identify, shape and support new threshold experiences.

Design thinking is unanimously acknowledged as an approach that promotes the use of methods for designing objects and services that match people's needs (Brown, 2009; Lockwood, 2010; Martin, 2009; Verganti, 2013) and sees things from users' perspectives (Ward et al., 2009, pp. 78–84). Dong (2014, pp. 1–16) underlines how design-inspired innovation in industry and organisations is strongly driven by the fulfilling of the desired qualities of the final product or service in terms, for example, of high emotional value, degree of newness, and being more socially responsive. After all, is not the satisfaction of visitor needs, emotions and expectations one of the most important drivers of innovation in twenty-first-century museums? (Bearing in mind that the growing adoption of digital technology is just a means to pursue this goal.)

At the core of these methods is *empathy*, which Brown (2009) defines as the 'effort to *see* the world through the eyes of others', '*understand* the world through their experiences', and '*feel* the world through their emotions'. Adopting an empathic approach essentially means to develop a deep understanding of the users in their real context (Rogers, 2011, pp. 58–62) by collecting qualitative data in order to understand people in the context of their experience. These techniques aim to obtain insights into the *why* and *how*, and know beyond the *what* users need, expect and desire. This approach can result in a rich source of inspiration for the design, beyond being an effective way to discover user needs (Lockwood, 2010, p. xi).

Nowadays, a main feature of innovation is the focus of attention on the quality of the user experience rather than on technology; this is to satisfy the needs and expectations of people who will use the final product or service (Dong, 2014, pp. 1–16). However, this attention on people is not a sufficient condition to guarantee innovation if it is not supported by an appropriate collaborative process that employs suitable design methods and tools (Lockwood, 2010, pp. xi-xvii).

70 *Marco Mason*

Multidisciplinary collaboration

The value in early exploration of opportunities and ideas is emphasised by the need for a collective approach to the problem of the threshold. Collaboration amongst different areas of expertise (and so different disciplines) becomes an essential boost for innovation (Bremner and Rodgers, 2013, pp. 4–13). It is not necessary to look outside our context to find confirmation of the value of a multidisciplinary approach to deal with new design challenges. The project that provided the theoretical foundation for this book – Transforming Thresholds[9] – started from the assumption that disciplines (apparently) far from exhibition design and architecture can influence and contribute to reframing museum thresholds. In particular, observers in the digital museum context (Freeman et al., 2016; Merritt, 2015) envision the integration of digital and physical worlds for configuring information spaces such as new museum thresholds; this requires collaborative practices that bring together skills and expertise from different backgrounds to inform design (Roberts, 2014, pp. 191–209).

Returning to our discussion, multidisciplinarity is much needed, for the transformation of actual threshold spaces as innovation cannot be driven by (technical) specialists alone; instead it requires the active participation of museum professionals and other stakeholders in the creative process because the nature of design problems presented by new threshold spaces is complex and, thus, dealing with those problems requires the integration of different knowledge domains (Adelson and Soloway, 1988, pp. 185–208). The solution of such design problems 'is not any longer in one silo of expertise but in the mix, as not one single discipline owns the solution' (Helsinki Design Lab, 2010). Design thinking promotes working at the intersections of different areas of knowledge as I will describe in the following sections, by defining the complex nature of threshold design problems and then making the case for an iterative process to support collaborative practice in tackling this complexity.

Defining threshold complexity

The problem of the Marriott hotel lobby space, as well as that of museum thresholds, disclosed a certain degree of complexity. Designing for museum thresholds is not only about the interactions necessary for performing particular visitor tasks – e.g. when a visitor touches buttons on a screen positioned in an multimedia kiosk in order to obtain information about an artwork – but also about designing workflows, experiences and interactions that weave together (digital) content, objects of display, information, visitor needs and expectations and both physical (indoor and outdoor) and digital spaces, while balancing these against the museum's objectives and strategy. According to Buchanan's 'four orders of design' (Buchanan, 2001, pp. 3–23) – in which the scholar proposes *symbols, things, actions,* and *environments* as four criteria to define design complexity – it is possible to situate thresholds in all the four orders. The museum threshold can present design challenges at the first order, for the design of *symbols* in form of 'visual communication' such as infographics; and/or at the second order, for example, to design *things* such as 'material objects' and multi-touch table interactives; and/or at the third order to design *interactions* for activities and organised services. Together the first three orders can form an *environment* (fourth order) integrating human, digital and material systems (Buchanan, 2001, p. 12).

As has been discussed at length by many design theorists (Buchanan, 1992, pp. 5–21; Coyne, 2005, pp. 5–17; Farrell and Hooker, 2013, pp. 681–705) these kinds of design issues are more specifically described as 'wicked problems', referring back to Rittel, who suggests that the term refers to a 'class of social system problems which are ill-formulated, where the information is confusing, where there are many clients and decision makers with conflicting values, and where the ramifications in the whole system are thoroughly confusing' (Churchman, 1967, pp. 141–142). To successfully deal with 'wicked problems', it is not possible to formulate all the problems and *then* find a final solution, as happens in some technical domains where it is feasible to reason from problems to solutions in a relatively controlled and orderly way (Dorst, 2006). On the contrary, because a 'wicked problem is not understood until after the formulation of a solution' (Conklin, 2006) and it is very hard to define all the problems at the beginning and *then* move to the final solution, design thinking proceeds by iterative steps in which there is a constant alternation of the understanding of a portion of the whole problem and testing a possible solution for that specific problem toward the final design that results from such evolution.

The need for iterative process in dealing with complexity

The creative design process repeats itself at different times as it moves toward the final best solution (Rittel and Webber, 1973, pp. 155–169). Dorst and Cross (2001, pp. 425–437), in their seminal experiment, showed that the problem-solving process of facing 'wicked problems' adopted in design thinking is non-linear and can be described as a 'co-evolution of problem and solution spaces'. According to the authors, the design process facing 'wicked problems' is a continuous process of testing and learning (pp. 425–437):

> It seems that creative design is not a matter of first fixing the problem and then searching for a satisfactory solution concept. Creative design seems more to be a matter of developing and refining together both the formulation of a problem and ideas for a solution, with constant iteration of analysis, synthesis and evaluation processes between the two notional design 'spaces' – problem space and solution space.

As we saw in the Marriott threshold project, the analysis essentially consisted of the understanding (and not the definition) of the problem space, the synthesis reflected on the problem by generating ideas for a possible solution, and the evaluation tested the idea for a solution. This co-evolutionary process allowed our team to advance and refine the design – from an abstract level to a more concrete form – throughout different levels of design by undertaking successive iterations of problem/solution cycles (from the early vision to the granular detail of the final design). In the same way, the design process adopted for transforming museum thresholds should move through successive levels of design – from experience to service to interaction to graphic interface components – adopting consecutive cycles of analysis-synthesis-evaluating.

In such 'co-evolutionary' design processes, where problems and solutions evolve together, prototyping plays a fundamental role in deepening the understanding of a solution throughout each iteration. Prototyping allows for the evaluation of a possible solution and then the use of the feedback to create a new prototype, advancing the design toward the final best solution (Mason, 2015, pp. 394–426).

Prototyping

Prototyping is an essential practice in collaborative design thinking, since it is a catalyst for the different voices involved in the project: museum practitioners, designers, developers and other stakeholders (Mason, 2015, pp. 394–426). Prototypes facilitate conversation amongst members of the team by translating ideas through more tangible examples. Museum and design team members have different types of prototypes at their disposal to explore possible solutions and their suitability, according to the particular problems faced during the design process. This can happen in any phase of the design, even in the generation of early concepts, as prototyping does not always require the creation of complex and expensive artefacts (Brown, 2008, p.84). For example, creating low-fidelity prototypes does not require any particular skill, encouraging the participation of professionals with different backgrounds, even those without specific digital development skills (i.e. curators, conservators and educators). This represents one of the strategic values of design thinking: the possibility to experiment early, fail early and explore a lot of possible solutions early (Mitroff Silvers et al., 2013).

The 'culture of prototyping' is at the basis of design thinking (Curedale, 2013, p. 39) as it is related to the 'continuous learning' that takes place during the entire design process, from the very early phase to the final product. During the iterative process of the co-evolution of problems and solutions (as described above), team members go through a learning process as they gather knowledge by experimenting with solutions (Dorst, 2011, p. 521) as happened in the design thinking process followed in the Marriott project, in which prototypes were utilised from early steps through to the conclusion of the project: from prototyping ideas (e.g. low-fidelity prototypes) to testing advanced interactive artefacts (e.g. high-fidelity prototypes).

Generally speaking, a low-fidelity prototype consists of an unfinished and sketched draft used to test design concepts (Figure 4.5). A low-fidelity prototype does not have an advanced degree of definition, and it usually looks different from the final design. A low-fidelity prototype can be anything from a storyboard sketched on paper, to sketchy wireframe drawings, to functional 'quick and dirty' drafts of the final design. For example, in the Marriott project we saw that an effective way to explore and develop concepts for the visitor experience can be through the creation of stories. Design scenarios and storyboards are effective ways to visualise the 'experience framework' by drawing a sequence of both events and actions visitors may perform during their journey while moving between the physical space and the digital media system. On the other hand, a high-fidelity prototype for digital interactives has a great level of definition (Figure 4.4), which can appear very similar to the final digital artefact – a prototype may even evolve into that solution. A high-fidelity prototype is a digital artefact and has different functionalities implemented. It is not always possible to opt for a low- or high-fidelity approach, because there are situations during the design process that require team members to make a compromise between these two kinds of techniques; however, it is possible to take advantage of the characteristics of both approaches through mixed-fidelity prototypes (Figure 4.6), that combine low- and high-fidelity techniques within the same artefact.

Visualisation to accelerate learning and foster collaboration

In the Marriott example, our team employed a range of visual techniques that offered a common language to increase communication within our multidisciplinary team, and with the client and other teams. This enhanced collaboration, encouraged participation, and boosted creativity, hence fostering innovation (Carlgren et al., 2014, pp. 403–423). Design thinking promotes the extensive use of visualisation for understanding and sharing (Curedale, 2013, p. 36). According to Ogilvie and Liedtka (2011, p. 49), 'visualization is the mother of all design tools' as visual tools support design activities during the entire process – from the exploration of the context to the experience framework to the interface flowcharts. Team members can use visualisation tools either internally or externally. In the former case they help to stimulate and spark idea generation; for example, during brainstorming sessions as the members of the team can see what others are thinking and build on top of this. Explaining ideas only with words or text exposes the risk that each member forms their own mental pictures which can substantially differ from those of others, especially in a multidisciplinary team – as individuals see things from their own perspective which is influenced by their own background. In the latter case, when different teams cross-collaborate or communicate with the client, visualisation considerably reduces the risk of misinterpretation because verbal or textual explanations are more subject to diverse interpretations than images (Brown, 2010). For example, Vavoula and Mason (2017, p. 251) use the term *intermediary design deliverables* to distinguish the type of visual communications delivered by the designer to the client from other design representations that may be used only internally within the design team. According to the authors, intermediary design deliverables' primary purpose is to communicate design progress, process and outcomes to external partners; they are 'the progressive objectification of the exhibit-idea throughout the series of intermediary deliverables, with the process culminating in a fully-fledged, tangible object: the exhibition itself'.

Conclusion

The Marriott project has offered the opportunity to describe how the team went through a design thinking process that has revealed six main tenets. Design thinking is a *strategic* asset to increase innovation by bringing in a design mindset from the beginning and fostering generation of concepts. It is a *human-centred design practice* that aims to develop a deep and empathic understanding of visitor experience. Also, it is a *collaborative practice* carried out by multidisciplinary teams (often, with users) which follow an *iterative process* that helps them to move from generating insights about end users to idea generation and testing and finally, to implementation and an approach. *Prototyping* is considered an integral practice within the iterative process, in which a large-scale *adoption of visualisation methods* accelerates learning and fosters collaboration.

In the museum world, as in other settings, the contribution of embracing a design thinking philosophy consists of innovation that originates from multidisciplinary processes; methods to foster teamwork and creativity and advanced prototyping practices in which different human-centred design methods are employed to address the visitors' needs and pursue twenty-first-century museums' objectives.

Acknowledgements

I would like to express my gratitude to Professor Federico Casalegno, director of the Experience Lab at the Massachusetts Institute of Technology, who afforded me the possibility to attend the Designing Interactions course, spring 2013, as part of my Marie Curie Actions training.

The Marie Curie research project (started October 2012) was funded by the European Union – Marie Curie Actions International Outgoing Fellowships for Career Development (IOFs). The outgoing stage of the fellowship (October 2012 – October 2014) took place at the Massachusetts Institute of Technology supervised by Professor John Durant from the

Science, Technology and Society Program; and the return stage (2015) took place at the University of Leicester supervised by Dr Giasemi Vavoula from the *School of Museum Studies*.

I would also like to express my gratitude to Ross Parry and Dana Mitroff Silvers for the stimulating conversations on digital heritage and design issues.

Notes

1 The Marie Curie research project titled 'Digital Media for Heritage: Refocusing Design from the Technology to the Visitor Experience' (started October 2012) is funded by the European Union – Marie Curie Actions International Outgoing Fellowships for Career Development (IOFs).
2 This activity was part of the research training required by and planed for the Marie Curie research project.
3 This MIT *Designing Interactions* course (https://architecture.mit.edu/subject/spring-2013-cms634) 'explores the future of mobile interactions and pervasive computing, taking into consideration design, technological, social and business aspects. [It] discusses theoretical works on human-computer interaction, mobile media and interaction design, and covers research and design methods. Students work in multidisciplinary teams (often in close collaboration with external partners to solve real problems) and participate in user-centric design projects aimed to study, imagine and prototype concepts illustrating the future of mobile applications and ubiquitous computing.'
4 The author, Kaitlyn Bailey, Kiranmayi Bhattaram and Sky Tien-Yun Huang.
5 This phase corresponds with the preparative work for the Laboratory. It involved only the MIT research team (led by Professor Federico Casalegno) and Marriott team.
6 This phase actually corresponded with the start of the MIT Laboratory. The MIT research team (led by Professor Federico Casalegno) and Marriott team had worked on the brief for the six months prior to this phase.
7 For an exhaustive description of experience journey maps see: Kalbach, J., (2016). *Mapping Experiences: A Complete Guide to Creating Value through Journeys, Blueprints, and Diagrams*. O'Reilly Media, Inc.
8 For an exhaustive description of touchpoints see: Halvorsrud, Ragnhild et al. (2014). 'Components of a visual language for service design', *Proceedings of ServDes* (2014), pp. 291–300 or Meyer, C. and Schwager, A. (2007), 'Understanding customer experience', *Harvard business review* 85(2), p. 116.
9 http://transformingthresholds.weebly.com.

References

Adelson, B. and Soloway, E.M. (1988). 'A model of software design', in Chi, M.T., Glaser, R. and Farr, M.J. (eds) *The nature of expertise*. New York: Psychology Press, pp. 185–208.
Baeck, A. and Gremett, P. (2011). 'Design thinking', in Degen, H. and Xiaowei, Y. (eds) *UX best practices: how to achieve more impact with user experience*. New York: McGraw-Hill, pp. 229–250.
Bremner, C. and Rodgers, P. (2013). 'Design without discipline', *Design Issues*, 29(3), pp. 4–13.
Brown, T. (2008). 'Design thinking', *Harvard business review*, 86(6), p. 84.
Brown, T. (2009). *Change by design*. New York: Harper Collins.

Brown, D.M. (2010). *Communicating design: developing web site documentation for design and planning* (2nd edition). Berkeley, CA: New Riders.
Buchanan, R. (1992). 'Wicked problems in design thinking', *Design Issues*, 8(2), pp. 5–21.
Buchanan, R. (2001). 'Design research and the new learning', *Design Issues*, 17(4), pp. 3–23.
Carlgren, L., Elmquist, M. and Rauth, I. (2014). 'Design thinking: exploring values and effects from an innovation capability perspective', *The Design Journal*, 17(3), pp. 403–423.
Carroll, J.M. (2000). *Making use: scenario-based design of human-computer interactions*. Cambridge, MA: MIT press.
Churchman, C.W. (1967). 'Wicked problems' (Guest Editorial), *Management Science*, 14(4), pp. 141–142.
Conklin, J. (2006). *Dialogue mapping: building shared understanding of wicked problems*. Chichester, UK: Wiley Publishing.
Coyne, R. (2005). 'Wicked problems revisited', *Design Studies*, 26(1), pp. 5–17.
Crabtree, A., Rouncefield, M. and Tolmie, P. (2012). *Doing design ethnography*. London: Springer Science & Business Media.
Curedale, R. (2013). *Design thinking: process and methods manual*. Topanga, CA: Design Community College Incorporated.
Dong, A. (2014). 'Design × innovation: perspective or evidence-based practices', *International Journal of Design Creativity and Innovation*, 2014, pp. 1–16.
Dorst, K. (2006). *Understanding design*, revised edition. Amsterdam: BIS Publishers.
Dorst, K. (2011). The core of 'design thinking' and its application. *Design Studies*, 32(6), pp. 521–532.
Dorst, K. and Cross, N. (2001). 'Creativity in the design process: co-evolution of problem–solution', *Design Studies*, 22(5), pp. 425–437.
Farrell, R. and Hooker, C. (2013). 'Design, science and wicked problems', *Design Studies*, 34(6), pp. 681–705.
Freeman, A., Adams Becker, S., Cummins, M., McKelroy, E., Giesinger, C. and Yuhnke, B. (2016). *NMC Horizon Report: 2016 Museum Edition*. Austin, TX: The New Media Consortium.
Hanington, B. and Martin, B. (2012). *Universal methods of design: 100 ways to research complex problems, develop innovative ideas, and design effective solutions*. Beverly, MA: Rockport Publishers, p. 90.
Helsinki Design Lab (HDL) (2010). *What is strategic design?* Available at: www.helsinkidesignlab.org/pages/what-is-strategic-design. [Accessed: 5 February 2018.]
Lockwood, T. (2010). *Design thinking: integrating innovation, customer experience, and brand value*. New York: Skyhorse Publishing.
Macdonald, S. (2007). 'Interconnecting: museum visiting and exhibition design', *CoDesign*, 3(S1), pp. 149–162.
MacLeod, S., Dodd, J. and Duncan, T. (2015). 'New museum design cultures: harnessing the potential of design and design thinking in museums', *Museum Management and Curatorship*, 30(4), pp. 314–341.
Martin, R. L. (2009). *The design of business: why design thinking is the next competitive advantage*. Cambridge, MA: Harvard Business Press.
Mason, M. (2015). 'Prototyping practices supporting interdisciplinary collaboration in digital media design for museums', *Museum Management and Curatorship*, 30(5), pp. 394–426.

Merritt, E.E. (2015). *Trendswatch 2015*. Available at: https://aam-us.org/docs/default-source/center-for-the-future-of-museums/trendswatch-2017.pdf?sfvrsn=2. [Accessed: 5 February 2018.]

Mitroff Silvers, D., Lytle-Painter, E., Lee, A., Ludden, J., Hamley, B. and Trinh, Y. (2014). 'From post-its to processes: using prototypes to find solutions', *Museums and the Web 2014*. Available at: http://mw2014.museumsandtheweb.com/paper/from-post-its-to-processes-using-prototypes-to-find-solutions. [Accessed: 10 February 2016.]

Mitroff Silvers, D., Wilson, M. and Rogers, M. (2013). 'Design thinking for visitor engagement: tackling one museum's big challenge through human-centered design', *Museums and the Web*. Available at: http://mw2013.museumsandtheweb.com/paper/design-thinking. [Accessed 1 October 2016.]

Moggridge, B. (2008). 'Innovation through design', *International Design Culture Conference – Creativeness by Integration*. Seoul, South Korea, 30–31 May 2008, pp. 1–12. Available at: www.ideo.com/images/uploads/news/pdfs/KDRI_BillM_Paper.pdf. [Accessed: 10 February 2016.]

Ogilvie, T. and Liedtka, J. (2011). *Designing for growth: a design thinking toolkit for managers*. New York: Columbia University Press, p. 49.

Parry, R. (2013). 'The end of the beginning: normativity in the postdigital museum', *Museum Worlds*, 1(1), pp. 24–39.

Parry, R., Moseley, A. and Kristiansen, E. (2014). 'On a new threshold: experiments in gaming, retail and performance design to shape museum entrances', *Museums and the Web 2014*. Available at: http://mw2014.museumsandtheweb.com/paper/on-a-new-threshold-experiments-in-gaming-retail-and-performance-design-to-shape-museum-entrances. [Accessed: 20 February 2016.]

Pruitt, J. and Adlin, T. (2010). *The persona lifecycle: keeping people in mind throughout product design*. San Francisco, CA: Morgan Kaufmann.

Rittel, H.W. and Webber, M.M. (1973). 'Dilemmas in a general theory of planning', *Policy sciences*, 4(2), pp. 155–169.

Roberts, T. (2014). 'Interpretation design: an integrative, interdisciplinary practice', *Museum and Society*, 12(3), pp. 191–209.

Rogers, Y. (2011). 'Interaction design gone wild: striving for wild theory', *Interactions*, 18(4), pp. 58–62.

Saffer, D. (2009). *Designing for interaction: creating innovative applications and devices*. Berkeley, CA: New Riders, p. 86.

Schneider, J. and Stickdorn, M. (2011). *This is service design thinking: basics, tools, cases*. Hoboken, NJ: Wiley.

Vavoula, G. and Mason, M. (2017). 'Digital exhibition design: boundary crossing, intermediary design deliverables and processes of consent', *Museum Management and Curatorship*, 32(3), pp. 251–271.

Verganti, R. (2013). *Design driven innovation: changing the rules of competition by radically innovating what things mean*. Cambridge, MA: Harvard Business Press.

Ward, A., Runcie, E. and Morris, L. (2009). 'Embedding innovation: design thinking for small enterprises', *Journal of Business Strategy*, 30(2/3), pp. 78–84.

Part II
Affordances and potential of the threshold

5 Suspended
Art in the threshold

Peter Ride

Gertrude Stein memorably quipped, 'I like museums. I like to look out their windows.' (quoted in Wright, 1988). Stein's cryptic quote can be read in many ways, starting with the description of the museum as 'a window onto the world'. But to expand on Stein's metaphor, windows not only offer transparency but also create ancillary spaces, or spaces of transition and connection. This chapter examines how the artwork in the threshold is a window in reverse – a window *into* the museum. Artwork allows the museum to enrich the visitor's experience, but in the manner of Stein's quote it is also ambiguous. This chapter explores how the creative language of artworks can augment the functionality of a museum threshold and contribute to the narrative that the museum visitor experiences.

The chapter explores a series of examples that illustrate ways in which artworks in the museum threshold[1] can also be seen to function as metaphors for the museum itself. From a projection of shadows on a white wall, the reclaimed wood of an old sailing ship and a granite table where visitors could take away a flower, to a tapestry made out of pins, these examples of artworks show how different strategies involve the visitor in complex ways. In some of the examples, artwork is literally suspended, but the significance lies in the way that artwork can metaphorically suspend meaning that the visitor then awakens and engages with as they journey through the threshold into the museum. The examples in the chapter are categorized as different types of metaphorical connection between the museum and the artwork. These categories are of course not exclusive, nor are they definitive; they are indications of the many ways that artworks can operate. The chapter also aims to show that by thinking of the artwork as having metaphoric qualities we can think of them as having a role beyond their material and aesthetic role.

The concept of 'artwork' is itself broad and is used in this chapter in a very inclusive way, covering works by artists commissioned by the museum, works by artists acquired or on loan, and works created by museum designers. Artworks could also be made by public participants. They could be incorporated within the building itself or they could be virtual. A fundamental part of most the examples featured in the chapter is that, when interviewed, curators and museum professionals were particularly interested in how visitors encountered the artwork and incorporated it within their own narratives. While visitors might be aware that the artworks might be a new creation by an artist, an object from the collection or a design product, in the context of their threshold experience what mattered to the curators was how the artwork facilitated the visitors' comprehension of the museum. Artworks that created metaphors could be seen as one of the elements that contributed to the 'authentic experience' (Lord and Piacente, 2014) of the visitor. In being open to interpretation, the artworks offered an ambiguous entry point to the experience of the museum, indicating that no one visitor's experience is more or less authentic than that of any other person, irrespective of what they might encounter or how they might respond to it. Not all artworks hang suspended in space, but a museum threshold can be seen as somewhere where many things are momentarily in suspension as the visitor moves from one environment into another. Of the many ways that the museum can facilitate this movement through the liminal space, the examples in this chapter show how artwork can be used in a powerful but non-didactic way to enable the visitor to make sense of the museum. In doing so the artworks can communicate important ideas about the way that the museum understands its relationship with its public.

The significance and potential of incorporating artworks within non-art museums is demonstrated by the continued importance of seminal projects that radically created interventions in the museum, notably that of artist Fred Wilson in *Mining the Museum* (Wilson, 1994), by curator James Putnam in *Time Machine: Ancient Egypt and Contemporary Art at the British Museum* (Putnam, 2001) and even as part of linked initiatives that connected different organizations, such as the 2007 bicentenary of the abolition of the transatlantic slave trade that was commemorated by museums in the UK by commissions and exhibitions of artworks.[2] Museums have used the arts as a means to demonstrate that there are many approaches to understanding what constitutes knowledge and to create alternative narratives to the dominant story being explored in the museum galleries. Artists have been used to offer ways to interpret and engage with empirical information (Redler, 2009); they have explored the notion of collective and personal memory; their practice has been used in laboratory environments where creativity can be seen to work 'in process' (Muller, 2011); and they have been used to help facilitate public interaction and enable voices from local or marginalized communities to be represented in the museum.

However, much of the literature on artworks in the museum takes an art historical approach, providing a critical 'reading' of the artwork in the context of artistic practice, the intentions of the artist and external cultural reference points. Of course these points are significant with artwork in the threshold, but to understand how it plays a part within the narrative of the museum it is also important to consider how it operates within a museum as a specific space. In this way, the artwork can be understood as part of a

Suspended: art in the threshold 83

series of relationships and interactions between the public and the institution. These issues around the way art operates within a space are akin to the way in which public art is discussed in terms of place-making, presence and the way that it facilitates community engagement (Doherty, 2015).

As the examples in this chapter show, artworks in the museum foyer also have an additional power. They draw attention to the importance of the visitor's own entrance narrative or subconscious expectations, as these are important to consider in the way that the visitors 'make meaning' during their journey though the museum (Doering and Pekarik, 1996). They also demonstrate how the threshold is a space where multiple narratives play out. The power of artworks often lies in their ambiguous meanings, and as such they also have complex roles, as writers such as James Elkins (2000) and Terry Barrett (2002) have argued. Yet their function can also be to operate as a device that helps transition the visitor into the gallery, and they do this in relation to other devices that could range from signage, to layout, to human contact. This could be thought of as something similar to the way that literary theorists describe the visual, graphic and written information contained from the cover to the introductions and prefaces of a literary text or cultural artefact as the paratext (Fludernik, 2009) that frames and orients the main narrative, a concept that has been adopted in other fields such as video games (Jones, 2008). As a paratext, an artwork in the threshold[3] therefore works with the museum's institutional metanarrative. But it also acknowledges that visitors needs to find their own way to engage with the museum space upon arrival and the artwork facilitates this by providing a metaphoric entry point.

Msheireb Museum: threshold artwork as consolidation

The Msheireb Museum in Qatar consists of four historic houses in the heart of Msheireb district, the 'Old Town' of Doha. Each house has been developed as a self-contained museum, each with its own subject area: three of them cover the social history of Doha, local archaeology, and the history of the petroleum industry. The fourth house, Bin Jelmood House, examines the history of the slave trade in the Indian Ocean, firstly within the context of the global slave trade and also as a form of human exploitation that played a crucial part in the history of the economic and social structures of Qatar. Visitors entering the Bin Jelmood House come in from the street up a small flight of steps, through the traditional heavy doors of a Qatari house and into a small foyer that is a square, predominantly white and unfurnished space. On the facing wall a projected image intermittently breaks the purity of the pale surface. It appears to show the shadows of a procession of individuals and small family groups in traditional Qatari clothing that walk from right to left; the shadow figures disappear heading towards the doors that open onto the museum's internal spaces. It is not clear if the figures are contemporary or historical. This artwork is an example of a piece created

84 *Peter Ride*

by the museum curators and design team and can be seen as a metaphor that responds to different elements of the museum concept, its spatial design and philosophy. Visually and thematically it draws the visitors into the museum space as they enter the threshold. Museum Manager, Colin Jones, describes this device as a 'shadowy conversation' that can invite people into the story of the museum without being didactic.[4] The artwork has the power to consolidate various threads of the underlying narrative of the museum and by being visual without any supporting text it can operate only as a metaphor.

Slavery in Qatar is a contentious subject and has a contemporary resonance. The Indian Ocean slave trade, under which people in East Africa were captured, trafficked and forced into slavery in the Middle East, continued until the late nineteenth century. However, the legal practice of slavery, including 'ownership' of people born into enslavement, was still in force while the country was a British protectorate and was only officially abolished in Qatar in 1952. Consequently, enslavement is still within the living memory of Qatari people.

The inhumanity of contemporary slavery in the Middle East is also given substantial coverage in the museum displays. It examines the situation of foreign workers trapped into work under contracts and conditions that deny their human rights and it addresses the subject of women forced into prostitution or trafficked through supply chains. Therefore, the museum is dealing with a subject that cannot easily be addressed at a historical distance.

Figure 5.1 Bin Jelmood House, Msheireb Museum, Qatar, showing the projection of moving shadow figures in the threshold

Source: Peter Ride

The shadow image in the foyer is also intended to evoke the idea of a community that could have occupied the house in previous generations. Original architectural details such as recesses and doorframes have been left to emphasize that the house is a historic building and pre-dates the development of modern Doha. The foyer leads onto a communal social area, the majlis. In a traditional Qatari house there are two majlis, one for men and another for women.

The museum approach aims to prompt a familiarity in visitors' minds with the social conventions of an Arab home where the interior is a very private space (Mahgoub and Theodoropoulou, 2014). Although visitors unfamiliar with Qatari culture would not necessarily understand the references, this would be very familiar to Middle Eastern audiences. Within the majlis families and social groups have the kinds of conversation that cannot easily be raised outside in a public space. 'We wanted people to feel that this is a safe space in which to have difficult conversations, to subtly allow people to engage without forcing it upon them [. . .] the subject of slavery was in the shadows', Jones explains.[5]

Additionally, the shadow is a motif that runs throughout the museum's displays. In the foyer, the minimal appearance of the projection forewarns the visitor that objects are not a key component in the museum's displays. The main exhibition in Bin Jelmood House primarily uses didactic panels and video, only occasionally punctured by historical artefacts, unlike the other museums in the Msheireb complex that are distinctly object-based. Mohammed Bin Jassim House, for example, exhibits objects uncovered during the construction of the site; Company House uses everyday objects and industrial items in displays on the pioneering petroleum industry workers; and Radwani House recreates domestic room environments from the house as it was when it was built in the 1920s. Many of the video installations are animations with a dramatic scenario that follows a family from East Africa as they are captured by slavers and traded along the slave routes of the African coast. Eventually they are sold to work for Bedouin tribespeople and to work in the pearl industry, the two main economies where people were made to work. The animations use silhouettes of human figures, which create a visual consistency with the shadow figures in the entrance, but the last video in the series is a filmed 'talking head' in which a Qatari woman of slave origin tells her life story. Crucially, the street entrance to the house is also the exit, which is a reminder that a threshold operates in many ways, not only facilitating a visitor's journey into a museum but also being a transition space where they leave the museum behind. Therefore the artwork provides the departing visitor with the opportunity for summative reflection at a point where the full effect of the different themes may resonate. The artwork not only provides an introductory metaphor but it also offers a concluding one.

The metaphor of the shadowy figures not only consolidates the themes of the museum but it can also be thought of as aggregating them, building and intensifying the idea that the story of slavery is one shared by everybody who enters the space. Its subtle suggestive quality works with the latency of its effect so that as it transitions the visitor from the threshold into the museum space it enables associations to be made with other aspects of the museum.

As a single artwork the piece itself is minimal and does not immediately demand attention as it is not at all self-explanatory. The effect of this artwork is to introduce and thread together complex and disparate themes that can lead the visitor on an emotional journey.

V&A: threshold artwork as declaration

The shadow procession of the Msheireb Museum draws together narrative threads that might otherwise be left unconnected, and it stands in contrast to the way that another museum might use artworks in the threshold to confirm core elements of the museum identity and make conclusive or definitive statements about the institution. Where the power of the Msheireb artwork as a metaphor lies in its subtlety, in other museums the metaphorical meanings of the artwork can operate as a bold statement, a declaration of what the museum is and what the threshold offers. These strategies operate effectively when the narrative of the museum is strongly established and the visitor could be expected to anticipate what they are likely to encounter. A declaration metaphor creates a singular and impactful threshold experience, announcing the presence of the museum, signifying its status, its function and the qualities it wishes to represent. The Victoria and Albert Museum in London presents itself as 'the world's leading museum of art and design'. Visitors entering the foyer of the V&A are confronted by a magnificent glass sculpture by Dale Chihuly (2001) that is nearly 30 feet high, suspended from a rotunda and hanging above the information (and visitor services) desk. This is a prestigious object that signals how the visitor's experience of the museum will emphatically be an aesthetic one in which they experience refined material objects. The presence of the sculpture celebrates masterful design and craft skills, and heightens the awareness that the V&A has a world-leading collection. Described as 'wonderfully dramatic in its effect, a real *coup de théâtre*' (Dorment, 2001), the artwork intensifies the drama of the entry into the museum space and the magnificence of the early twentieth-century architecture. It also signposts the museum's interest in modern design and craft. In this context, the artwork is used as a statement of contemporary panache in an institution that is very aware of the importance of the image that it conveys and also aware that the museum has a brand that is upheld and managed through key moments in the visit (Whitemore, 2013).

The artwork therefore communicates the presence of the museum, and endorsement or celebration of the visitor's expectations. Its purpose is not to make subtle suggestions in the manner of Bin Jelmood House or to provoke questions. The V&A is a national museum of a vast size and with

Suspended: art in the threshold 87

Figure 5.2 Dale Chihuly, V&A rotunda chandelier (2001) at the V&A, London
Source: Steven Smith

a huge amount of choice on offer and a potentially confusing number of directions in which people can turn when they are in the foyer area. An artwork that presents the visitor with a metaphor of certainty and belief in the

88 *Peter Ride*

resonance of objects is in line with many of the nineteenth-century values of the museum which upheld the scholarly interpretation of the collection as its key function and saw the museum as a space of enlightenment (Conn, 2010). The metaphorical power of the sculpture also suggests that while the visitor's journey may have been arduous, the bag check frustrating and the crowds disorientating, the spectacle of a dramatic artwork provides an aesthetic reward and is in keeping with the grand architecture of the foyer.

MOHAI: threshold artwork as metaphors of site

A sculpture at the Seattle Museum of History and Industry (MOHAI) demonstrates how an artwork can operate as site-specific. Created by artist John Grade, the sculpture *Wawona* (2012) is a vertical structure standing 65 feet from floor to ceiling as a tapered tower that recalls both a ship's mast and a tree. The work is made from the reclaimed Douglas fir timbers of a nineteenth-century windsail schooner, *Wawona*. The sculpture can be examined and 'read' critically in the context of art history discourse, as an aesthetic object with integrity and visual meaning, but it can also be seen as a site-specific artwork in that the space it occupies is crucial to what it communicates. It in turn gives added meaning to the threshold. It also demonstrates how a threshold can extend from the external environment

Figure 5.3 John Grade, *Wawona*. Seattle Museum of History and Industry (MOHAI), showing the positioning of the sculpture in the threshold
Source: Peter Ride

through which the visitor approaches the museum to the interior space, which in the case of MOHAI is a large atrium leading onto the galleries and which contains objects and displays.

The sculpture draws on many different themes of the museum. The Douglas fir timber industry dominated the early industry of the Seattle region. The *Wawona* ship itself had a history as an iconic object in Seattle's maritime and industrial history. Dating from 1897, it was one of the best examples of the ships that transported timber on the US north-western coast. Retired in the 1960s and later dry-docked, it became the first vessel to be placed on the National Register of Historic Places and, in 1977, was designated an official Seattle landmark. However, its condition made it unsalvageable and only the timbers that had been below the waterline could be restored. The owners, Northwest Seaport, offered the reclaimed timbers to the artist John Grade for his proposed project for the museum's competition for an artwork as part of the development of its new building, which opened in 2012. The sculpture was designed, computer-cut and hand-carved from the timber planks, with structural engineering provided by Arup Seattle and the incorporation of water-jet cut steel rib plates (Blomgren, 2012).

Wawona draws on and evokes the maritime industry of Seattle. The exterior of the sculpture has been re-hewn to create bobbles along its surface, often in line with the knots of the wood, giving the impression of plankton brushing against the surface of the vessel. It has also been engineered with a hollow interior large enough for people to stand inside and from this point of view it creates the impression of the interior cross-section of a ship's keel. The sculpture is suspended as a pendulum so that when visitors press against its exterior it starts to slowly move like a boat rocking in the water. When a visitor stands inside the object the pinpricks of light emerge through the knotholes of the wood in a mesmerizing starlight pattern. The sculpture uses a poetic sensibility and through its physical interactivity it enables visitors to have a sense of tactile engagement with the artwork. *Wawona* is supported by didactic information panels but allows visitors to explore and learn through touch, sight and imagination. The artwork also employs a constructivist approach to museum learning and engagement.

Once *Wawona* has been encountered, it becomes obvious that this artwork draws on all the narrative threads being explored in the museum: the historic industries of the region, natural ecology, human endeavour and resource management. Not only does the sculpture create connections to the subject areas of the museum, but it also addresses its physical site. The museum is in a historic harbour building, the former Naval Reserve Armory, on the shores of Lake Union. The sculpture extends through the building, starting below the floor of the museum, in the waters of the lake and rising through the roof. When visitors stand inside the sculpture they can see down into the waters of the lake below and up towards the sky where the sculpture punctures the fabric of the building. While the museum protects the main body of the sculpture from the climate, the extremities are revealed to

Figure 5.4 John Grade, *Wawona*. Seattle Museum of History and Industry (MOHAI), interior of sculpture, looking up

Source: Peter Ride

the elements and will weather over time. Therefore, as well as being housed in the museum, the artwork connects directly to the local environment.

The threshold of the museum covers a large area, from the entry point in the lakeside park. The foyer opens onto a central atrium of the building which houses a number of exhibits as well as *Wawona*, including major objects from the collection such as a dramatically suspended US mail aircraft. The museum's brief to the artist was broad, requiring that it dealt at least loosely with Seattle history and, in relation to the architecture of the building, that it could be located near the elevator shaft.[6] As visitors go up to the higher floors of the museum the sculpture becomes a constant reference point. A 2014 visitor survey showed that a quarter of museum visitors move around the exhibits on the ground floor starting from the direction of *Wawona*.[7]

The significance of this sculpture is that it exemplifies how an artwork resonates beyond the physical space of the museum and connects to local interests, stories and histories. Metaphorically it combines the spectacular power of the Dale Chihuly artwork at the V&A and the suggestive quality of the shadow projection in Qatar and in addition it has an additional

Suspended: art in the threshold 91

Figure 5.5 John Grade, *Wawona*. Seattle Museum of History and Industry (MOHAI), visitors interacting with sculpture
Source: Peter Ride

attraction as a site-specific work drawing an awareness of the location into the space of the museum.

Aga Khan Museum: threshold artwork as subtext

Threshold artworks such as those discussed already may be outstanding because of their dramatic quality and because of the way in which they relate with a context of the museum collection or displays. However, in many situations it is hard to consider the qualities an artwork brings to a space without considering it in relation to the architecture. Indeed, in some situations the architecture creates such a defining concept for the institution that what an artwork offers is a subtextual way of understanding the physicality of the museum. The artworks serve as a reminder that museum buildings can be conceptualized as dynamic spaces where meaning is not static but results from the interactions of the people and material within them (Jones and MacLeod, 2016).

The Aga Khan Museum in Toronto illustrates the way in which a threshold artwork can respond and contribute to the qualities of the building but can also address a subtext of the museum narrative. The Aga Khan Museum houses and exhibits some of the most important works of Islamic art in the world. Founded by His Highness the Aga Khan, the spiritual leader of the Shia Imami Ismaili Muslim community, the museum aims to celebrate the geographic, ethnic, linguistic and religious pluralism of Muslim civilization and the museum collection highlights 'objects drawn from every region and every period, and created from every kind of material in the Muslim world'.[8] A six-metre-long tapestry hangs in the café area of the museum outside the galleries housing the permanent collections and temporary exhibitions. Created by Pakistani artist, Aisha Khalid and titled *Your Way Begins on the Other Side* (2014) the work was commissioned to be part of the museum's opening exhibition *The Garden of Ideas* and designed specifically for the space. It was subsequently acquired for the permanent collection. From one side the tapestry appears to be delicately patterned in the style of a Persian carpet, but on closer inspection it is becomes clear that instead of stitching the artist has used gold and steel pin heads to puncture the velvet and silk to create outlines of animals and a garden. Looking at it from the reverse side, the pins protrude and form a shimmering, beguiling but dangerous surface. The tapestry was made in Lahore with skilled tapestry craftspeople and consists of over one million pins and weighs over 100 kilos.[9] The title of the work, drawn from the writing of the thirteenth-century mystical poet Rumi, alludes to the connection between the spiritual and everyday life.

However, the use of artwork in the Aga Khan Museum demonstrates that it can be complicated for artworks to have an independent presence when the architecture defines the mood and feel of the building. The museum opened in 2014 in an elegant, white granite modernist building designed by Fumihiko Maki, and the entrance is approached through an open square where formal gardens are placed amongst shallow granite-lined pools. The entrance leads past a restaurant and bookshop to a dramatic central courtyard. This internal open space within the building is the climactic part of the threshold approach, and is lined with glass panels that are decorated with repeating designs based on traditional Islamic designs. Beyond the courtyard are the galleries housing the museum collection and temporary

Suspended: art in the threshold 93

exhibitions. However, there are no museum objects or images on show as visual evidence of the collection at this point in the visitor's journey. The only exception to this is the tapestry *Your Way Begins on the Other Side*. Its positioning is a reminder that what constitutes the threshold experience is not defined by architecture but by the way in which the building is used. The threshold area at the Aga Khan Museum is not only extensive but free, whereas entry is charged to the main galleries that lie beyond the lobby and courtyard area, thereby fostering a different type of visitor engagement.

The key visual element in this area, and throughout the building, is light. The central well of the courtyard throws patterned shadows that move across the adjacent walls and floor throughout the day, reproducing the patterns on the glass that are inspired by Islamic Jali screens. Skylights also cast delicately patterned shadows onto the floor. The use of light is typical of the architect's practice but it is also symbolically important within the institution, the museum's mission being to foster knowledge and understanding within Muslim communities and between these societies and other cultures. The museum uses light as a metaphorial concept shared by many faiths and a metaphor of tolerance and understanding (Monreal, 2014). The tapestry by Aisha Khalid, *Your Way Begins on the Other Side*, picks up the theme of light by having a surface that glistens and glimmers, reflecting light from

Figure 5.6 Aga Khan Museum, Toronto, exterior looking towards the main entrance
Source: Peter Ride

different directions. Linda Milrod, Head of Exhibitions and Collections at the Aga Khan Museum, identifies that the light patterning is a crucial creative element in the museum threshold that other artworks or displays would disrupt. From the perception of the museum staff, light is crucial for the mood of the museum, contributing directly to the ambience of the interior space and making it comfortable for visitors. Because it is not a large building, visitors are always aware of the dimensions of the light from the courtyard.[10] Additionally, it was recognized that as well as the light patterning, the scale and height of the lobby would diminish the impact of anything other than very large works. Therefore, as a threshold artwork the tapestry differs considerably from the way that a declarative artwork such as the Chihuly operates at the V&A by making a grand statement. In an architectural space such as the Aga Khan Museum an artwork is required to have a subtle presence so that it provides subtext rather than an explosive impact.

However, the power of the tapestry as a metaphoric artwork also lies in the way that it works with the subtext of the museum's narrative. Principally, the museum collection focuses on the history of Islamic Art from the seventh century until the seventeenth. It deals with creativity across the art and with artefacts that relate to a variety of cultural practices as well as material from different geographic communities. This emphasis on historical work is not unusual with collections of Islamic art and is justified by the excellence of the material on show, much of which has been contributed from the family collection of His Highness the Aga Khan. However, the tapestry by Aisha Khalid represents a contemporary approach to a traditional subject and suggests a relationship between the history and the present. The museum has been committed to a vision of plurality from the outset, of interaction between faith groups and communities, Muslim and non-Muslim:

> In a world in which some speak of a growing clash of civilizations we hope and believe that the museum will help to address what is not so much a clash of civilizations as it is a clash of ignorance.
> (His Highness the Aga Khan, 2014)

The modernist architecture places the museum in a contemporary milieu but the tapestry contributes a missing element that is the visible contribution of contemporary Islamic culture. It provides the necessary representation that the museum has a self-declared role as an agent of social engagement and interaction and engages in current debate as well as showing and studying historic material. The tapestry at the Aga Khan Museum is an example of the way in which institutions use artworks to offer visitors different ways of experiencing the building and allow an entry point into the museum's concepts and concerns. Like *Wawona* at MOHAI and the shadow projection at Msheireb Museum, the tapestry prompts metaphors in a way that is open-ended, offering suggestions

Suspended: art in the threshold 95

Figure 5.7 Aisha Khalid, *Your Way Begins on the Other Side* (2014). Aga Khan Museum, Toronto, interior

Source: Ian Rashid

rather than fixed meanings. Its placement recognizes that the threshold can be a liminal space where the many threads of the museum's narrative are suspended, and the visitors' interaction with the space can be subtle as they progress on their journey into the museum.

Brooklyn Museum: threshold artwork as participation

Brooklyn Museum is another museum that shows how the interaction of architecture and artwork lets the visitor approach the museum in ways that might not otherwise come about. Like MOHAI in Seattle, it also shows how artworks can emphasize the connection between the museum and its physical location but furthermore it emphasizes its place within the public realm by enabling and facilitating public participation.

In 2012 Brooklyn Museum commissioned Taiwanese-American artist Lee Mingwei to re-present his artwork *The Moving Garden*. The artwork was a process-based, conceptual art project and consisted of a 45-foot-long granite table with a jagged channel along its length and from which over 200 flowers appeared to grow. It stood in the lobby area of the museum. Visitors were invited to take a flower as they left the museum but on the condition that they made a detour in their journey to give it to a stranger before they reached their next destination.[11] As each day progressed, the stock of flowers was depleted but was then replenished the next day. Although the table and flowers existed as an object in the museum, the real activity was in the interaction of the visitor. This interaction then put them into the role of a protagonist, first in taking the flower and second in making a gift of the flower to another person, in a location outside the museum. The artist was inspired by the concept of gift-giving but also by a fascination with the conscious or unconscious deliberations that people make when deciding to whom they would offer the flower.[12] The artwork therefore shifts the role of the museum visitor from being a passive viewer to an active participant in the artwork. It also suggests that the foyer is not only an entry and exit point but also a transitional space that links the business of the museum with people and their daily lives. In a museum environment where objects cannot often be touched, it is highly memorable when an object can not only be handled but becomes something that can be transferred to another context, and in doing so can acquire any number of personal or evocative meanings.

On a metaphoric level, the artwork is not only concerned with site, and with participation, but it also embodies metaphors of social engagement. It demonstrates how the museum can intensify the visitor experience through the use of artwork. *The Moving Garden* was also part of a visitor engagement strategy by the Brooklyn Museum to include works from the collection and present temporary works in the threshold area. It reflects an acute awareness of the importance of bridging the museum with the surrounding area and its social dynamic and of exploring the opportunities provided by the architectural space.

An extensive visitor experience evaluation that took place over three years addressed how the institution could create a dynamic and responsive museum that fostered dialogue and sparked conversation between staff and all its visitors. Using focus groups, discussion forums and observation, the

Suspended: art in the threshold 97

Figure 5.8 Artist Lee Mingwei, *The Moving Garden* (2009/2011). Brooklyn Museum
Source: Brooklyn Museum

evaluation included the part played by the museum threshold.[13] Opened in 1895, the museum is an imposing Beaux Arts building with a classical

98 Peter Ride

portico. In 2004 the ground floor entrance was redesigned to expand the lobby area and to create an extensive glass pavilion coming out from the building. This meant that the doors of the museum seamlessly connected onto a large open plaza.[14] Through its evaluation, the museum examined the contrast between the way that the plaza could be a vibrant and exciting community gathering point and the visitor's entry into the museum threshold. The museum's audience engagement team found that public feedback showed that visitors identified that they would walk in from the outside where the mood felt relaxed and hip with people playing, reading, and kids on skateboards, but when they approached the beautiful glass front door the mood became silent, imposing and sterile. Consequently, the museum's engagement team took on the challenge of how to take the mood that existed outside and bring it indoors.[15]

In response to the challenge, changes were made in the spatial arrangements of the lobby area by moving visitor information desks and changing signage but the evaluation also resulted in a commitment to use the space to present art. As well as temporary projects like *The Moving Garden* that could be located in the pavilion area other artists' projects, for example *Stephen Powers: Coney Island Is Still Dreamland (To a Seagull)* (2015) were programmed so that work was displayed in both the gallery space and the plaza,

Figure 5.9 Brooklyn Museum visitor interacting with sculptures by Auguste Rodin, *Burghers of Calais* (1889), in the pavilion

Source: Peter Ride

thereby bridging the interior of the museum with the outside. The museum also continued an existing strategy of displaying significant works from the collection in the threshold area making key works from the permanent collection accessible and aiming to ensure that visitors did not feel intimidated by the artworks they were encountering. For example, Auguste Rodin's sculptures *The Burghers of Calais* (1889) were placed in the pavilion area for an extended display. Significantly, these iconic works of European modernism were not placed on plinths but were placed at ground level so people could move in and among them, match their body size to that of the sculptures and take selfies in front of them.

The relationship between Brooklyn Museum and its local community is an indicator of this approach. A 2016 survey indicated that 70 per cent of the museum's visitors were from New York City and 50 per cent were local to the Brooklyn area. The social media engagement also showed that the people who were the most engaged on digital platforms were also local audiences.[16] This information underscores the importance of the threshold because not only is it the space where the visitor's journey begins and ends but it is also the point at which the community accesses the museum. The use of art in the threshold, inside and out, is therefore an important part of the way in which Brooklyn Museum can reflect upon its community role. It illustrates its commitment to social engagement by making the threshold a place of performance, shared ownership and social activity. Brooklyn Museum demonstrates how artworks can help address some of the barriers to participation that exist with museums. The example indicates that it is not only relevant who crosses the line into the museum but also how they are then facilitated to engage with it. Lee Mingwei's project *The Moving Garden* is not only an example of the way that a museum can support its relationship with its community but it also shows that the threshold is a space of two-way traffic. While on the one hand it is the space where the public comes into the museum, it is also the space where the museum can take itself out, even symbolically, into the community.

Museum of London: threshold artwork as wayfinder

Another aspect of the part played by artwork in the threshold is that it provides non-directional guidance to the visitor. This is demonstrated by artworks in the lobby of the Brooklyn Museum but also more specifically in museums where the movement of people through the museum space is a particular concern. As in the Brooklyn Museum, artwork can be used to facilitate the visitor experience, but in these museums the artwork has a role both as a wayfinder that orients people through their approach and entry and to enable to them to transition through the space. These examples also illustrate that wayfinding is more than creating directions through text and graphics, it is about enabling visitors to understand the complexity of their

100 *Peter Ride*

journey. Contemplating the way that artworks can contribute to wayfinding also recognizes that different audiences need different experiences. The Museum of London shows how artworks in the museum are not just single items but they can operate as a suite that gives a range of different opportunities to the visitor. The entrance to the Museum of London is positioned above street level as part of the Barbican inner city complex that is connected by walkways, which means that although it is in the heart of London's financial district it has no street traffic and few passing pedestrians. The threshold of the museum could be said to start from the point at which the visitor approaches the stairs and escalators that will take them from the street to the overhead walkways and from there to the museum's entrance. The museum foyer is a large square area that houses the visitor information desk and bookshop and has exit points to the café and the museum galleries on the same level. It also includes a stairwell which leads to galleries on a lower level, including the exhibition gallery which houses the high profile temporary shows. The foyer has two wall spaces, one used for promoting museum activities and the other a temporary display space for commission or small scale projects. The programme team at the Museum of London describe the foyer as being a complex transition zone, where it is important to manage how visitors pass from being in one state to being in another as they begin to be involved with the content of the museum.[17]

In October 2014, the Museum of London launched a major temporary exhibition *Sherlock Holmes, The Man Who Never Lived And Will Never Die* and created a trail of related displays going from street level to the exhibition itself. On a large wall in the centre of a traffic roundabout were placed large-scale stick figures of 'dancing men'; above ground level where a rotunda leads to the entrance of the museum a short story by Arthur Conan Doyle, 'The Adventure of the Dancing Men', was reproduced in its entirety. This explained that the figures below were a code that spelt out 'come at once'. Inside the foyer was an installation consisting of brightly coloured doorways. Titled *Mind Maze*, and designed by Seán & Stephen and Neu Architects, each was a version of the famous front door at 221B Baker Street, with clues and illustrations relating to a Sherlock Holmes case.[18]

Encountering the artwork in the extended threshold area in this instance was not just part of a physical entry into the museum space but an entry into a whole season of activities and displays. Elsewhere in the museum, apart from the major Sherlock Holmes exhibition itself, was a display of photographs of Holmes-inspired menswear. In addition, the museum commissioned an online performance audio work that audiences could download before taking part in a 'walk' of the neighbourhood streets. Described as a site-specific, 'cinematic, walking, theatrical experience' the piece was titled *A Hollow Body* by the art collective Circumstance.[19] The final crescendo point of the visitor's journey was the exhibition itself which

Figures 5.10–5.13 (continued)

(continued)

Figures 5.10–5.13 Museum of London, following the visitors' entrance from the external rotunda, inside the rotunda to the foyer display (Images: Peter Ride)

included original manuscripts, historical objects that related to the fictitious clues from the Holmes stories, and artworks of London from the period. Entry to the museum is free but temporary exhibitions are significant revenue earners for the museum, so as well as delivering a high-quality and rewarding cultural experience the museum also needs to reach attendance targets. The visitor's journey, and their satisfaction, therefore needs to be thought of as operating on a number of levels.

The *Mind Maze* installation in the foyer was itself a playful pun on the concept of the threshold, using the doorway of 221B Baker Street as a motif because the consulting room is the starting point of most of the Sherlock Homes stories. The installation was designed as a game, but one that required detailed knowledge of the Conan Doyle stories. The museum employs a very detailed and precise form of audience segmentation when planning its programmes[20] and the Sherlock Holmes exhibition was primarily designed for the segment typified as 'London Insiders', who are trendsetters and cultural advocates. The *Mind Maze* was therefore designed to be appropriate for this group. Ironically, this was not the audience segment that spent most time at the display. The museum's visitor research looking at overall museum experience showed that a minority of 'London Insiders' who visited the exhibition paid attention to the foyer installation.[21] However, additional university research through observation confirmed that although adults as individuals or groups did not often appear to spend sustained time solving the puzzle it was very popular with family visitors as a play space, because of its interactive, physical nature, so that it served multiple roles and audiences.[22]

The example of the Museum of London demonstrates the complexity of the physical boundaries of a threshold and how artworks can be used to facilitate the visitor's journey not only through the physical building but into the heart of the programme. The non-directional guidance it provides emphasizes that the 'paid' exhibition is at the heart of the experience, and furthermore it rewards the visitor who wants to engage deeply with the museum across a number of platforms or cultural offers and possibly across different visits.

Conclusion

These examples have illustrated what happens when an artwork is one of the features of the museum that visitors encounter in the threshold. They demonstrate how the multiple roles of the threshold space go well beyond the utilitarian functions. Alongside introductory or wayfaring signage, invitations and instructions on how space is to be used and negotiated or suggesting the social mores that are in place, and promotions for exhibitions, events, products and income-generating activities, there are many other ways in which the threshold conveys meaning to visitors. Artwork gives the museum visitor a nuanced and complex way of understanding what the museum has to offer.

Artworks contribute to the meaning of the museum threshold in ways that are ambiguous and diverse by offering a creative experience to the museum visitor. They can be impactful or resonant, experimental or playful and they can deconstruct or interpret the experience of the architecture. These examples have shown how artwork can offer metaphoric meanings that play a part in the museum narrative, either framing it as a paratext, working as a subtext or extending the connections of the museum's narrative with its physical and social sites of engagement. Ultimately, the study of artworks shows that museums operate as flexible spaces where the meaning that the visitor takes with them on their journey comes about through a complex interaction of space, materials, objects and other people. To return to the metaphor with which this chapter opened, we can think of the artworks in the threshold as openings that create windows for the imagination.

Notes

1 Within the chapter I have used a range of terminologies for 'threshold', depending on the terms the curators use or how the literature for each museum describes it, and because each museum has specific spaces: foyer, lobby, pavilion, atrium, entrance, forecourt, hall, etc.
2 www.history.ac.uk/1807commemorated/discussion/present_past.html.
3 'Genette's study of paratext – the "undecided zone" between the interior and the exterior of the text occupied by prefaces, epigraphs, notes, interviews, etc. which constitutes a space of transaction between author and reader – is titled *Seuils* (thresholds), the very term employed to describe the transitions between narrative levels.' Didier Coste and John Pier (2011) *The Living Handbook of Narratology*, Hamburg University Press, http://wikis.sub.uni-hamburg.de/lhn/index.php/Narrative_Levels.
4 Colin Jones interview with Peter Ride, April 2016.
5 Colin Jones interview with Peter Ride, April 2016.
6 Mark Gleason, Exhibits Manager, MOHAI, interview with Peter Ride, 2016.
7 Mark Gleason, Exhibits Manager, MOHAI, interview with Peter Ride, 2016.
8 His Highness the Aga Khan quoted in (2013) *Aga Khan Museum Project Brief*, p. 6, www.akdn.org/publications/akm_project_brief.pdf.
9 www.facebook.com/aishakhalid72/.
10 Linda Milrod interview with Peter Ride, July 2015.
11 www.brooklynmuseum.org/exhibitions/moving_garden/. Accessed 29 May 2014.
12 Lee Mingwei 'The Moving Garden' <https://www.youtube.com/watch?v=VUcEDVZQigw>
13 The visitor experience evaluation was a Bloomberg Connects project www.brooklynmuseum.org/community/blogosphere/2014/09/09/responsive_museum/ <accessed February 2016.
14 www.brooklynmuseum.org/features/building. Accessed March 2016.
15 Sara Devine Manager of Audience Engagement & Interpretive Materials, Brooklyn Museum, interview with Peter Ride, 2016.

16 Sara Devine Manager of Audience Engagement & Interpretive Materials, Brooklyn Museum, interview with Peter Ride, 2016.
17 Annette Day, Head of Programmes at the Museum of London, interview with Peter Ride, February 2016.
18 http://seanandstephen.com/projects/. Accessed 8 February 2018.
19 http://wearecircumstance.com/a-hollow-body/. Accessed 8 February 2018.
20 www.research-live.com/article/opinion/segmenting-a-cultural-audience/id/4012189.
21 Annette Day interview with Peter Ride, February 2016.
22 Observational research conducted by University of Westminster students February–March 2015.

References

Barrett, T. (2002) *Interpreting Art: Reflecting, Wondering, and Responding*, London: McGraw-Hill.
Blomgren, H. (2012) 'Realizing the Wawona Sculpture: An Engineer's View on Collaborating with the Artist John Grade', *ARCADE* 30:4 Available: http://arcadenw.org/article/realizing-the-wawona-sculpture-1.
Conn, S. (2010) *Do Museums Still Need Objects?* Philadelphia, PA: University of Pennsylvania Press.
Doering, Z. D. and Pekarik, A. J. (1996) 'Questioning the Entrance Narrative', *The Journal of Museum Education*, 21:3.
Doherty, C. (2015) *Public Art (Now): Out of Time, Out of Place*, London: Art/Books.
Dorment, R. (2001) 'The Mind-blowing Gift of a Master', *Daily Telegraph*, 24 July 2001 Available: www.telegraph.co.uk/culture/4724668/The-mind-blowing-gift-of-a-master.html. Accessed 29 May 2014.
Elkins, J. (2000) *The Object Stares Back*, London: Routledge.
Fludernik, M. (2009) *An Introduction to Narratology*, London: Routledge.
His Highness the Aga Khan (2014) Foreword, *Aga Khan Museum Guide*, Toronto: Aga Khan Museum, p. 8.
Jones, P. and MacLeod, S. (2016) 'Museum Architecture Matters', *Museum & Society*, 14:1, p. 208.
Jones, S. E. (2008) *The Meaning of Video Games: Gaming and Textual Strategies*, London: Routledge.
Lord, B. and Piacente, M. eds. (2014) *Manual of Museum Exhibitions*, London: Rowman & Littlefield.
Mahgoub, Y. and Theodoropoulou, I. (2014) 'Investigating Qatari Traditional Architecture from an Interdisciplinary Approach', *Humanities and Social Sciences Review*, 3:4, pp. 477–485.
Monreal, L. (2014) 'Wisdom Begins with Wonder: The Aga Khan Museum in Context'. In Kim, H. ed. *Pattern and Light: The Aga Khan Museum*, Toronto: Aga Khan Museum.
Muller, L. (2011) 'Learning from Experience'. In Candy, L. and Edmonds, E. eds. *Interacting: Art, Research and the Creative Practitioner*, Faringdon, UK: Libri, pp. 94–106.
Putnam, J. (2001) *Art and Artifact: The Museum as Medium*, London: Thames and Hudson.

Redler, H. (2009) 'From Interventions to Interactions: Science Museum Arts Projects' History and the Challenges of Interpreting Art in the Science Museum', *Journal of Science Communication* 8:2.
Whitemore, D. (2013) 'Branding the Museum', *V&A podcast*. Available: www.vam.ac.uk/content/articles/v/v-and-a-podcast-branding-the-museum/. Accessed 29 May 2014.
Wilson, F. (1994) *Mining the Museum: An Installation*, New York: Folio.
Wright, S. (1988) *Koviashuvik*, San Francisco, CA: Sierra Club Books.

6 Curation at the threshold
Making museum meanings through new interfaces

Angelina Russo and Philip Pond

In this chapter, we explore how the architectural threshold has become a significant concept for curators and for museum studies, as digital technologies increasingly shape the interaction between visitors and exhibitions. In recent years, the way in which visitors first arrive in a museum has changed profoundly, as have the technologies that those visitors bring with them. The photographing and social sharing of images taken within museums have extended the museum into digital space, so that for many visitors, the 'curated experience' begins well before they set foot within the physical architecture of the museum. These changes require news ways of conceptualising the museum, most particularly, the notion that these highly connected visitors create a new threshold by curating and publishing their personal experiences, thus making meanings through new interfaces.

In the first part of this chapter we attempt to draw together some of the discourses that link architectural thresholds to museum communication by exploring notions of liminality, connectedness and transparency. Then we seek to describe the influence of digital communication technologies on museum visitation and we define how these fit within the notion of the 'connected museum' – that is, the museum in an age of increased mobility and access to digital technology. We suggest that software and digital cultures shape the interaction between visitors and museum objects, and that this interaction can be conceptualised as an emergent threshold. In order to explore this threshold, we report on a study of visitor engagement with the exhibitions held in the Nicholson Museum, which is part of the Chau Chak Wing Museum at Sydney University. We look at how visitors to the museum have used Instagram to document their visits, and discuss the implications of these practices for the digital threshold and for the connected museum more broadly. In doing so, we make two substantive observations. First, we note that Instagram users curate a threshold that is both personal and public and that this has both practical and conceptual implications for curators. Second, we recognise the considerable complexity of the digital threshold. While researchers are beginning to develop a suite of conceptual and technological tools to explore this complexity, we describe how privatisation and restrictions on data access threaten this work.

The conceptual threshold

> If anything is described by an architectural plan, it is the nature of human relationships, since the elements whose trace it records – walls, doors, windows and stairs – are employed first to divide and then selectively to re-unite inhabited spaced. But what is generally absent in even the most elaborately illustrated building is the way human figures will occupy it . . . [W]hen figures do appear, they tend not to be substantial creatures but emblems, mere signs of life . . . Take the portrayal of human figures and take house plans from a given time and place: look at them together as evidence of a way of life, and the coupling between everyday conduct and architectural organisation may become more lucid.
>
> (Evans, 1997)

In this way, the late Robin Evans (1944–1993) framed his discussion of the representation of people in architectural drawings. Evans, an architectural historian, explored the lack of fit between the stated intention of housing and the impact on those who inhabited it. Evans was known for scrutinising plans, searching for characteristics that could 'provide the preconditions for the way people occupy space, on the assumption that buildings accommodate what pictures illustrate and what words describe in the field of human relations' (Mostafavi, 1997).

Decades earlier, and with a similar enthusiasm for scrutiny of those moments of spatial and temporal change in architecture, Gordon Cullen offered that 'no sooner do we create a HERE than we have to admit a THERE, and it is precisely in the manipulation of these two spatial concepts that a large part of urban drama arises' (Cullen, 1971). In essence, Cullen was describing the threshold. In his lyrical prose and delightful sketches, Cullen remarked on the how space is captured and made infinite; how deflection and projection come to be used; how the inside extends out; and how space is made continuous while it shifts from public to private, external to internal. All the while, he explored the physical characteristics that operate together to complete the physical and conceptual transition from 'here to there'.

Both Cullen and Evans spoke of the interface between building and occupation, between the now and future, a transitional space that we have come to understand as the threshold.

In these analyses, spatial sequences and geometries of form provided the interface for engagement and encounter. Boettger (2014) describes how the design and construction of major public buildings is underwritten by guiding themes such as transparency, clarity and openness. Museums are 'expected to develop a sense of identity among the inhabitants by exhibiting cultural works and providing a platform for discussion', their thresholds become places of communication and representation, cultivating imagination and offering transparent, open and accessible spaces which, in turn become showpieces of the institutions' understanding of culture (Boettger, 2014, p. 59). The threshold becomes imbued with cultural and social significance well beyond its formal geometry and provides insights into both the spaces that await the visitor and the transformative experience that transcends their visitation.

Sfinteș (2013) suggests that through the treatment of the threshold, the museum 'introduces its visitors into a parallel reality in which time and space have other meanings and dimensions than in everyday life, being experienced differently. The building becomes a transitional space, a thirdspace in-between.' Sfinteș seeks to understand what Smith (2001, p. 1) describes as liminality in architecture, a process she defines as the 'precarious threshold between a person's previous role in society and his new, evolved existence'. It is this liminality between existing and future relationships that enables us to explore the possibilities of the threshold as a testing ground for both communication technologies and architectural intention, particularly in ways that connect with the questions that Strobel (2014) poses for future interactions between architecture and technology. He asks whether new typologies will be formed as conflicts between transparency and separation develop and whether architecture, technology and communication can be separated at all in these increasingly important cultural spaces.

As we have seen, the threshold is a complex space explored through multiple discourses and presented as an important place of encounter in architectural theory and praxis. Throughout these discussions the liminality of the threshold and the ways in which the encounters between space and visitors occur are increasingly central to the future museum. Even so there is still some way to go to create a seamless journey from architectural transition to museum communication through the threshold. Many of the concepts and theoretical frameworks which have been offered to the museum sector over the past twenty years have been challenged with similar issues of liminality at the threshold. Stuedahl (2015) more fully analyses a number of concepts and theoretical frameworks which describe encounters between visitors and museums. From the 'responsive museum' (Lang, Reeve and Woollard, 2012) through the 'engaging museum' (Black, 2005) and the 'participatory museum' (Simon, 2010), she describes how each conceptual framework shifts the discussion further from inward and often collection-focused discussions, and outward towards museum communication and the public role that it occupies in delivering education, social inclusion and development (Stuedahl, 2015). This is in keeping with Sfinteș (2013) who suggests that visitors are now considered heterogeneous rather than undifferentiated and that, as a result, their experiences may not be those intended by curators, nor then can learning be conceptualised as a one-way process; rather, visitors and their experiences come to extend the social role of the museum well beyond its formal setting.

Through concepts such as liminality, connectedness and transparency, we can find critical discourses that help us to link architectural thresholds to museum communication, and to illustrate the challenges associated in understanding heterogeneous visitor encounters within the museum, and the ways in which the conceptualisation of these encounters is itself changing. Consequently, we can assert that our visitors' experiences of the threshold are as complex and as subtle as their experiences of the collection.

The threshold of the 'connected museum'

Visitors are encountering the museum in both physical and conceptual ways. We must consider and explore, therefore, how it is that they come to cross the conceptual threshold and enter the museum afresh. If the dynamics of encounter have indeed changed, then we too must extend our notions of the threshold to create a conceptual mapping of these encounters. For instance, one way in which the encounter has changed irrevocably is the ways in which visitors arrive at the museum and the technologies that they bring with them. Kelly (2014) reminds us that mobile technologies afford the museum visitor a richer, deeper and more interesting way of interacting with the physical museum. This is due primarily to their ability to provide layered information and rich media but more importantly, mobile technologies enable visitors to contribute in ways that are meaningful to them (Kelly, 2014). Since the beginning of widely available social media, much of the research has focused on the ways in which museums drive engagement and participation through their emergent social media programs. It is important to remember that in the early days of social media visitors rarely had smartphones (the first iPhone was released in 2007), mobile wireless was not readily available in most institutions and platforms such as YouTube, Facebook, Flickr and Twitter were predominately desktop rather than mobile applications. Today visitors have easy access to multiple network platforms and carry both the device and the enabling technology to become autonomous 'live' agents. This has changed the way in which museums encourage visitors to engage within their buildings, with the traditional 'No Photography' signs increasingly replaced by greater tolerance for individuals sharing and tagging their visits – not least via memes such as #Museumselfie.[1] Salazar (2010) suggests that the rise of mobile technologies has allowed audiences to become 'relevant cultural brokers', contesting current understandings of the complex interfaces and intersections between, in this case, science, media and citizenship, and offering insights into how museums could engage with local communities. We contend that at the same time, these social and technological changes shift some aspects of authority away from the museum, giving agency to individual ambassadors or influencers who develop discursive yet autonomous relationships with the museum. Each of these shifts takes us closer to the recognition that conceptual thresholds related to audience experience are based on communication where the visitor is no longer an active cultural participant (Russo et al., 2006), nor a consumer or pro-sumer, but rather a cultural broadcaster with, in some instances, a significant currency as cultural influencer within a value network. Stuedahl argues that the framework that best captures the compelling characteristics of museum visitation in an age of increased mobility and access to digital technology is that which Drotner and Schrøder (2013) describe as the 'connected museum'. At the heart of the connected museum are museological traditions that share a focus on segmenting their objects of study while analysing visitation as contextualised practices of meaning-making that emerge through interactions between collections and visitors. The scholarly adoption and analysis of these two frameworks provides the focus for the connected museum (Drotner and Schrøder, 2013). This emphasis on the convergence of existing theoretical and conceptual discourses is no accident at a time when audience expectation and visitor engagement are increasingly central to the discourses of the future of our cultural institutions.

It is through the conceptual lens of the 'connected museum' that we draw together here the practices of architecture and communication to allow them to inform the discussion of the threshold. Parry, Moseley and Kristiansen (2014) provide a backdrop for the work carried out by Drotner and Schrøder, pacing through the typologies and nomenclature which allow us to connect architecture and communication in a precise, visitor-focused way. Importantly, they formalise the continued importance of the physical threshold, describing it as a space which 'remains historically resonant, sociologically complex, interpretatively meaningful, and pivotal to the visit event'. In their own research into the museum threshold, they use three experimental interventions – ambient media, augmented signage and invisible performance – to conclude that the '"threshold" might better be understood in terms of intention and action, rather than as a physical parameter'. In making this assertion they strengthen the convergence of the traditions described above in that intention (segmenting objects of study) and action (meaning-making) describe the very preconditions for both the threshold and the connected museum.

Here we use Stuedhal's propositions to anchor our discussion of the threshold in the connected museum. Specifically, Stuedhal (2015) proposes several key areas concerning the author of these connections, as well as how they are made and maintained: the transition to cultural heritage activities; the question of democratic education; the question of collaboration; and collaborative methods and involvement. In the rest of this chapter we seek to contextualise our discussions within these four key areas in order to test the validity of our claim that as a result of increasingly heterogeneous audience engagement, the museum threshold must extend beyond the physical site and into new cultural spaces.

Instagram and #NicholsonMuseum

We have chosen to explore how Instagram can enable the making of meaning through new interfaces at the threshold. We are particularly interested in how the dynamics of the communicative system (Instagram) shape the construction of the threshold. Our proposition is that the peculiar characteristics of different software tools will have particular significance for the interaction between visitor and museum space. The effect, we posit, is that the threshold becomes something shaped partly by curators, partly by visitors and partly by the technological systems that are increasingly used to make and share meaning around museum objects.

Instagram (an online mobile photo-sharing, video-sharing, and social networking service) was purchased by Facebook in 2012, thus reducing the barriers to content-sharing across applications. Instagram is a useful technology through which to follow this discussion as it exposes the complex relationships between audiences and collections, and it introduces new relationships between audiences and their discrete publics. In doing so it creates conceptual thresholds that enable audiences to make sense of and communicate their experiences across multiple networks.

As part of the Sydney University Museums relocation project, and the establishment of the new Chau Chak Wing Museum, we have sought to understand how social media technologies like Instagram can make visible the construction of new conceptual thresholds. By focusing on visitors who share their experiences via Instagram using the hashtag #NicholsonMuseum, we are able to observe the textual–material interaction between technology, users and the curated objects within the Chau Chak Wing Museum.[2] As a university museum, the Chau Chak Wing Museum offers an excellent case to explore the conceptual threshold. It exists as a democratic, educational space that is reliant on collaborative cultural heritage activities for its collections and collaborative methods and involvement for the dissemination of knowledge surrounding those collections. When visitors post and tag their photos they create an extended conceptual threshold for the museum. These images become the extensions of the museum foyer, a site which itself will soon become virtual as the reconstruction begins. We have sought to understand this digital extension of the physical space using a range of methods, and we advocate that a diverse analytical approach is necessary to explore these complex thresholds. There are two observations that we wish to make about these emergent practices; both draw from that wider analysis but can be illustrated in quite specific contexts.

Users who post photographs to Instagram are able to add hashtags to their images, which are searchable, and which Instagram uses to curate tag-specific pages of supposedly similar images.[3] In October 2016 the tag #NicholsonMuseum returned 440 posts dating back four and a half years. Instagram displays these posts chronologically but, in addition, it selects a limited number of 'top posts', which it displays always at the top of the page. For visitors using the hashtag to explore the digital threshold, these top nine posts represent a visual introduction to the Nicholson Museum on Instagram (see Table 6.1).

Table 6.1 Top nine posts on Instagram on hashtag #NicholsonMuseum

RANK	IMAGE DESCRIPTION	LIKES	FOLLOWERS	URL *as originally posted*
1	Lego Venus	235	197,000	www.instagram.com/p/BHJIOLpgKGH/
2	Peacock in stone! A Roman mosaic from Sicily 300–500 BC	35	140	www.instagram.com/p/BGDVmCFCOW4/
3	Woman posing in front of mummies	633	829,000	www.instagram.com/p/BEWcfxoE0SE/
4	Egyptian pencil tips (merchandise)	10,200	385,000	www.instagram.com/p/BCj70s5viW1/
5	Woman pointing to mummies in exhibition case	44	1.964	www.instagram.com/p/BHwrBpmDPtZ/
6	Egyptian Goddess Hathor	23	572	www.instagram.com/p/BJm9BEGjvJR/
7	Lego Venus in exhibition space	26	139	www.instagram.com/p/BHWwvL9AhHA/
8	Lego Pompeii	28	121	www.instagram.com/p/BAwWU0WnZZW/
9	Lego Acropolis	46	32	www.instagram.com/p/BEO7O2hLAiD/

Our first observation is that through the #NicholsonMuseum tag, Instagram users curate a threshold that is both personal and public, both collective and additive, but also one that hints at fragmentation and the instability of shared cultural practices. There are nine different users responsible for the nine top posts, and it is immediately evident that there is huge variety between these user accounts. For instance, Instagram users can follow each other to receive updates of image posts, and this following capability enables individual users to 'broadcast' their uploads to an audience of personalised content subscribers. This following 'connectivity' – the personal public (Schmidt, 2014) – is seen as a key dynamic of social media logic (van Dijck and Poell, 2013). Social media software tends to reward popularity, pushing traffic towards accounts, pages and software objects that are already popular, with the result that there tend to be huge discrepancies between the average size of these personal publics, and a few accounts become extremely popular (van Dijck and Poell, 2013). This is evident in the top posts: there are three accounts with fewer than 200 followers, three with a few thousand followers and the most popular account has 385,000 followers. These huge numerical differences suggest different communicative relationships between Instagram users and their followers; these communicative differences imply quite different forms of threshold construction and highlight a tension between private and public forms of meaning-making.

Of the nine images selected as top posts, seven are 'object-centric': the image represents the curated object much as we might imagine it exists in physical space. The user is interpreting the object, of course, perhaps focusing on a particular aspect (some figurines within a Lego Pompeii) or directing the viewer's gaze in a particular way, but the object remains the focus of the image and it is possible to connect the Instagram representation more or less linearly with a first-person experience of the physical threshold, even if that experience is an imagined one. In two of the posts, however, the Instagram user replaces the object as the focus of the image – the curated object is a prop, subordinate to a user-centric interpretation of the physical threshold experience. This subordination of shared cultural experience to the type of personal 'lifestyle curation' is something for which Instagram is particularly known (Fisher, 2016).

We are not suggesting that there is a correlation, or even a theoretical connection, between the size of the personal public and the type of threshold construction that a given public might expect or reward in Instagram-specific culture, but simply that there are divergent structures for communicating content on Instagram and divergent forms of meaning-making through images. These differences shape a digital threshold that is complex, varied and dynamic but the images and their descriptions, their tags and comment threads, define a lexicon of experiences that is generally available for study. To illustrate what we mean by this, it is worth looking at a couple of images in greater detail, and in considering how these images are represented as computable data.

Instagram enables users and their followers to 'interact' with images in different ways. One way is to 'like' a post – effectively a one-click recommendation – and another is through leaving a comment, which will be displayed as part of a sidebar list on the Instagram website and beneath the image on the mobile application. These comments enable an additive dynamic at the threshold – users and their followers can respond to images and to each other – and lists of comments can be used to explore private and public meaning-making around individual images. For instance, it is worth noting that the tension between object and user-focus and between personal and public culture is evident in how users frame their images with text. For some users, comments are explanatory or informational. The comment attached to image 6 labels the object in the image – as a historical and cultural item – and locates it using the hashtag: 'Egyptian Goddess Hathor #nicholsonmuseum'. Such commenting reflects an assumed publicness – it suggests that the value in the image is evident on its own terms – as a noteworthy object within a shared cultural framework.

This type of threshold construction is quite different from the commenting attached to image 3: 'One more before I go to bed. Have a sweet dream loves, I'll be here dreaming about mummies, vampires, and dragons. Good night! . . . #mummies #NicholsonMuseum'. In this example, once again, the focus is the visitor to the physical exhibition, rather than the exhibition itself. The narrative revolves around her experience of the museum – an experience that is situated within a continuous, personally curated image stream. The threshold is still a shared space, but in order to share it fully, a viewer must be able to translate the ongoing discourse between this Instagram user and her followers.

These contrasting commenting cultures illustrate the complexity and discontinuity of the digital threshold – individual social media users are empowered to interpret their visits to the Chau Chak Wing Museum as they wish, and to share these interpretations with structurally diverse audiences. In one sense, then, the digital threshold represents a challenge to museums: the diversity on display in the #NicholsonMuseum hashtag may represent a loss of control, both in terms of the objects themselves and also in terms of the carefully curated physical threshold. In another sense, though, the digital threshold represents a unique opportunity to explore empirically the construction of the threshold. Museum visitors have interpreted meaning around objects on their own terms – here, at least, that interpretation is encoded in text and made visible.

One issue is that the complexity evident in this limited sample of posts suggests that the full digital threshold is likely to remain unknowable to curators and to museum researchers. At the time of writing there were 440 images on the hashtag page, but Instagram has other ways of representing the digital threshold, and there are other social media platforms and other channels that are less visible to researchers. The conceptual mapping necessary, then, is a daunting task. As researchers, we are better prepared for this endeavour if we can access and understand the data structures and the algorithms through which the digital threshold is constructed. Images, comments, likes and user-specific data are stored in repeating data structures on Instagram, which makes it easier to search, sort and study these thresholds. These images and their descriptions, their tags and comment threads define a lexicon of experiences – a visual and conceptual mapping that, with further investigation, should allow us to make assertions about the future boundaries and obstacles which must be examined in order to create the conceptual threshold of the museum. It is particularly important for researchers and for curators, then, that social media services continue to provide some level of access to this data and to the shared, curated threshold. During the course of our work with Sydney University Museums, Instagram – which is owned by Facebook – changed the terms of access to its application programming interface (API), effectively preventing the type of research that could help elucidate the emergent digital threshold. This change reflects a broader trend across the industry to commercialise data generated through shared cultural endeavour. While these arguments may seem tangential for museums, it is important to recognise that the digital threshold is being privatised as part of this process.

Instagram has created the opportunity for new curatorial activities related to cultural visitation and in doing so is creating a new type of democratisation of collections – enabling broader audiences to be involved in viewing and trading images. Davis (2014) suggests that Instagram 'has so democratized image-making that it has put the artistic power once mainly associated with aristocrats – to stylize your image and project yourself to an audience as desirable – into everyone's hands'. This conceptual threshold may not yet have a direct counterpart in today's museum but it is worth considering that it shares many of the characteristics of the connected museum and must, at the very least, be considered as part of the lexicon.

There is, of course, unevenness in the creation of this conceptual threshold. While visitors are able to upload and publish their experiences, the ways in which those uploads are viewed, shared and remarked upon are ambiguous and widely varied. This leads to a genuinely expansive and distributed threshold where meaning is created both between the visitor and the museum, and the visitor and multiple publics. Future development of museum experiences will need to acknowledge the ways in which this distributed meaning-making impacts on traditional curatorial practices. As distributed platforms and services continue to evolve it is inevitable that visitors will bring an ever more complex and sophisticated set of interfaces into the museum and through the process of sharing, commenting and tagging, they will forge new meanings both personally and within a broader network of viewers.

This in turn will shape the way that we shape our physical environment, presenting new ways of considering digital cultures, digitality and information-gathering. Our understandings around the role of visitor, along with expectations of what the visitor might do in the space, will, in time, come to shape how space itself is designed and arranged. Considered in this way, these digital experiences are important to the museum encounter; not only at the threshold but embedded throughout the visitor experience, ensuring that our digital encounters will continue to affect the way that we understand the physical threshold.

Conclusion

In this chapter we have taken what might be an inventive step from tectonic space to digital communication and back again via the notion of the conceptual threshold in the museum.

We have explored the use of social media as an interface between the visitor and the museum, beginning the process of conceptually mapping the connections between visitor experience and curatorial practice. We have drawn these thoughts together to formalise our position that software and digital cultures shape the interaction between visitors and museum objects and that this interaction can be conceptualised as an emergent threshold.

Throughout this chapter we have contended that it is imperative that the threshold and the threshold experience be considered in tandem; and that the wider context of the museum encounter underpins our understanding of audience visitation irrespective of whether visitors ever enter the physical foyer. The mechanics of that threshold, the proposition that the connected museum embeds the conceptual threshold, allows us to plan for future social experiences; in some ways to rehearse, in a rudimentary way, the basis for the future programming. By delving more deeply into the use of Instagram we begin to create a broader understanding of both the ways in which visitors make meaning through sharing their experiences and the ways in which these new conceptual thresholds spread out organically across the web.

We accept that there is more to be discovered, particularly if we explore the shaping of physical space in ways that do not follow conventional architectonic tropes. Perhaps through the convergence of the digital and the social we can create a statement about how visitors come together and collectively share their experience of the conceptual threshold. There is a possibility that if the threshold is approached in this way we will discover a new idiom, one that does for the future threshold what Evans suggested the architectural plan did in dividing and selectively reuniting inhabited space in order to understand the nature of human relationships.

Notes

1 www.instagram.com/explore/tags/museumselfie/.
2 http://sydney.edu.au/museums/ccw-museum/news-2015-sep.shtml.
3 There are other ways in which Instagram curates context-specific images. For instance, it is also possible to search the platform for 'places' which are computed using a user's geolocation on point of upload. The decision to focus on tagged curation, here, reflects the desire to focus on users who exhibit a higher degree of intentionality – the tag implies a deliberate attempt to share and to collectivise a Nicholson Museum experience. The Nicholson Museum place page is available at www.instagram.com/explore/locations/213209/.

References

Black, G., 2005. *The Engaging Museum: Developing Museums for Visitor Involvement*. Abingdon, UK & New York: Routledge.

Boettger, T., 2014. *Threshold Spaces: Transitions in Architecture – Analysis and Design Tools*. Basel: Birkhäuser Verlag.

Cullen, G., 1971. Here and There. In *The Concise Townscape*. London: Architectural Press, pp. 182–188.

Davis, B., 2014. Ways of Seeing Instagram. *Artnet News*, 24 June 2014. Available at: https://news.artnet.com/exhibitions/ways-of-seeing-instagram-37635. Accessed 1 December 2016.

Drotner, K. and Schrøder, K., eds., 2013. *Museum Communication and Social Media: The Connected Museum*. New York and Abingdon, UK: Routledge.

Evans, R., 1997. Figures, Doors and Passages. In *Translations from Drawing to Building and Other Essays*. London: Architectural Association Publications, pp. 55–58.

Fisher, J., 2016. Curators and Instagram: Affect, Relationality and Keeping in Touch. *Journal of Curatorial Studies*, 5:1, pp. 101–123.

Kelly, L., 2014. The Connected Museum in the World of Social Media. In K. Drotner and K. Schrøder, eds. *Museum Communication and Social Media*. New York and Abingdon, UK: Routledge, pp. 74–92.

Lang, C., Reeve, J., and Woollard, V., eds., 2012. *The Responsive Museum: Working with Audiences in the Twenty-First Century*. London: Routledge.

Mostafavi, M., 1997. Paradoxes of the Ordinary. In *Translations from Drawing to Building and Other Essays*. London: Architectural Association Publications, pp. 5–9.

Parry, R., Moseley, A., and Kristiansen, E., 2014. MW2014: On a New Threshold: Experiments in Gaming, Retail and Performance Design to Shape Museum Entrances. *MW2014: Museums and the Web 2014*. Published 2 April 2014. Consulted 10 February 2018. Available at: https://mw2014.museumsandtheweb.com/paper/on-a-new-threshold-experiments-in-gaming-retail-and-performance-design-to-shape-museum-entrances/.

Russo, A., Watkins, J., Kelly, L., and Chan. S., 2006. How Will Social Media Affect Museum Communication? *Nordic Digital Excellence in Museums conference (NODEM 06)*. Oslo, Norway, December 2006. http://www.tii.se/v4m/nodem/nw_06/papers/pa pers.htm.

Salazar, J. F., 2010. 'Mymuseum': Social Media and the Engagement of the Environmental Citizen. In F. Cameron and L. Kelly, eds. *Hot Topics, Public Culture, Museums*. Newcastle upon Tyne, UK: Cambridge Scholars Publishing, pp. 265–280.

Schmidt, J.-H., 2014. Twitter and the Rise of Personal Publics. In K. Weller, A. Bruns, J. Burgess, M. Mahrt and C. Puschmann, eds. *Twitter and Society*. New York: Peter Lang.

Sfinteş I. A., 2013. Rethinking Liminality: Built Form as Threshold-Space. Available at: www.researchgate.net/publication/283328321_RETHINKING_LIMINALITY_BUILT_FORM_AS_THRESHOLD-SPACE.

Simon, N., 2010. *The Participatory Museum*. Santa Cruz, CA: Museum 2.0.

Smith, C., 2001. Looking for Liminality in Architectural Space. *Limen*, 2, pp. 1–9. Available at: http://limen.mi2.hr/limen1-2001/catherine_smith.html.

Strobel, P., 2014. Threshold Spaces. *Architecture at the Threshold, Siedle Magazine*, 3, pp. 140–143.

Stuedahl, D., 2015. The Connective Museum. *Museum Communication: Practices and Perspectives*. Royal Danish Academy of Sciences and Letters, Copenhagen, 27–28 August 2015.

van Dijck, J. and Poell, T., 2013. Understanding Social Media Logic. *Media and Communication*, 1:1, pp. 2–14.

Conversation 2
Birmingham Museum and Art Gallery

Ruth Page [RP] interviews Lauren Deere [LD], Visitor Experience Manager with the Birmingham Museums Trust.

RP: *Lauren: can you tell us a little bit, please, about Birmingham Museum and Art Gallery?*

LD: Of course. Birmingham Museum and Art Gallery is part of a larger charitable trust which runs nine museums across the city of Birmingham. This museum, Birmingham Museum and Art Gallery, is the largest of all of the nine sites. It is based right in the city centre, next to the Council House, in Victoria Square, Birmingham.

    The museum opened in 1885. And in 2015 we celebrated our 130th anniversary. The museum's been around a long time with multiple extensions and changes, and it has a really varied collection. Our art collection, for example, covers medieval art all the way up to contemporary. We are lucky enough to have one of the largest collections in the world of public Pre-Raphaelite art, which is one of the highlights of a visit here. We have a large portion of the Staffordshire Hoard, and we also have artefacts from the Greek and Roman era. And we also have a large gallery committed to reflecting the history of Birmingham.

RP: *How many visitors do you get here? What kinds of visitors come to Birmingham Museum and Art Gallery?*

LD: We have approximately 600,000 visitors a year. So it is very busy, particularly at peak times. Demographics are quite varied as well: I would say probably about a third of our visitors are families; we have some overseas visitors; we have older adults that come, independent adult students. Birmingham's a really young city, so we try and encourage as many of the students living in the city to come in.

    About 45 per cent of our visitors are first-time visitors. But it's really important to understand that actually, just over half of them come from outside Birmingham. So even though we do have a local contingency

within our visitors, we do have people coming from within the larger west Midlands, and more regionally and internationally.

RP: *In terms of thinking about the threshold and their entry to the museum, can you tell us a little bit about what it would actually be like for a visitor to find their way into Birmingham Museum and Art Gallery, please?*

LD: Birmingham Museum and Art Gallery is based in two separate buildings, the Council House and the Council House Extension.

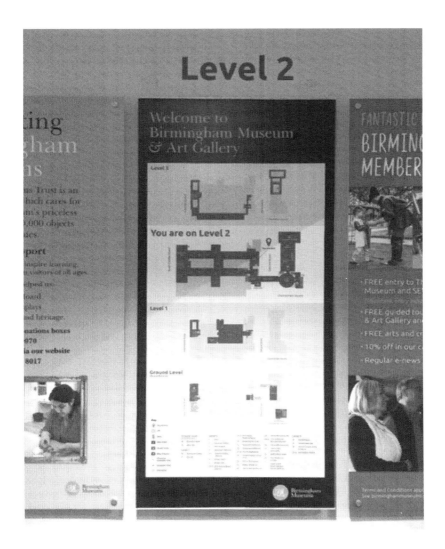

The main entrance and the Water Hall entrance are attached to the main Council House Building, and the Council House extension has three different entrances. Two of the entrances are quite close to the main entrance, just around the corner. The other one is a bit further away, on the opposite side of the building.

When we were thinking about our main entrance, I would say that the main complexity concerns how the entrance is staged. Visitors have a short flight of stairs that take them into the physical building.

Then within that space, it's really glorious. The immediate entrance has many of the original features of the building, including the foundation stone. Once inside, you have to go up a further two flights of stairs to be able to come to a space in which you can really orientate yourself. So the threshold is staged a number of times as visitors enter the building.

Because of all the stairs, obviously, there's an accessibility issue. Unfortunately, the separate lift entrance is at a short distance from our main entrance. You have to go to the [neighbouring] Gas Hall to be able to enter if you have pushchairs or wheelchairs or individuals with mobility issues. That creates a problem in itself: the orientation to the museum has to be in multiple areas.

We find that our members of staff are a great resource when it comes to orientation. We always have a member of staff in the area to welcome visitors and also to provide directions. We get a lot asking for directions to places outside as well, which is quite a nice service to provide. We also have maps and other promotional material available.

RP: *So Lauren, can you tell me a little about some of the practical changes that you've made in your approach to your complex threshold spaces?*

LD: The wayfinding project we did for the Staffordshire Hoard is one example: there are physical directional signs you can see all over the museum, which aim to bring visitors from our main entrance through to the Staffordshire Hoard gallery, which is at the rear of the building. The gallery is quite far, so it was going to be a challenge for us to try and bring people through the museum using the most direct route.

We changed our website as well: being able to have one central website for all the sites has been really great. We've also designed a new map. We conducted a visitor study that was really important for us in producing that map, which we're hoping visitors will find much easier to use: it includes visual clues, rather than just words. So we've incorporated some of the highlights of our collection and used them as trigger points so visitors can see them and they can see where they are on the map.

RP: *Are there any other changes that Birmingham Museum and Art Gallery are anticipating in the future around your thresholds?*

LD: Well, Birmingham Museum and Art Gallery is going to have some huge improvements in the future, especially when we're looking ten years on. We're really starting to think about a master plan for a museum in the twenty-first century.

However, in the next twelve months we are working on a project to improve the general visitor facilities. And we've been lucky enough to get a grant from the DCMS [Department for Culture, Media and Sport] Wolfson Galleries and Museums Improvement Fund to be able to incorporate some of these improvements, as well as being able to update the facilities and improve accessibility in general to the museum. We're also looking at a signage project for our nine entrances and throughout the museum, particularly focusing on our entrances and orientation.

Lauren provided an update to our conversation in August 2017, revealing some of the work that has already been done:

LD: Each entrance without a staff member, including the lift that opens out onto three levels, has a map of the internal museum so that visitors can see where they are arriving. We also have new orientation plinths placed around the museum to help guide visitors once in the museum as well as new directional signage throughout the galleries. Great Charles Street (which was an entrance at the time of interview) is no longer an entrance. Other temporary external signage has been necessary at times, such as a larger building and redevelopment project adjacent to the museum that closed off one of our main exits.

7 Using 3D visualisation technology to improve design and visitor orientation

David Burden

The use of 3D visualisation technology is becoming a part of everyday life, from film and computer-game effects to kitchen design. But how can this technology be applied cost effectively to the design and improvement of the threshold experience? This chapter looks at a number of different ways that 3D technology can be used to conceptualise and design museum and gallery entrances and thresholds. It offers an additional lens to add to the range of new methods presented in this volume in order to provide alternative ways of reflecting upon the museum threshold experience.

After a brief review of 3D visualisation technology, and in particular how it has begun to be democratised, this chapter will look at the elements which make up a 3D immersive environment, how the user experience of the 3D space can be structured, and how the user experience can be evaluated in order to inform real-world decisions. Issues will be considered in a non-technical way as far as possible. Effective research and planning using 3D environments can contribute to the success of any physical build, from its initial opening to any later-life changes and retro-fits. A full case study of the design of the new Library of Birmingham will be presented to show the use of 3D visualisation in context.

Key to this chapter is the way that the use of 3D tools can help to create environments in which ordinary users – be they staff or visitors – can immediately connect with a space, and understand it in a similar way to how they relate to the physical space. This can give users a level of input to design decisions and a sense of ownership of the space that has hitherto been inhibited by the complexities of the tools used by architects and builders.

The development of 3D visualisation

Computer-based 3D visualisation has been around since the late 1950s (Hao, 2006; Carlson, 2007). Through the 1950s and 1960s until well into the 1970s most 3D computer visualisations were wireframe models (see Figure 7.1a), showing only the edges of walls and floors. Solid surfaces (see Figure 7.1b) started to emerge in the 1970s (Gouraud, 1971; Hao, 2006).

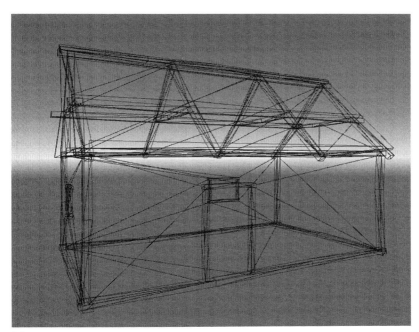
(a)

(b)

Figure 7.1 (continued)

(continued)

(c)

(d)

Figure 7.1 Developments in computer model rendering: (a) Wire-frame image; (b) Single-colour surfaces; (c) Image-based surfaces (aka 'textures'); (d) 'Bump-map' to give sense of surface material

Since then there has been a steady improvement in a computer's ability to create a digital model of the physical world. Principal developments have been in the use of images (called 'textures') to replace solid colour (see Figure 7.1c), and the creation of the algorithms to enable objects to more realistically produce the reflections, shadow and texture of real surfaces (see Figure 7.1d). However, the computation required to do this well led, during the past few decades, to a split between systems that would render the scene offline (e.g. overnight) in order to create a high-resolution image or video, and those that were happy to run at a lower resolution in order to create the scene in real time as the user explores it. This led to a bifurcation of the market between 3D design tools that had a high degree of complexity, visual quality and costs to match (e.g. AutoCAD, Maya, 3D Studio Max), and game-engine based systems offering lower-level quality real-time experiences for hobbyists and game creators (e.g. Unity3D, Unreal).

Democratisation of 3D

The past 15 years have seen an increasing democratisation of the ability to create high quality interactive 3D environments. This change has been driven by three main factors: increases in computer performance as illustrated by Moore's law (Schaller, 1997), the growing interest in making, as well as playing, computer games – resulting in cheap and easy to use tools such as Unity3D, and research into visualisation techniques for movies trickling down into these consumer tools, such as the ability to more realistically model skin and hair, and motion capture for character animation.

One of the biggest steps in this democratisation was the emergence in the late 1990s and early 2000s of social virtual worlds. Whereas game engines such as Unity3D provide the developer with a blank canvas on which they have to build all the buildings and create avatars (digital representations in the environment) and interactions, a virtual world (such as Second Life: Foth et al., 2009) provides the user from the very start with a world (albeit rather empty) and an avatar, and the way to define interactions, so that the user can focus on just building the parts they need. In contrast with a game engine where you are God (you need to build everything from scratch), with a social virtual world you are just you – ready to build a house in a world which already exists, using tools and materials which already exist, or to go out to earn the money to pay a builder to build it for you!

Second Life in particular enabled a whole new group of computer users to start creating and interacting with 3D environments. Since Second Life was an open, persistent virtual world it meant that as soon as a user built something everyone else in the world could see it – just as in the physical world. And since the object creation tools did not need any real computer programming expertise, a large number of artists, teachers, social scientists, curators

128 *David Burden*

and librarians started to experiment with how they could use the world. This included virtual museums (Urban, 2007) (e.g. the Virtual Spaceflight Museum, The Second Louvre Museum), interactive explorations of works of art (e.g. Virtual Starry Night), libraries (e.g. the Alliance Library System's Info Island), unique works of art (such as by the artist Starax), studies into issues

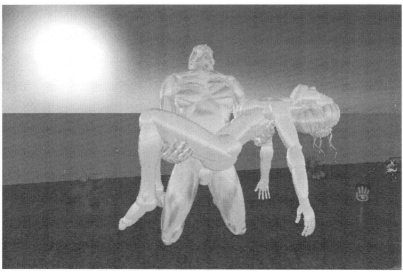

(a)

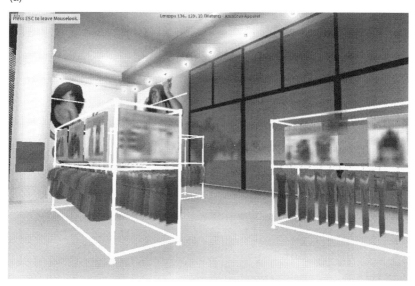

(b)

(c)

(d)

Figure 7.2 Example Second Life builds: (a) An early Starax sculpture in Second Life; (b) American Apparel store in Second Life – one of the first to look at reproducing the physical world retail experience in a virtual world; (c) The Second Life Rossell Hope Robbins Medieval Library; (d) A reproduction of St Paul's Cathedral

of identity (Martey and Consalvo, 2011) and liminal spaces (Gottschalk, 2010), and the modelling of historic and artistic spaces (Kuksa and Childs, 2014; Eduserv, 2009).

To the surprise of many, Second Life is still an active place for teaching, socialising and cultural exploration (e.g. Gallego et al., 2016 and Berger et al., 2016). However, many developers have moved on from Second Life to game engines – although typically driven by practical issues of software development and distribution and user security rather than any lack of core capability in the platform. Another key driver for the move to Unity3D (in particular) has been the ability to support a range of different user devices, from the PC and Mac, to iOS and Android phones, and even some games consoles. Indeed, Unity3D has even been making inroads into the architectural community (Boeykens, 2013) as the environments it can generate begin to reach the high level of realism which that profession demands.

It should be borne in mind that although technologies in this space are changing rapidly, and many of those described may soon become outdated, most of the approaches presented here are technology-neutral and could be implemented using most current, and many future, technologies.

Architectural use of 3D

Whilst computers had been used for creating 2D technical and architectural plans and drawings by large corporations in the 1970s it was the launch of AutoCAD in 1980 that revolutionised the market and by 1984 it was almost ubiquitous. By the mid-1990s CAD packages such as AutoCAD, ArchCAD and 3D Studio supported a variety of techniques, including 2D and 3D design, accurate colour rendering and lighting effects. However, these were tools designed for, used by, and only affordable by, professionals. Even at this early stage, though, Senyapili (1997, p. 260) argued that:

> [the] possibilities offered by visualization do not fit into the paper-based way of architectural thinking. In order to benefit from the potential of visualization it is required to redefine architecture, architectural design process and architectural terms with respect to the virtual environment.

Three Ring Model

From the author's work in social virtual worlds since the 1990s, and talking to clients and contacts in the Architecture–Engineering–Construction (AEC) community, three communities of people can be identified who have an interest in the 3D visualisation of any built-environment project. These are the architects, the builders, and the people who are actually going to use the space (as residents, employees or visitors). However, each of these groups has very different demands of any 3D building model:

For architects it is the look of the visualisation that seems to be paramount. Their 3D visualisations typically use non-real-time rendering in order to ensure that reflections and surfaces all show the building and its local environment off in the best possible way. These 3D models are then used to generate either 2D images or 3D fly-throughs. Given the non-real-time nature of the rendering, though, the images and fly-throughs will only show what the architect wants to show, and the user can't just ask to look around the corner.

For builders the model is there to inform the actual construction of the building, working out the bill of quantities, the order to build, and of course ensuring that the building stays up. Until relatively recently the building trade relied on 2D blueprints rather than 3D models, and even when 3D was adopted it was initially used to generate 'wire-frame' type models with no actual surfaces or lighting shown. Recent years have begun to see a merger of the tools used by architects and builders (or at least a pipeline between them) (Steel et al., 2012) so rendered 3D models are now far more common within the building trade, encouraged in part by the move towards the Building Information Modelling (BIM) standard (Bille et al., 2014, and below).

Users are very much the poor relation. They typically have limited access to the builder's and architect's models, and usually then only in the form of 2D plans and rendered videos or stills. The user, however, wants to not only see the building but use it. They want to know what it's like to navigate its corridors, how long it takes to get from office to toilet, whether doorways will allow equipment to be moved around, where signage is best placed, and how accessible the building is to those with disabilities. Whilst the architect's and builder's model(s) include most of the information needed to answer these questions they do not present it in the best form. From experience there are four key elements missing:

1 The users' model needs to generate a rendered model in real time, so that the user can navigate through it at will.
2 The users' model needs to be interactive – lifts and escalators need to work, and so ideally do lights and other environmental controls and building systems (e.g. security) so that the user has a sense of agency.
3 The user needs to have a sense of self within the space, either from a first-person viewpoint based around the movement of a walking person, or possibly better a third-person representation as an avatar.
4 Ideally there need to be other users in there, also represented by avatars, with whom the user can interact and navigate and use the building as a social space.

These diverse needs are summarised in the Three Ring Model (Burden, 2013).

132   *David Burden*

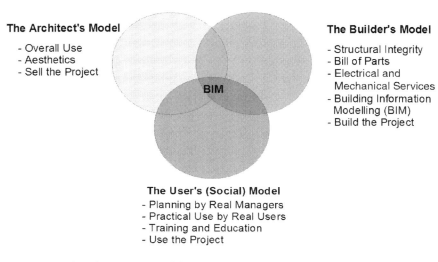

The Architect's Model
- Overall Use
- Aesthetics
- Sell the Project

The Builder's Model
- Structural Integrity
- Bill of Parts
- Electrical and Mechanical Services
- Building Information Modelling (BIM)
- Build the Project

The User's (Social) Model
- Planning by Real Managers
- Practical Use by Real Users
- Training and Education
- Use the Project

Figure 7.3 The Three Ring Model

Whilst 3D modelling applications are well suited to the needs of architects, and 3D CAD tools are well suited to the needs of builders, it is virtual worlds that come closest to meeting the needs of the users. This immediately highlights the biggest problem in creating a user model: how to move the (data-based) representation of the space from the 3D Design and CAD tools into a more user-focused tool such as a virtual world. However, as will be described later, various changes are happening in the industry, which are beginning to overcome this problem.

Virtual Library of Birmingham

An example of how virtual worlds can be used in support of heritage spaces, and specifically threshold experiences, is the Virtual Library of Birmingham project. In early 2010 Daden (a 3D visualisation company) were engaged by Birmingham City Council to create a user model of the new 20,798m^2 Public Library. Whilst the architects, Mecanoo, already had their high-gloss model, and the project managers (Capita Symonds) were creating their builder's model, the City and library management saw the advantage in having a user model in order to:

- Support the outreach activities for the new library.
- Enable the library staff to plan how to use and lay out the new library, and in particular manage the threshold experience.
- Ensure a smooth opening experience once the library formally opened to the public.

Using 3D visualisation technology 133

(a)

(b)

Figure 7.4 The Virtual Library of Birmingham: (a) Virtual Library of Birmingham – external view from Centenary Square; (b) Physical Library of Birmingham – external view from Centenary Square

The build

Given the need for a publicly accessible, multi-user model it was decided to build the Virtual Library of Birmingham (VLOB) in the Second Life

134 *David Burden*

virtual world. Virtual construction, based on 2D plans supplied by Mecanoo, started in January 2010.

For VLOB it was decided that as well as building the library the model had to include the whole of the surrounding location in Birmingham's Centenary Square, as well as a backdrop representing the whole city. This was to ensure that users understood the full context of the building, and so that the full threshold experience could be provided from almost the moment that the Library first came into view.

The virtual build was completed in the Autumn of 2010, and the virtual model handed over to the Library staff in January 2011, the same month as the two-year above-ground construction of the physical library started.

Interaction systems

From the start the intention was to make the Virtual Library an interactive experience. To that end a number of interactive systems were created to

(a)

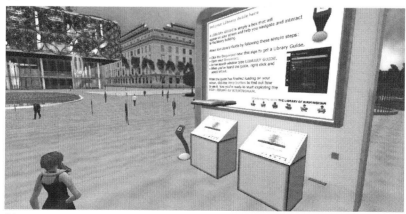
(b)

Using 3D visualisation technology   135

(c)

(d)

Figure 7.5 Interaction systems in the Virtual Library of Birmingham: (a) User interface, with animated tour guide top left, and options voting for the display panels in the Library threshold space; (b) Flying book dispenser at the arrival point on Centenary Square; (c) The layout option selection and voting tool; (d) Explaining how to use the 'annotated spaces' comment smileys

both enhance the user experience and increase the amount of feedback that the staff could get on proposed designs. These systems included:

- A virtual tour guide who could tell users what each space was to be used for, and who could also answer basic questions about the build.
- A 'flying book' tour, where users could sit on a giant book and be taken on a magic-carpet style narrated tour of the library.

- A voting system which let staff provide two or three different layouts for an area and let users switch between them and vote on their favourite.
- Large feedback spheres which users could place in the build and make a comment on. Other users could then vote the comment up or down, and the sphere's colour and smiley face changed accordingly.
- Footfall tracking, so staff could examine routes and dwell time of visitors as they moved through the library.

Orientation

It was understood that for many visitors this would be their first experience of Second Life, and so it was important that the experience was as smooth as possible. As was common in Second Life an orientation zone was created: essentially a threshold to the threshold experience! This space consisted of two parts: a 'hamster trail' intended to get the user used to the Second Life controls for movement and interaction, and a 'Marketing Office', explaining the background to the physical and virtual builds, and letting users try out the various interaction systems. Visitors were then transported to Centenary Square, arriving where a user would typically get off a bus or taxi if visiting the library so as to fully replicate the threshold experience.

Public engagement

One of the key roles of the Virtual Library was to support public engagement. There were two models for this. The first was open-access: since the Library was on a public space in Second Life any Second Life user could get access to it, as well as members of the public registering via the VLOB web page. Indeed the Library attracted a large number of overseas visitors from

(a)

Using 3D visualisation technology 137

(b)

Figure 7.6 Virtual Library of Birmingham orientation: (a) The orientation 'habitrail' to get users familiar with Second Life controls; (b) The scale model in the orientation space, along with videos and photos of the physical construction

amongst the general Second Life community, and formal visits were also organised for some Second Life groups – such as the active Librarian group.

The open-access uptake from the citizens of Birmingham was less than hoped for. This was probably due in part to the relative complexity of installing and setting up the Second Life software and opening an account, and also the need at that time for a relatively powerful PC to run it. However, as PC and tablet power has increased performance is becoming less of a barrier, and the move to a more app-based culture is making more immediate methods of public engagement with 3D environments more viable.

The second model, of facilitated access, was far more successful. Here the Virtual Library was shown off at various arts and cultural events in the city, and in local libraries. Central and local library staff were trained on how to give virtual tours and to show people how to explore the Virtual Library.

The response to these facilitated sessions was overwhelmingly positive, as John Marsh, Project Manager, Service Birmingham remembers:

> I ran a session at Yardley Library and the effect was astonishing. Got one of the kids out of the audience to drive himself around the Virtual Library while his Mum and Dad were watching on the big screen and they were absolutely staggered. There were 40–50 people at a time in those sessions, and to try and have the same impact other than through a 3D model, it would be really, really difficult. This had much more impact than the public doing it themselves.

Tom Epps, Development Project Manager, Birmingham Library Service, also acknowledged the value of this public outreach, saying, 'The opportunity to reach more people, more quickly and in a more meaningful way, was extremely important to the planning for the new Library.'

Staff usage

During the 18 months between handover of the Virtual Library and the opening of the physical library the library staff were able to use the model on an almost daily basis to try different layout ideas, and also to keep the library model up to date with finalised layouts. Just navigating their way as avatars from the external plaza into the entrance area and then on to the different parts of the building by foot, travelator, escalator or lift gave the staff a good idea of the visitor threshold experience and helped to identify potential choke-points, and where additional information might be needed. In particular, the staff found that the model was useful for agreeing layouts for items such as signage and AV displays. Tom Epps recalled that 'The virtual model showed us areas where we needed to review our existing plans, and was a huge help in planning the layout of the facilities that were installed.' John Marsh added:

> There is a fairly unique screen arrangement to the left of the lifts, where we decided to use two double portrait orientation screens to display the information. Which is weird, but we tried it out in the Virtual Library first and put an image on there and thought 'blimey that's good!' And it is such an unusual shape, we probably wouldn't have had the nerve to position the screens that way if we had not been able to test out first in the virtual build.

Unexpected uses

One unexpected use of the model was by companies bidding for work as subcontractors on the physical build. Whilst they are well versed in reading 2D plans, the fact that they had a 3D model that they could walk through gave them a significantly better idea of what the library was actually going to be like, and of how their systems would fit in. The model could then be used by the successful subcontractors and library staff to place systems such as AV screens and WiFi points in agreed places with a far higher level of confidence than would have been possible with the 2D plans.

Phil Hewson, Senior Wireless Consultant, Lan2Lan, one of the Library subcontractors reported that:

> Due to the unique nature of the building, practical and serviceable physical locations for the Wireless Access Points would be a challenge and important to get correct. This challenge was greatly assisted using the Virtual

(a)

(b)

Figure 7.7 (continued)

(continued)

(c)

(d)

Figure 7.7 Virtual Library of Birmingham orientation – Physical and Virtual comparisons: (a) First floor in the Library of Birmingham – 3D model; (b) First floor in the Library of Birmingham – physical build; (c) Virtual Library of Birmingham reception area – note comment sphere; (d) Library of Birmingham reception area – 2016

Library of Birmingham in Second Life. Having calculated the locations required to provide the Library with the WiFi coverage they need, the virtual build helped us verify the practicalities of establishing these positions.

Using 3D visualisation technology 141

The sense of déjà vu that people get when visiting a physical space that has become virtually familiar was also reported by Phil:

> Having recently visited the Library to carry out some post-installation RF tests, I felt I was more than familiar with the building having spent so many hours in Second Life during the design stage. The likeness and detail felt almost surreal.

Case study conclusion

Overall the Virtual Library of Birmingham was a very positive experience for all concerned. The lessons learnt by using the model, particularly in the design of the threshold space, helped to contribute to the success of the physical build, and also to smoothness of the opening. As Brian Gambles, the Library Director, said:

> We opened the doors of the Virtual Library in 2011, two years before the real building opened in 2013, for the public to come in, explore and share their comments and ideas and encourage people to explore it for themselves . . . This has proved a powerful tool for the project team and staff as we develop[ed] the new library, enabling us to get a really good feel for how the spaces in the new building will work that would not otherwise be possible.

Creating the digital threshold environment

Having established the efficacy of using virtual environments to help in the design of threshold spaces it is worth considering the practicalities involved, and the extent to which the features of a threshold space can be modelled within a 3D immersive environment. This section will consider seven key elements: the wider environment, building structure, heritage assets, visual media, sound, lighting, other people and the user/visitor themselves. Note that this discussion is completely platform-independent, and most of the issues discussed are common whether the immersive environment being used is a social virtual world such as Second Life or OpenSim, a game engine such as Unity3D or Unreal, native web platforms such as WebGL, or one of the new emerging social virtual reality environments such as vTime or AltSpaceVR – although each platform is likely to have its strengths and weaknesses.

The environment

Decisions need to be taken about how much of the area surrounding the location needs to be included. At what point does the visitor's physical threshold experience start? As with the VLOB example there is no need to model this wider area to the same detail as the main location, but it could be useful to think through the visitor's journey by car, bus, train, cycle or on foot and think about when the threshold experience should commence, and begin the model there. It may even be possible to mix systems, for instance using 3D photospheres, Google Earth or Streetview to help with the wider area, and then moving the visitor into the fully immersive environment as they get in sight of the location.

The building

Creating the 3D model of a threshold (or whole) space is currently the biggest challenge in using virtual environments to support the design and transformation of threshold spaces. Whilst tools such as Second Life, and even Unity3D, can provide relatively quick (less than one day) and simple ways of modelling a space to a low level of visual fidelity (which may actually be enough for many purposes), users often want a higher fidelity model, and the creation of that does require significant expertise in 3D modelling, design and CAD tools. For existing buildings, models can be created from simple measurement and photography or more advanced techniques such as photogrammetry (where hundreds of photos are automatically stitched together to make a 3D model), or Lidar (where a laser scans the environment around it taking accurate measurements of distances to automatically create a model). However, both Lidar and photogrammetry can have issues as they typically produce a single model that cannot necessarily tell the difference between a concrete wall, a movable partition, an exhibition case or an exhibit. The time taken to 'deconstruct' the model in order to be able to change it is likely to exceed the time taken to build the model from other sources, even from simple direct measurement. Whatever the method used to create the gross features of the location there are likely to be many days or weeks of work in optimising the build so that it reflects the current physical environment.

For new builds, and in due course for renovation work, the Building Information Modelling (BIM) initiative (Bille et al., 2014) promises to make it easier to pick up a 3D building model used for one purpose (e.g. the architect's or builder's model) and use it for another purpose (e.g. the user model). The UK Government is mandating BIM for most new government build projects, and it seems that industry is already seeing the benefits of BIM and applying it to other projects. At its core BIM provides a set of standard definitions for the digital representation of a building, and if design and CAD tools can export and import to this standard then the model can be passed along the production line in the architectural and building community, with each user drawing from it what they need. There are issues, though, in using such models within the types of environment described here (such as reducing the level of detail so it works on consumer devices), but it is certainly a move in the right direction.

Using 3D visualisation technology 143

The next stage, as in VLOB, is then to clearly define in software which elements of the build are fixed, and which can be changed (in position and texture), and to also provide a virtual warehouse of potential new items, and the ability for the user (not the 3D designer) to easily place them to try out different combinations. The ability to strip the building back to its 'white room' state is also useful when considering changes to layout, as shown in Figure 7.8.

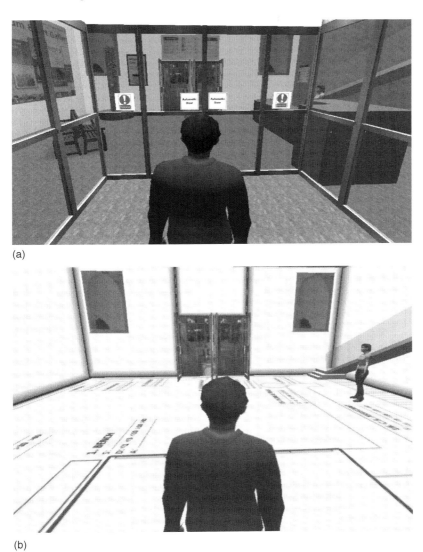

Figure 7.8 As-is and 'white room' models of the New Walk Museum threshold space: (a) New Walk – as-is model; (b) New Walk – 'white room' model

Heritage assets

Making digital copies of key heritage assets that might be displayed or used within a threshold space is becoming easier and easier. The two key technologies are again Lidar and Photogrammetry, but as with buildings both methods are likely to need some tidy-up of the model afterwards (Barrile et al., 2015). Also, both methods can generate models into industry-standard formats, so there should be no problems with using the models across a multitude of platforms over the coming decades.

Visual media

All immersive environments support the use of images in world, so it is easy to take scans of photos of existing or proposed signage and posters (or save them directly from Photoshop or Powerpoint) and move those into the virtual space. Almost all immersive environments also support video (and audio) in world, so existing video screen assets can be brought in. More problematic are surfaces such as touch screens or digital information display screens. If users do not need the interactivity then a sense of the device can be replicated by video recordings. If users do need the interactivity then a developer can probably create this as a bespoke item. The holy grail of immersive worlds is having a fully functioning web browser in world – not only to reproduce web access terminals but also to speed the creation of any interactive terminal lookalike – but implementing has proved problematic and not many platforms offer this.

Sound

Whilst immersive environments do not offer a completely realistic sound model (e.g. reverb in a big hall or down a stairwell), they do offer a variety of tools to enable a convincing sound model to be created. Spatial audio emitters can be placed all around the model, and their fall-offs defined – so an ambient sound can be set for a whole room or a sound bubble set under a single speaker. Sounds can also be keyed to interactive exhibits so that they are activated by a button press (or even just on approach). Global sounds, independent of the environment, can also be used to model items such as audio-tour devices.

Lighting

As with sound, the lighting model of a real-time, interactive, immersive environment will not match that of a system designed expressly for the purpose – such as an architect's 3D renderings. However, with the steady improvement in computing power, and the growing sophistication of immersive environment platforms, the visual look of an immersive environment can get very close to reality. There is, though, definitely a law of diminishing returns. It will be budget as much as anything that determines the overall visual look of the model, and whether it includes shadows (almost default now), surface roughness, or reflections and refractions. For standard museum tropes, though, such as spot lighting, downlights and uplights, immersive environments are more than up to the task.

Other people

Whilst a well-modelled space can look very realistic it usually doesn't feel 'real' unless there are people in there. It is perfectly possible to create virtual people within these environments who can make the space feel 'lived in', and who can conduct basic but natural interactions with visitors.

A useful model when thinking of modelling people in the environment is this three-tier approach drawn from the film industry:

> **Extras** – background characters with whom the visitor does not interact, but who are there to make the place look busy. They don't need a high degree of visual detail or programmed intelligence.
>
> **Walk-ons** – characters with whom the visitor may have a fleeting interaction: perhaps dropping off a coat, someone they bump into on the stairs, a security guard in a chair, etc. A slightly higher level of visual detail is required, as is the ability to answer some basic questions.
>
> **Stars** – characters that are visually as good as the visitor's avatar and which have the ability to conduct an extended conversation and to move about the environment as required.

Characterising the non-player characters (NPCs) in this way allows any budget to be focused in the most important areas. Work by Gilbert and Forney (2015), inspired by an earlier paper describing how virtual worlds provide a more level playing field for the Turing Test (Turing, 1950; Burden, 2009), showed how with modern technology a virtual shop assistant fooled 78 per cent of users into believing that it was human. The software that drove this virtual shop assistant was not especially complex, and shows that creating virtual characters within an environment, as guides, virtual visitors, or virtual staff, is a distinct possibility, and opens up the way to using virtual spaces to explore the human as well as the physical dimension of a threshold space.

'Other people' may also include other human visitors, and a key design decision will be whether the environment is intended to be used in single-user (or solo) mode (each user is in their own copy of the space and doesn't see other users) or in multi-user mode (every user can see, and possibly interact with, every other user). The decision will be very much driven by how users are intended to use the space, and what questions need to be answered, but note that a system designed for multi-user can often also be used for solo exploration, but a system designed for solo use will need a lot of work to make multi-user.

User

The final element is the user and their avatar. There is a decision point about whether the user's viewpoint should be first person (they don't see their own avatar, they are looking out through its eyes), or third person (their viewpoint is always just above and behind their avatar). Users vary in which they prefer, and there is also conflicting evidence about which generates the most realistic experience (Black, 2015). It is, though, easy to switch in and out of first-person view if the system has been built for third-person use, whereas if the system has been built for first-person use it is hard to then add a third-person view.

If the choice is for third person (or if it's a multi-user system so users will have to see each other's avatars) then the issue of avatar dress and look also needs to be considered. Some users find it hard to identify with an avatar that doesn't in some way look like them (Lee, 2004), and this may cause them to not take the experience seriously and could invalidate any results. At a minimum it is sensible to ensure that a range of culturally and demographically appropriate avatars are available.

Finally, it is important to consider how the avatar moves and interacts with objects and to make this as natural as possible. Avatars are normally steered just by using the cursor keys on a keyboard, but joysticks are also a possibility, as is point-and-click navigation (where the avatar walks itself to whatever part of the screen the user has clicked on). It is also possible for the system to take control of avatar movement and even gaze, which can let the user experience an automated ride. Another aspect to consider is modelling the experience of disabled users. Whilst visual impairment can be hard to model (but not impossible) it is relatively easy to set features such as step height limits for an avatar in order to reflect the challenges facing users with mild mobility problems, or to force the user to explore the whole space in a wheelchair.

Structuring the user experience of the digital threshold

Having created the environment it is sensible to structure the experience that the user will have in it, for instance in order to assess and improve the threshold experience. This is likely to start by replicating the current user experience, and then trying out different ideas in the relatively cheap virtual environment before trying them in the physical world. Four aspects are considered here: signage, interactive systems, design with intent and gamification.

Signage

Signage is the most traditional way to structure the threshold experience. Signs guide users on where to go and what to do, and the virtual environment can be a good way to explore the use of different styles, types and positioning of signs, both passive and digital (as in the VLOB example).

Interactive systems

Audio tour guides and mobile phone guides are very prevalent in heritage spaces (Wacker et al., 2016). Whilst the audio guide picked up at reception has already missed the threshold experience, the mobile application downloaded before visitors travel enables the threshold experience to be guided from the very beginning of the journey. Both audio tour guides and smartphone experiences can be modelled inside the virtual environment so that these 'assistive' technologies can be trialled and assessed.

Interactive systems could also include some of the 'virtual only' systems described in the Library of Birmingham project which were used to actively solicit feedback on the virtual model in order to inform the physical design.

Design with Intent

Design with Intent is based on Dan Lockton's description (Lockton et al., 2010) of how spaces, particularly public spaces, can be designed to promote or discourage certain types of behaviour. Layout and other non-literal cues in the space can be used to guide people as to how they should interact with the space. The positioning of doors, information desks, exhibits, seating, and even the style of each, can all affect whether, for example, the user sees this as a space to be hurried through or one to dwell in. The digital model can provide a useful test bed to try out different design options and to track user responses.

Gamification

There is an important distinction between gamification and the use of games technologies. The 3D immersive environments so far described have been typically built using games technologies, but there is no reason why the experience should be at all game-like. Likewise, gamification is about structuring an experience in either the virtual or physical world so that it draws on game design elements (that may or may not create a true 'game-like' experience) in order to achieve a specific goal. There is potential in using a gamification approach to structure the physical world threshold experience, and to trial this within a game-technology-based virtual environment (Johnson et al., 2015; Döpker et al., 2013; Sanchez and Pierroux, 2015).

Assessing the user experience of the digital threshold

All of this virtual work will be wasted if the user experience is not assessed and then learnt from in order to inform the physical design. Any project is likely to use a wide variety of traditional assessment techniques including interviews (structured and semi-structured) and questionnaires, but there are also some additional methods which can be used inside the virtual space, many of which have physical world counterparts.

User tracking

Whilst technologies such as Bluetooth and WiFi are only just beginning to make it feasible to track everyday users moving around a physical museum or gallery space (Chianese et al., 2013) it is very easy to track users' avatars moving around a virtual space. Data can be obtained at a sub-metre resolution and tracked at least every second, the limit often being how to manage and analyse all the data that the tracking will generate. More typically, though, all that is needed is information on which signs, doors, or exhibits the user approached, which route they took, etc. The resulting data can be shown not only in 2D heat and track maps, but also in similar forms within the 3D model itself, or even as 'replays' of their avatars moving through the space. Tracking can readily be extended to tracking user interactions with exhibits and systems, and there is also the potential for virtual eye-tracking (Tanriverdi and Jacob, 2000).

Probes

Since the user is already interacting with a computer it is possible to generate 'probes' – quick questions at any point in the interaction (Loiterton and Bishop, 2005). For instance, if the user stops in one space for a while, but away from an exhibit, possibly randomly turning their avatar, then a quick probe question could be asked to understand why and whether they are looking for some particular direction – capturing feedback on an event that may be lost in a debrief an hour later. An alternative approach would be to use screen-capture technology to video the whole experience from the user perspective and then get the user to do a talk-aloud exercise at the end, although they themselves may have forgotten, or post-rationalised, some of their at-the-time thinking.

Interactive systems

As described in the Library of Birmingham project, specific interactive systems can be developed within the environment to get user feedback on particular items – such as choice of layout, colour schemes, or even which exhibits should be shown in which order to get a particular point across. At the most extreme level the whole lobby space could become a set of interactive choices allowing each user to build their own best threshold experience.

Conclusion

3D visualisation techniques are far more available, affordable and accessible to those involved in the creation of threshold experiences than they have been in the past. These tools need no longer be the domain of the architect or the builder but can be used by almost any IT-literate user to create representations of the physical environment (at a wide variety of different levels of visual fidelity). These virtual environments can provide a fresh and useful insight into how people relate to, navigate through, and interact with a threshold space; and this knowledge can then be transferred to the physical world.

The last few years have seen significant developments in immersive environments, not least in the rise of consumer virtual reality (VR). Headsets such as Google Cardboard make the VR experience available to almost anyone. Since the environments described above are all based on full 3D models it is relatively trivial to make them available on a VR headset, and indeed since Second Life has Oculus Rift compatibility the Library of Birmingham model discussed earlier could be explored with the Rift headset (Figure 7.9).

This ability to immerse a user in the 3D model is likely to provide an even higher level of immersion and engagement for the user when testing out potential threshold spaces. However, there are undoubtedly issues of familiarisation, comfort and disorientation that need to be addressed if a user is to have a pleasant and seamless experience, and one where the novelty of VR does not override the exploration of the target environment.

(a)

Figure 7.9 (continued)

(continued)

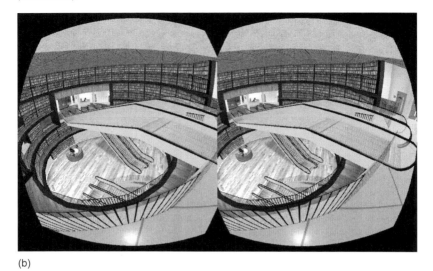

(b)

Figure 7.9 Virtual reality examples: (a) A 3D photosphere tour of a new building; (b) Virtual Library of Birmingham in a VR headset

Whilst advanced techniques such as VR, Lidar and photogrammetry, AI characters and emerging standards such as BIM can all help with the visual fidelity, much of the benefit of the virtual space can be achieved just by having people interact within the virtual environments: using virtual cardboard boxes to do a virtual planning-for-real, or having users try out a variety of layout and signage options within a threshold space. 3D virtual environments are ultimately social spaces, bringing people together to share experiences and to explore environments.

References

Barrile, V., Bilotta, G., Lamari, D. and Meduri, G.M. (2015) 'Comparison between techniques for generating 3D models of cultural heritage'. Recent Advances in Mechanics, Mechatronics and Civil, Chemical and Industrial Engineering, Mathematics and Computers in Science and Engineering Series, 49, in *Proceedings of the 2015 International Conference on Civil Engineering* (CIVILENG 2015), Zakynthos Island, Greece, July 16–20, 2015, pp. 140–145.

Berger, M., Jucker, A.H. and Locher, M.A. (2016) 'Interaction and space in the virtual world of Second Life', *Journal of Pragmatics*, 101, pp. 83–100.

Bille, R., Smith, S.P., Maund, K. and Brewer, G. (2014) 'Extending Building Information Models into game engines', in *Proceedings of the 2014 Conference on Interactive Entertainment* (pp. 1–8). ACM.

Black, D. (2015) 'Why can I see my avatar? Embodied visual engagement in the third-person video game', *Games and Culture*. Doi/abs/10.1177/1555412015589175.

Boeykens, S. (2013) *Unity for Architectural Visualization*. Birmingham, UK: Packt Publishing.
Burden, D.J. (2009) 'Deploying embodied AI into virtual worlds', *Knowledge-Based Systems*, 22(7), pp. 540–544.
Burden, D.J.H. (2013) *Buildingscapes: A White Paper*. Available from www.daden.co.uk. (Last accessed 9 September 2016.)
Carlson, W. (2007) *A Critical History of Computer Graphics and Animation*. Available at http://design.osu.edu/carlson/history/lesson4.html. (Last accessed 9 September 2016.)
Chianese, A., Marulli, F., Moscato, V. and Piccialli, F. (2013) 'SmARTweet: A location-based smart application for exhibits and museums', in *Signal-Image Technology & Internet-Based Systems (SITIS), 2013 International Conference on Signal Image Technology & Internet Based Systems* (pp. 408–415). Kyoto: IEEE.
Döpker, A., Brockmann, T., Stieglitz, S. and Campus, L. (2013) 'Use cases for gamification in virtual museums', in *Proceedings of die Jahrestagungen der Gesellschaft für Informatik 2013*, Koblenz, pp. 2308–2321.
Eduserv. (2009) *THEATRON Final Report*. London: King's College London. Available from www.heacademy.ac.uk/system/files/theatron_final_report.pdf. (Accessed 1 September 2016.)
Foth, M., Bajracharya, B., Brown, R. and Hearn, G. (2009) 'The Second Life of urban planning? Using NeoGeography tools for community engagement', *Journal of Location Based Services*, 3(2), pp. 97–117.
Gallego, M.D., Bueno, S. and Noyes, J. (2016) 'Second Life adoption in education: A motivational model based on uses and gratifications theory', *Computers & Education*, 100, pp. 81–93.
Gilbert, R.L. and Forney, A. (2015) 'Can avatars pass the Turing Test? Intelligent agent perception in a 3D virtual environment', *International Journal of Human–Computer Studies*, 73, pp. 30–36.
Gottschalk, S. (2010) 'The presentation of avatars in Second Life: Self and interaction in social virtual spaces', *Symbolic Interaction*, 33(4), pp. 501–525.
Gouraud, H. (1971) 'Continuous shading of curved surfaces', *IEEE transactions on computers*, 100(6), pp. 623–629.
Hao, W. (2006) 'Virtual Reality – improving the fidelity of architectural visualization'. MSc thesis. Texas Tech University. Available at https://ttu-ir.tdl.org/ttu-ir/bitstream/handle/2346/12601/hao_wu_thesis.pdf. (Accessed 9 September 2016.)
Johnson, L., Adams Becker, S., Estrada, V. and Freeman, A. (2015) *The NMC Horizon Report: 2015 Museum Edition*. New Media Consortium. 6101 West Courtyard Drive Building One Suite 100, Austin, TX 78730.
Kuksa, I. and Childs, M. (2014) *Making Sense of Space: The Design and Experience of Virtual Spaces as a Tool for Communication*. Oxford: Chandos Publishing, Elsevier.
Lee, K.M. (2004) 'Presence, explicated', *Communication Theory*, 14(1), pp. 27–50.
Lockton, D., Harrison, D. and Stanton, N.A. (2010) 'The Design with Intent Method: A design tool for influencing user behaviour', *Applied Ergonomics*, 41(3), pp. 382–392.
Loiterton, D. and Bishop, I.D. (2005) 'Virtual environments and location-based questioning for understanding visitor movement in urban parks and gardens'. Conference paper presented at *Real-time Visualisation and Participation*, Dessau, Germany.

Martey, R.M. and Consalvo, M. (2011) 'Performing the looking-glass self: Avatar appearance and group identity in Second Life', *Popular Communication*, 9(3), pp. 165–180.

Sanchez, E. and Pierroux, P. (2015) 'Gamifying the museum: A case for teaching for games based learning', in *Proceedings of the 9th European Conference on Game Based Learning*. Reading, UK: Academic Conferences and Publishing International Limited, pp. 471–480.

Schaller, R.R. (1997) 'Moore's law: Past, present and future', *IEEE Spectrum*, 34(6), pp. 52–59.

Senyapili, B. (1997) 'Visualization of virtual architecture', in *Proceedings, 1997 IEEE Conference on Information Visualization*. London: IEEE, pp. 260–266.

Steel, J., Drogemuller, R. and Toth, B. (2012) 'Model interoperability in Building Information Modelling', *Software & Systems Modeling*, 11(1), pp. 99–109.

Tanriverdi, V. and Jacob, R.J. (2000) 'Interacting with eye movements in virtual environments', in *Proceedings of the SIGCHI conference on Human Factors in Computing Systems*. ACM, pp. 265–272.

Turing, A.M. (1950) 'Computing machinery and intelligence', *Mind*, 59(236), pp. 433–460.

Urban, R.J. (2007) 'A Second Life for your museum: 3D multi-user virtual environments and museums', in *Proceedings of Museums and the Web 2007*. Archives & Museum Informatics. Toronto, 2007.

Wacker, P., Kreutz, K., Heller, F. and Borchers, J. (2016) 'Maps and location: Acceptance of modern interaction techniques for audio guides', in *Proceedings of the 2016 CHI Conference on Human Factors in Computing Systems*. ACM, pp. 1067–1071.

8 Difficult thresholds
Negotiating shared and embedded entrances

Steven Kruse

What happens when a museum does not have an entrance of its own? What happens when the method of visitor entry is drawn out through a wider (or separate) institution, or when the site is focused in a different way, with a different orientation towards visitors? What does a situation like this do to the visiting process, and what are some of the issues that are brought to the fore? This chapter is concerned with museums that are, in many ways, hidden, or at least nested in such a way that entering is not a straightforward process. As we shall see, at these types of sites, the act of entering is complicated and challenging, but often in senses that are not immediately obvious. Besides the difficulties of access for the visitor (knowing where the museum 'begins' or ascertaining what is or is not appropriate behaviour) the whole entrance area, with its multiple thresholds and mixed signals, can be host to internal contestations and compromises. It is suggested here that these issues are not only rooted in particular histories and institutional relationships, but have ongoing ramifications for the character of those entrance spaces.

The discussion is based around case studies of three embedded or nested museums in the UK: the Museum of Archaeology and Anthropology (MAA) in the University of Cambridge; the Stained Glass Museum in Ely Cathedral; and the Hunterian Museum in the Royal College of Surgeons. These sites illustrate how museum entrances can be embedded in different ways, both in terms of the variety of physical entrance types, but also in the nature of the relationship they have with their host institutions. The range of institutional contexts is also notable – university, church, medicine; not least in the way that these specific examples might indicate how these particular kinds of embeddedness may not necessarily be unusual for that particular institution. It is suggested here that by looking at some of the issues at these sites, our understanding of museum entrances in general can be enriched – not just through widening our view to encompass under-researched entrance types, but by alerting us to the potential effect that institutional contestations and compromises may have, even at apparently straightforward thresholds.

Openings and impositions

There are two chief theoretical assumptions that inform this chapter. First, that the entrance is an important element in the presentation and structure of meaning. Second, that the spaces at these sites can be analysed with special attention to social relationships. In terms of this first assumption, museums are often encouraged to develop or maintain narratives for their visitors (Bedford, 2001), even if sometimes it is unintended (Macdonald, 1998, p. 133). In fact, if we take the process of constructing narrative as, in a sense, inevitable, part of the normal functioning and meaning-making of the human experience (Austin, 2012, p. 107; MacLeod, 2012, pp. xxi–xxii), then not only can we overlay the concept onto whole museum visits, but also onto human relationships to landscapes (Furse-Roberts, 2012), houses (Austin, 2012, p. 113) and personal histories (Falk and Dierking, 2000, pp. 48–49). We could imagine the museum's entrance threshold as the end of one narrative (reaching the building's threshold), the beginning of another (the museum visit), as well as a midway point for a further kind of narrative (the visit as a whole), and a microscopic slice of an overarching narrative (one's personal life-journey). In short, the entrance may be at the intersection of a number of journeys, not just for visitors, but for other users too. This provides a framework for understanding some of the ways in which the building intervenes at these embedded museums. The position of the threshold of the museum in relation to other thresholds, the galleries, and any enveloping institutions will have an impact on the sequential experience of users and ultimately the meaning(s) of the museum (Psarra, 2009; Duncan and Wallach, 1978). At sites where the building is entered before the museum itself, the host institution may in effect frame the museum experience. Although external to the museum this nevertheless conditions the museum narrative(s), leading to potential tension or confusion – which may in turn necessitate negotiation with other institutions.

This leads onto our second theoretical assumption, that space can be fruitfully analysed multi-dimensionally, with social relationships considered a crucial aspect. There is a rich literature that sensitises us to the cultural and social aspects of museums and their buildings; they may be potential filters for class (Bourdieu, Darbel and Schnapper, 1990), or manifestations of the operations of the state (Bennett, 1995), ritually capitalistic (Duncan and Wallach, 1978), or otherwise implicated in the (re)production of social conditions (MacLeod, 2011). The influence of Lefebvre (1991) encourages us to note that social relations, mental conceptions and the physical are all involved in producing space. This is especially pertinent if we are to consider the entrance area not just as a pattern of physical objects, but as an 'information space' (Mortensen et al., 2014, p. 331). Museologist Suzanne MacLeod (2013, p. 182) helps us here by demonstrating that museum architecture is a dynamic social and cultural production: physical material deeply rooted in and produced through the lives and politics of multiple groups, agencies, governments and individuals and active, at every level, in the production of (unequal) social relations, (varied) social experiences and the formation of (specific) social networks and identities.

Turning to shared entrances explicitly, examining the institutions that administer this space, and have interests invested in it, should help us understand its character. At an entrance area to multiple institutions (or sub-institutions), we would wish to pay attention to crossovers of function, jurisdiction, ethos and use. In addition, we ought to be aware that the multiple users of the space, including the visiting public, may all perform an active role in this interaction and production (Fraser, 2007, pp. 294–296).

Here it may be useful to turn to concrete examples from a range of contexts to examine how this use of space might play out in practice. Through the following examples, it is argued that the museum entrance (whether placed within another entrance, shared or, indeed, separate) embeds distinctive meaning, and both enacts and affects the specific relationship between museum and host institution – with the visiting public playing a key role. More specifically, in the university context, a refurbishment at the Museum of Archaeology and Anthropology that bypassed a complicated triple entry through university property (courtyard, shared corridor, museum proper) has partially enacted a shift in presentational emphasis; in a church context, the placement of the independent Stained Glass Museum within a predominant ecclesiastical institution has ramifications for visibility and control over narrative, meanings and identity; and in the medical context of the Hunterian, the rich history that has resulted in the museum's position deep in the building has ongoing consequences for security and the operations of a functionally complex venue.

A museum entrance in a university

The University of Cambridge is vast. It physically dominates the city, the patchwork 'gown' of colleges, campuses, departments and administrative buildings impressing on what is an essentially provincial 'town', while it intellectually contributes heavily to countless disciplines, consistently rating as one of the world's preeminent higher education institutions. Its buildings reflect both the functional variety necessary to operate such an institution, and the sprawling historical development of a decentralised and ancient university. They run the gamut from imposing to modest to anonymous, often arranged in constellations that deepen these characteristics, and frequently interspersed with the shops, homes, and public amenities of the conurbation. There are thus, necessarily, myriad portals into the university: courtyard gates, site archways, departmental front doors, loading bays, tight windowless back entrances, anonymous alleys. The Museum of Archaeology and Anthropology (MAA) sits on the Downing Site, a discrete series of twentieth-century buildings and courtyards close to the centre of the city. Much of the site was acquired from the nearby Downing College, and the Law School, geology labs, the Sedgwick Museum (of Earth Sciences) and MAA itself moved to the site in the first decade of the twentieth century (Brooke, 1993, pp. 90–91). The collections of archaeology and anthropology that made the move to the site in 1913 had their origins in material gathered from around the city and colleges (MAA, 2016a) and in major expeditions to the Torres Strait; see for example Herle (2012). Today, the collection comprises over a million objects and the public galleries are spread over three floors: the ground floor Clarke Hall (dedicated to British Archaeology) and Lia Ka Shing Gallery (for temporary exhibitions), the first floor Maudslay Hall and second floor Andrews Gallery, dedicated to world anthropological and world archaeology collections respectively.

Compared to many other British universities, the University of Cambridge is relatively decentralised: students and academics belong to colleges that are highly independent, and study in specialised departments that are organised into schools, ultimately part of the General Board (University of Cambridge, 2016b). It is the university that is the outermost container institution for MAA. However, more directly, the museum is sited with a department that grew around it physically and institutionally: the Department of Archaeology (formerly Archaeology and Anthropology), which is also part of the Faculty of Human, Social and Political Science and the School of the Humanities and Social Sciences (University of Cambridge, 2016a). The museum is used extensively as a resource by the department, providing material and expertise for practical elements of both teaching and evaluation (Gunn, 2016; MAA, 2016b). Although a large proportion of the museum's activities are therefore entwined with the functions of the wider university, there is a degree of independence in its work. Researchers from further afield also make extensive use of the collection; and the museum is proud of its ongoing connections to source communities (Harknett, 2016; Herle, 2012).

Before 2012, the only way for a member of the public to get to the museum was through an entrance shared with the rest of the department, accessible through the Downing Site. This entrance is still in use, primarily by large groups and those who have also visited the Sedgwick Museum of Earth Sciences, also on the Downing Site. It involves passing through an archway from the street, and continuing through the university courtyard (often populated with students), with little signage until the door is almost reached. Once through this, visitors find themselves in a departmental corridor – one of thousands that usually run hidden through Cambridge (Harknett, 2016).

From late 2010 until 2012, the museum closed for redevelopment. The downstairs galleries were significantly changed in look and ethos: whereas

Negotiating shared and embedded entrances   157

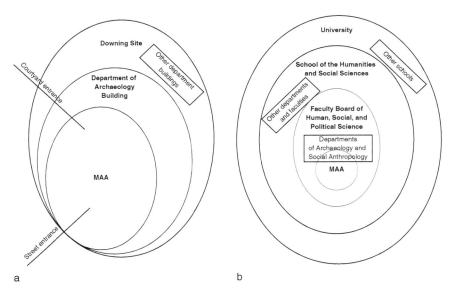

Figure 8.1 Simplified plans of the museum within the university showing (a) the **physical** position of the museum within the department and site and (b) the **institutional** position of the museum within the university

the pre-2010 archaeology gallery was set up to follow undergraduate (Part I) teaching, the new Cambridge Gallery focused more self-consciously on appealing to the wider public (Harknett, 2016; Gunn, 2016). In contrast to the courtyard entrance, accessible only through entering the university's Downing Site, the museum took advantage of more direct access through a wall that was external to the whole site. An integral part of the refurbishment was therefore converting a large window into a new entrance onto Downing Street, a reasonably busy public road. A large door, in keeping with the general style of the building, was installed (Harknett, 2016). Upon completion, this opened into an initial area containing a reception desk towards the centre of the area, a prominent shop near the front external wall, and immediate access to the Cambridge Gallery, the Lia Ka Shing Gallery, as well as stairs (still shared with the rest of the department) and a lift to the upper galleries. The new entrance area was conceived as an initial point for many different routes or narrative arcs through the building, and the first display case attempts to encourage this openness by presenting a summary of the whole collection: both the archaeological and the anthropological (loosely speaking), both the immediately accessible and the deeply researched.

Figure 8.2 Courtyard entrance of the museum and department

Contrasting the new entrance to the (still extant but less used) shared courtyard entrance is striking. MAA's pre-2012 main entrance required a triple entry through courtyard, department and museum. Unlike some college sites that are advertised as heritage venues, the courtyard of the Downing Site is not a tourist attraction. Entering through the rear entrance required negotiating difficult implicit barriers, causing the visitor to question whether they were in the right place. The symbolic power of the university estate – in the case of the Downing Site, involving courtyards, Edwardian buildings, the grassy areas that are subject to seemingly arcane rules (Harknett, 2016) – was therefore layered onto the usual exclusory and filtering effect of buildings. In other words, the museum was very much 'within' – institutionally, conceptually, physically and narratively – the university.

The renovation of the museum and the moving of the main entrance to Downing Street, a public thoroughfare, allowed the public to largely bypass non-museum university property. Entering the university through this portal is certainly not value-free, but the transition from public space to university interior was now both quicker and managed in a more self-consciously public-facing manner: the courtyard entrance literally facing back into the university; the new entrance facing town. The museum has, therefore, both increased its visibility and underlined a change of emphasis. That this has occurred hand in hand is no accident and illustrates how entrances can be used in the management of presentation, meaning and ethos.

A museum entrance in a church

Thirty miles from Cambridge, a short distance from where the River Cam runs into the Great Ouse, sits the small city of Ely. Approaching this historic settlement (by road, by river, by foot across the fens) it is Ely Cathedral that first emerges into view. The cathedral's dominant size, indeed, once had a wayfinding role for pilgrims, with unbroken views possible over the flat landscape, pointing the way to journey's end (Broughton, 2008, pp. 13–15). Today's travellers may flock here for a variety of reasons, religious and secular, and have no trouble locating its spiritual centre. Within this centre, however, there is a separate institution that is a little more hidden from view. This is the Stained Glass Museum, a heritage venue (fully open to the public) embedded within another publicly accessible site.

One way of looking at the history of the cathedral is through convulsions of collapse, disrepair and renewal. Dating from the eleventh century, its most iconic feature (the spectacular central 'Octagon') was built after the catastrophic collapse of the original 'crossing tower' in 1322 (Maddison, 2003, p. 124). Another collapse of the north-west transept 'during medieval times' was never fully replaced (Ely Cathedral and Sills, 2016). The impact of both the English Reformation and the Civil War had a significant effect on the fabric; and the following centuries involved a continual struggle against disrepair (Cocke, 2003). By the 1980s, income generation became vital to the cathedral, and with great reluctance, from 1986 admission charges were levied for all days but Sunday (Higgins, 2003, p. 374, Anon., 2016a). Ely Cathedral's purpose – its reason for being – may be worship but 'there cannot be worship without a roof' (Higgins, 2003, pp. 363–364).

160 *Steven Kruse*

The Stained Glass Museum is an independent museum that is committed to 'raising the profile of the medium [stained glass] as an historic and contemporary art form' (Stained Glass Museum, 2011, p. 2). This is a secular aim for what has been, and is perceived as being, a religious form of expression and teaching. It therefore seems appropriate for this 'leading national centre for the display, research, interpretation, and enjoyment of stained glass' (ibid., p. 2) to be set in this major Christian centre of worship and heritage. However, it is perhaps surprising to learn that the museum actually has no formal connection to the cathedral (Anon., 2016b; Anon., 2016a). It is a separate institution leasing a distinctive and historic portion of the estate. Founded in 1972, the museum spent some years assembling its collection before opening in 1979. It was originally located in a part of the cathedral called the north triforium, before moving to its current location in the south triforium in 2000 (Stained Glass Museum, 2016), reachable through the West Entrance of the cathedral and up one hundred steps. Entering the museum therefore requires entering the cathedral, and the functioning of the museum is conditioned by the goals and practices of its host institution (Anon., 2016b; Anon., 2016a).

The cathedral sets itself the role of 'joyfully proclaiming the love of God in worship, outreach, welcome and care' (Ely Cathedral, 2016). Although community and pastoral care is considered of primary importance to the institution, the estate must also be cared for (and general visitors welcomed)

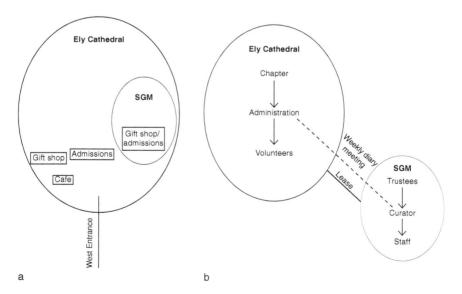

Figure 8.3 Simplified plans of the museum within the cathedral showing (a) the **physical** position of the museum within the cathedral and (b) the **institutional** position of the museum in relation to the cathedral

with a professionalism that requires extra-ecclesiastical assistance. The responsible body for the cathedral is the Cathedral Chapter, a mixture of clergy and external members with secular expertise. The estate itself may be used for filming (for example) to generate income to support the upkeep of the building. Religious life takes priority, however, and services take place several times a day (Anon., 2016a). The museum's smaller hierarchy of trustees, curator and specialist staff are independent of this, and are not formally involved with the running of the cathedral. A weekly diary meeting involving the curator allows some coordination between institutions (Anon., 2016b).

Figure 8.4 West Entrance of Ely Cathedral

Visitors to the cathedral and the Stained Glass Museum must pass through the West Entrance of the cathedral (under the external Galilee porch, through the West Door) and into the narthex (or West Tower). Once they open the heavy wooden door (often closed due to the blustery wind) visitors are immediately afforded a spectacular view of the internal space. This entrance may once have had a processional and symbolic role: passing into the interior signalling a new journey and a movement into a new life, mirroring Christ's own procession into Jerusalem, the dramatic opening up from the relatively crouched porch area adding to the drama and awe (Broughton, 2008, pp. 31–36). The pull of the central nave (the shape, the sightlines) is designed to encourage an onward journey towards the Octagon's heavenly light (ibid., pp. 78–80). At the narthex, the visitor must select (knowingly or not) whether they will proceed in the direction of the nave to the cathedral's admissions desk, enter the cafe or cathedral gift shop, or ascend the stairs to the Stained Glass Museum, which has a modest way finding presence in the entrance area. On the north wall, there is a modern sculpture *The Way of Life*; to the south is a prominent font, access to St Catherine's Chapel, and of course the stairs to the museum. Volunteers (the Ministry of Welcome) are stationed in the narthex to welcome and help direct visitors. It is not surprising that visitors, although often exploring this initial narthex and south-west transept area in advance of official admission, rarely choose to enter the museum before visiting the rest of the cathedral: it seems counter-intuitive in narrative terms to ascend to the next level (especially through a dark stairway) without investigating the rest of the building first.

If, and when, the museum is entered it must therefore present a narrative within a narrative: the history and practice of stained glass embedded within the general sweep of the cathedral. Nevertheless, despite its institutional separation, and its marginal position, the museum is often perceived as part of the cathedral in a fuller sense than mere tenant (Anon., 2016b). And with its secular and improving technology of historicising, labelling, arranging, it augments the sense of the cathedral as not only a religious space, but also a heritage venue, an institution that takes its heritage – its fabric – seriously. One of the filtering functions of the cathedral admissions desk is to allow those who have come to the cathedral purely to pray to do so without charge (Anon., 2016a). In a similar vein, on Sundays, admission is free. This is in line with the cathedral's primary goal: proclaiming the word of God. The Stained Glass Museum also has an admission fee, although joint tickets can be purchased at the cathedral desk. Not having the same religious mission, it charges on Sundays – a policy which can lead towards some confusion for the visitors.

Overall, the West Entrance is undoubtedly seen, and largely experienced, as the entrance to one institution – the cathedral. This makes sense from a comparison of the relative external pull of both institutions (Anon., 2016b) and from the ecclesiastical meanings that can be attached to the entrance procedure for the church (and that are woven into the fabric) (Broughton, 2008). The cathedral as 'institution' and the cathedral as 'building' are clearly entwined in a way that the Stained Glass Museum, as an independent entity without its own eponymous building, is not. The museum is thus in a curious position: it is perhaps more prominent, accessible and relevant than it otherwise would be, but is somewhat obscured within the building itself.

The Stained Glass Museum does not have, in other words, control over its entrance experience, and the effect of its independence is double-edged. While a good deal of control can be exercised within the museum itself, participation in decision-making within the estate is limited, conditioning the visibility and meanings of the museum during the entrance act. We also see the embeddedness of history and purpose within the architecture and symbolism of the cathedral threshold and entrance area, something that the much younger, institutionally separate, museum must accept, work with, and work around. The devotional message, in this sense, frames the museum-going experience. That said, the cathedral itself, with its secularised functions (cafe, admissions desk, gift shop) has also, to a certain degree, an internal tension. The narthex dramatises the cathedral's own compromise between dominant religious concerns and the necessities of tourism, a compromise that the museum, in a modest way, participates in.

The position of the museum deep (indeed, on an upper level) within this historically rich building complicates the entrance process, and contributes towards a mixed-use zone involving heritage, devotion, fundraising and museum-going at, and around, the narthex. A similar position within the host building exists at our next museum, but within a context that does not have the same openness to the public: a professional membership organisation within the medical community. Here, historical vectors within the profession, as well as trends in museum access and historical contingencies, have coincided to produce a challenging entrance.

A museum entrance in a medical institution

In order to reach the Hunterian Museum – to experience, as its poster-board puts it, the 'best kept secret in Holborn' and place oneself in the bluish light of its spectacular crystal gallery – one must find Lincoln's Inn Fields, slip between the six pillars of the college façade and enter, temporarily at least, a space also used by college employees, students and professional members. To enter the Hunterian as a museum visitor, one must also enter the Royal College of Surgeons, which as a building is grand, neoclassical and somewhat austere, and as a membership body is entered only by expertise and qualification.

This is a building of several different functions involving different categories of user (e.g. Welch, 2016). The museum is one, much valued, element, but it is impossible to usefully disconnect it from the history and work of the college as a whole. This is not just because of a physical quirk of proximity, or a historical accident of ownership, but because of the way the collection has been, and continues to be, used by the college, and by the role the museum plays in representing the function of the college to the public (Alberti, 2016).

The Royal College of Surgeons of England is, as a body, a membership organisation of surgeons (including dental surgeons) committed to 'enabling surgeons to achieve and maintain the highest standards of surgical practice and patient care' (Royal College of Surgeons of England, 2015, p. 13). It offers training courses for all stages of a surgeon's career; membership of the college (as with membership of its Scottish and Irish equivalents) indicates that one has fully qualified as a surgeon. As a professional organisation it also offers guidance to other organisations (including the government) and advice to the public (Royal College of Surgeons of England, 2016). The college developed out of previous surgeon and barber-surgeon organisations, becoming the Company of Surgeons in 1745, prior to the issuing of the Royal Charter that formally established the college in 1800 (ibid.). At about the same time, the government had finally (with some persuasion) decided to purchase the anatomical specimen collection of the recently deceased John Hunter (1728–1793), in accordance with his wishes. The company (soon to be college) was charged with its care (Royal College of Surgeons of England, 2011, p. 21). A complicated web of ownership and guardianship still continues to this day, with an independent Hunterian advisory board (composed of some members external to the college) having some formal powers over the founding collection. The college must perform its custodial duties towards this collection appropriately or face the unlikely prospect of the government removing this collection (Alberti, 2016).

The college building had, in many ways, been constructed, and indeed enlarged, around the Hunterian and its expanded collections; and, until the Second World War the museum was located on the ground floor – much more prominently than it is now (Dobson, 1961; Alberti, 2017). Disastrously, the college was bombed in 1941, resulting in a halving of the Hunterian Collection and the devastation of the site. Post-war changes in the relationship between the medical discipline and museum collections influenced subsequent rebuilding, resulting in the museum's relocation to its current upstairs position (Annals of RCS England, 1963; Alberti, 2011, pp. 201–2). In addition the teaching and research collections were hived off into what is now the Wellcome Museum of Anatomy and Pathology, a restricted museum for medical professionals and trainees – also located at the college (Royal College of Surgeons of England, 2011, p. 30). The degree of openness permitted to museum medical collections in general has waxed and waned over the last century – in line with moral concerns or concerns over, for example, the 'titillating' effect of morbid specimens (Alberti, 2011). In fact, it was not until a major refurbishment in 2005 that the museum was officially open to all. Before then, arguments and fashions moved one way

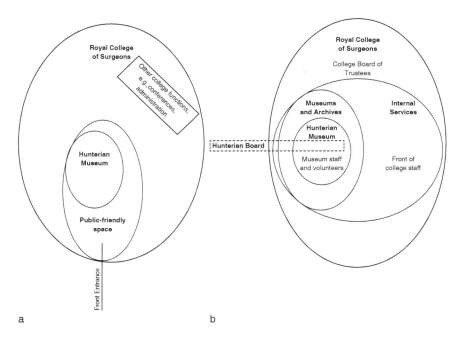

Figure 8.5 Simplified plans of the museum within the college showing (a) the **physical** position of the museum within the college building and (b) the **institutional** position of the museum within the college. Hunterian board has some external members

and then another; after 1963 'seventeen categories of people' had a right to visit; although the curator could use their discretion to allow access (and mostly, of course, did) (Alberti, 2016).

Within the internal hierarchy, the museums and archives department sits within the Directorate of Internal Services, taking up around about ten per cent of the estate and about ten per cent of the budget of the college. Ultimately the Directorate reports to the Board of the Royal College of Surgeons, which is largely made up of surgeons (Alberti, 2016). The receptionists at the front of the building do not report to the museum director's department, but to the Head of Facilities whose duties also include college events and functions management. These members of staff, understandably, are not employed as museum greeters, but as front-of-house staff for the college, dealing with the different categories of people who wish to access the building – staff, surgeons, students, conference-goers and so on. The primary goal for the receptionists is that they make sure that each category of user finds the correct area and that security is not compromised (Welch, 2016; Alberti, 2016).

166 *Steven Kruse*

Figure 8.6 Front of the Royal College of Surgeons

In order to pass under and through the college's portico, visitors approach through stark black railings and the front car park. Entering the building they pass into the first of two general use rooms, the reception, a small, observed space. At the far end of the reception there is a mechanised barrier operated by the receptionist(s) on duty, who attempt to politely expedite visitors' progress, essential for security (e.g. Welch, 2016), and, indeed, the enjoyment of the visitors.

Visitors are asked whether they wish to go to the museum – if so, they are given a badge to wear, identifying them as a museum visitor before being allowed to pass into the lobby area, through the barrier. A kind of openness in this lobby area sets up a challenging dialectic: it is a wide room with several exits, but only the stairs up (to the museum and library) or down (to the cloakroom and toilets) are permissible options for the visitor. The badges may function as a method of implicit control in this open space. Visitors sometimes still get confused (Welch, 2016), leaving staff with the very difficult task of ensuring that visitors do not go into inappropriate areas, while sitting in a space cut off from the hall. At times this area is used for conference reception functions, further adding to the challenge. The route upstairs to the museum itself is lined with the portraits of former college presidents. There the visitor is greeted a second time, this time by one of the volunteers at the museum desk and gift shop.

Negotiating shared and embedded entrances 167

This is clearly a challenging entrance procedure that involves the visitor in more of the life of the college than perhaps is intended. A rich historical story involving the position of the collection within the building and the subject helps explain why the museum is now no longer in a preeminent position at the primary threshold (Alberti, 2016). But the openness of access to the modern Hunterian Museum is in line with what one would expect of a contemporary museum, that is, it is open to all, not merely the qualified or those considered appropriate. This is not, understandably, the general ethos of the wider college or building. Museum visitors are not encouraged, or indeed allowed, to wander around and enjoy the administrative, training and corporate functions of a professional membership organisation – although users of these latter functions require access to be as straightforward as possible. This complicates the threshold area: museum visitors must be managed while an appropriate openness is maintained. Visible security and signs of identification become a necessity. As with the other 'shared' entrances, museum visitors are exposed to a series of cues, choices and modes of access that are not designed for them, but are rather a glimpse into the social life of other functions of the institution. The result is a contested zone, with various functions and affordances in tension.

The entrance as tension and disruption

These examples illustrate the ways that shared or embedded entrances can complicate both the physical act of visiting, as well as the process of narrative meaning-making that characterises the experience of a museum visit. The host institution, experienced in advance of the museum, frames the experience of the galleries, and compels the visitor to make sense of another transitional space within the overall sequence of events. However much museums work on internal coherence, this extra layer of significance is something the museum cannot fully control, in a similar manner to a surrounding landscape. The visitor encounters wider institutions that have their own historical, social and political meanings; these journeys themselves may be structured (as with cathedral architecture), or potentially fragmentary (as with a series of unexplained portals through a courtyard).

Bound up with the welcoming and orientation procedure, therefore, is a tension concerning, if not control, then management of meaning. In the Museum of Archaeology and Anthropology, the courtyard entrance involves visitors in a kind of triple entry through the estate of the university; the refurbished entrance simplifies and softens this for the public, itself telling a story of reorientation. The Stained Glass Museum, as a heritage venue within a heritage venue, inevitably tells a part of the cathedral's story while aspiring to a more general exposition; is bound up with the religious priorities of its host (and indeed the cathedral's own compromises concerning visiting), with entry achieved through an architectural journey that has the museum on the periphery. And the Hunterian Museum, as one function of the college among many (its role and position changing over the years) inevitably involves the visitor in the multi-functional life of the college while attempting to propel them through it. The specific institutional relationship (the corporate structure and degree of independence) as well as the physical relationship, rooted in architectural and historical contingencies, sets important conditions in the framing and management of these narratives.

In the sites chosen here, either the museum is embedded within the overall structure as one function among many, or it has (relative or absolute) independence in a clearly junior position. Either way, the museum plays a subsidiary role, its activities either explicitly (through operations) or implicitly (through context) supporting the host's activities. We see this, in practice, within the physical site. In the university setting, the buildings or estate are set up primarily to cater for the student and teaching faculty; in the cathedral setting, devotional practice; in the Royal College of Surgeons' setting, the needs of the professional organisation. Where the entrance is shared, it serves multiple functions reflecting the breadth of activities within the site, with the container institution's priorities predominating. Seen through this prism, a shared entrance becomes a manifestation of relative power and priorities, dramatising the social relations of the site (Fraser, 2007).

However, the entrance and its challenges also, in turn, seriously affect the structures of, and relationships between, institutions. Concern with access to the museum can generate tension or compromise; the entrance area can be a point of contact between otherwise relatively autonomous functions; it can encourage cooperation (or contestation) over shared concerns with security, welcome or meaning. All of which may lead to re-evaluation of relations and a reconception of the threshold. In short, there is a dynamic interplay of the institutional and the physical. We can begin to conceive these entrance spaces as a fabric of meaning, relationships and physicality that can both stand for the wider institutional milieu and play a key part in it (Lefebvre, 1991, pp. 26–27).

The visiting process enacts the various tensions and compromises that characterise much of the relationship between museum and host. Where visitors are, in a sense, a shared audience, their attention is to be contested or cooperatively catered for. In other words, they not only enter into this complex fabric, but partially constitute it. They may, in response to potentially mixed signals, creatively (mis)read environmental cues and act in ways that affect the potential overlap in institutional jurisdiction. This might have ramifications for consequent perceptions of security, or simply inadvertently interfere in the smooth operations of other functions. Visitors' reading of the narrative of entering and their subsequent behaviour can itself upset institutional balances of power. In short, visitors inevitably find themselves tangled in, performing and disrupting a set of relations between pre-existing institutions in what is clearly a contested area.

Taking this to its fullest extent, therefore, and noting the interrelation of physicality, relationships and meaning, at the shared entrance we have an example of use reconstituting architecture (MacLeod, 2013, p. 27). Besides any overt disruption of space, the visitor is reappropriating a building or site designed for a particular use (perhaps with a more restricted access) within the context of their privately motivated visit. They are a disruptive element to a more general contestation between the institutions at the entrance area.

Although the museums we have considered here are situated in very distinctive circumstances, the institutional pressures, tensions and compromises have echoes within all museums. Any change to the threshold – physical or procedural – will be modulated through sub-institutions and (potentially) competing functions or concerns. By attending to the whole fabric of the space (the interrelationships of its various attributes) we can perhaps be more sympathetic to the challenges facing staff at difficult thresholds, and better able to identify what changes to make when change is needed.

In summary, we have examined the phenomenon of small museums embedded in separate or wider institutions (a situation that often necessitates a shared or nested entrance) remaining alert to its potential impact on meaning, and paying special attention to the institutional relationships involved. These relationships have been seen to have physical and conceptual dimensions, both of which are at play in the entrance area. With the help of three case studies (from a university, a church and a medical context), we have seen how the entrance frames the presentation of museum narratives and therefore plays a part in institutional shifts; how the nature of the host institution can condition visitor experience, particularly in advance of the museum; and how strategies are deployed to deal with these spatial and jurisdictional overlaps.

References

Alberti, Samuel J.M.M. (2011) *Morbid curiosities: medical museums in nineteenth-century Britain*. Oxford: Oxford University Press.

Alberti, Samuel J.M.M. (2016) *Interviewed by: Kruse, S. at the Hunterian Museum (13 January 2016)*. Interview. Unpublished.

Alberti, Samuel J.M.M. (2017) 'This post mortem palace: accommodating the Hunterian Museum', in Berkowitz, C. and Lightman, B. (eds.) *Science museums in transition: cultures of display in nineteenth-century Britain and America*. Pittsburgh, PA: University of Pittsburgh Press.

Annals of RCS England (1963) 'Completion of the Hunterian Museum', *Annals of the Royal College of Surgeons of England*, 33:1, pp. 1–7.

Anon., E. (2016a) *Interviewed by: Kruse, S. at Ely Cathedral (11 February 2016)*. Interview. Unpublished.

Anon., S. (2016b) *Interviewed by: Kruse, S. at Ely Cathedral (25 January 2016)*. Interview. Unpublished.

Austin, T. (2012) 'Scales of narrativity', in MacLeod, S., Hanks, L.H. and Hale, J. (eds.) *Museum making: narratives, architectures, exhibitions*. London: Routledge, pp. 107–118.

Bedford, L. (2001) 'Storytelling: the real work of museums', *Curator: The Museum Journal*, 44:1, pp. 27–34.
Bennett, T. (1995) *The birth of the museum: history, theory, politics*. London; New York: Routledge.
Bourdieu, P., Darbel, A. and Schnapper, D. (1990) *The love of art: European art museums and their public*. Stanford, CA: Stanford University Press.
Brooke, C. (1993) *A history of the University of Cambridge*. Vol. 4, Cambridge: Cambridge University Press.
Broughton, L. (2008) *Interpreting Ely Cathedral*. Ely, England: Ely Cathedral Publications.
Cocke, T. (2003) 'The history of the fabric from 1541 to 1836', in Meadows, P. and Ramsay, N. (eds.) *A history of Ely Cathedral*. Woodbridge, Suffolk; Rochester, NY: Boydell Press, pp. 213–223.
Dobson, J. (1961) 'The architectural history of the Hunterian Museum', *Annals of the Royal College of Surgeons of England*, 29:2, pp. 113–126.
Duncan, C. and Wallach, A. (1978) 'The museum of modern art as late capitalist ritual: an iconographic analysis', *Marxist Perspectives*.
Ely Cathedral (2016) *Home page*. Available at: www.elycathedral.org/ Accessed: 26 March 2016.
Ely Cathedral and Sills, P. (2016) *A descriptive tour of Ely Cathedral*. Available at: www.elycathedral.org/visit/a-descriptive-tour-of-ely-cathedral Accessed: 26 March 2016.
Falk, J.H. and Dierking, L.D. (2000) *Learning from museums: visitor experiences and the making of meaning*. Walnut Creek, CA: AltaMira Press.
Fraser, J. (2007) 'Museums: drama, ritual and power', in Knell, S.J., Macleod, S. and Watson, S.E.R. (eds.) *Museum revolutions: how museums change and are changed*. London; New York: Routledge, pp. 291–302.
Furse-Roberts, J. (2012) 'Narrative landscapes', in MacLeod, S., Hanks, L.H. and Hale, J. (eds.) *Museum making: narratives, architectures, exhibitions*. London: Routledge, pp. 179–191.
Gunn, I. (ed.) (2016) *Interviewed by: Kruse, S. at the Museum of Archaeology and Anthropology, Cambridge (16 March 2016)*. Interview. Unpublished.
Harknett, S.-J. (2016) *Interviewed by: Kruse, S. at the Museum of Archaeology and Anthropology, Cambridge (12 February 2016)*. Interview. Unpublished.
Herle, A. (2012) 'Objects, agency and museums: continuing dialogues between the Torres Strait and Cambridge', in Dudley, S.H. (ed.) *Museum objects: experiencing the properties of things*. London; New York, NY: Routledge, pp. 295–310.
Higgins, M. (2003) 'Ely Cathedral: 1980–2000', in Meadows, P. and Ramsay, N. (eds.) *A history of Ely Cathedral*. Woodbridge, Suffolk; Rochester, NY: Boydell Press, pp. 363–385.
Lefebvre, H. (1991) *The production of space*, trans., Nicholson-Smith, D. Oxford and Cambridge: Blackwell.
MAA (2016a) *Museum history*. Available at: http://maa.cam.ac.uk/category/about-the-museum-of-archaeology-and-anthropology-history-governance-job-opportunities-staff/museum-history/ Accessed: 21 March 2016.
MAA (2016b) *Research and teaching at the Museum of Archaeology and Anthropology*. Available at: http://maa.cam.ac.uk/category/research/ Accessed: 25 May 2016.

Macdonald, S. (1998) 'Supermarket science? Consumers and "the public understanding of science"', in Macdonald, S. (ed.) *The politics of display: museums, science, culture*. London; New York: Routledge, pp. 118–138.

MacLeod, S. (2011) 'Towards an ethic of museum architecture', in Marstine, J. (ed.) *Routledge companion to museum ethics: redefining ethics for the twenty-first century museum*. Abingdon, UK; New York: Routledge, pp. 279–292.

MacLeod, S. (2012) 'Introduction', in MacLeod, S., Hanks, L.H. and Hale, J. (eds.) *Museum making: narratives, architectures, exhibitions*. London: Routledge, pp. xix–xxiii.

MacLeod, S. (2013) *Museum architecture: a new biography*. New York: Routledge.

Maddison, J. (2003) 'The Gothic cathedral: new building in a historic context', in Meadows, P. and Ramsay, N. (eds.) *A history of Ely Cathedral*. Woodbridge, UK; Rochester, NY: Boydell Press, pp. 113–141.

Mortensen, C.H., Rudloff, M. and Vestergaard, V. (2014) 'Communicative functions of the museum lobby', *Curator: The Museum Journal*, 57:3, pp. 329–346.

Psarra, S. (2009) *Architecture and narrative: the formation of space and cultural meaning*. Abingdon, UK; New York: Routledge.

Royal College of Surgeons of England (2011) *Hunterian Museum at the Royal College of Surgeons: guidebook*. London: RCSENG.

Royal College of Surgeons of England (2015) *Royal College of Surgeons annual report 2015*, London: RCSENG – Council.

Royal College of Surgeons of England (2016) *About the College*. Available at: www.rcseng.ac.uk/about (Accessed: 28 March 2016).

Stained Glass Museum (ed.) (2011) *Collections development policy*. Governance document. Unpublished.

Stained Glass Museum (2016) *History of the Stained Glass Museum*. Available at: http://stainedglassmuseum.com/about_history.html (Accessed: 26 March 2016).

Welch, D. (ed.) (2016) *Interviewed by: Kruse, S. at the Royal College of Surgeons (21 January 2016)*. Interview. Unpublished.

University of Cambridge (2016a) *School of the Humanities and Social Sciences: institutions in the School*. Available at: www.cshss.cam.ac.uk/institutions-in-the-school.

University of Cambridge (2016b) *University of Cambridge structure*. Available at: www.cam.ac.uk/about-the-university/how-the-university-and-colleges-work/structure.

Part III
The threshold rethought

9 Games in the lobby
A playful approach

Erik Kristiansen and Alex Moseley

Themes of play and gaming can impact on threshold spaces in a number of ways. In this chapter we will show how a game or play perspective might help or change our understanding of threshold and the lobby. The gaming perspective will also provide new ways of working with the threshold. Based on the classical understanding of games and play by Huizinga (1949) and extended with new research on pervasive games and alternate reality games (ARGs), games can be used as a research tool, a design tool, or as a game with a purpose. The lobby can be analysed as a game with respect to different game types, it can be designed using specially prepared design games, and it can be staged as a game with the visitors as the players. Theories of pervasive games and alternate reality games are particularly interesting as they address the challenges and benefits from playing in public spaces. We will explore questions such as: Which features of games can inform design decisions in the lobby space? How can a game support the functions (ticketing, queueing, waiting, etc.) of the lobby? How can games facilitate a seamless threshold transformation? How can games be used as a tool for analysing the functions of a particular lobby? We will review the possibilities for gamification of the lobby, discuss case studies and preliminary results and discuss how gaming the lobby might develop our understanding of the threshold at museums.

Playing the lobby

There are numerous examples of the use of play and gaming within museum contexts (see Beale, 2011, for a snapshot of over 40 recent case studies), yet the vast majority of these are focused on particular objects, galleries, installations or overarching museums or narratives. The lobby, the interface between 'inside' the museum and the 'outside', is ignored as a playful location – indeed is often seen as the most serious part of the museum: untouched by changing design themes or creative interpretations, a sense often reaffirmed by its architecture (which may in some cases appear grand, austere, cold). In this chapter we argue that a playful approach to the lobby, informed by game design principles, could recast the lobby as a welcoming and engaging part of the visit: starting or augmenting stories and experiences for the visitor, and helping them to overcome the challenges that Gurian signals in her concept of 'threshold fear' (Gurian, 2005).

Game and play theory

Play is often seen as fun activity: non-serious, non-pressured (in free time); belonging to the realm of children or those behaving as children. Such perceptions make its use within adult spheres, and particularly traditionally 'serious' places, problematic. Yet museums cater both to free time, and to children: play already exists either in defined spaces (such as activity areas, or activities) or in approaches to galleries or exhibitions.

But what does it mean to be 'playful'? Carse (1987) provides a thoughtful yet simple rule which draws on the 'non-pressured' requirement: 'whoever must play, cannot play': if one is forced, one cannot really be playing. Huizinga (1949) defined play as different from, and distinct from, 'ordinary' or 'real' in every way: it has no material interest or gain. Play is therefore a sheltered or safe place to be, with whatever happens during play separated from the 'real' world before and after play. Those studying or using play as a learning experience, of course, have since countered this argument by noting how play can develop a number of pervasive skills (problem-solving, social, organisational skills and so on: see Erickson, 1985 and Pellegrini and Smith, 1998) and many parents know how decisions, power struggles and arguments within play by children can spill out into the 'real' world.

Huizinga suggests a 'magic circle' into which players willingly step when they want to play: inside the circle they accept certain rules (or maybe the lack of rules), which they might not normally accept outside the circle. This acceptance of 'non-normal' rules helps to define what makes a *game*: a subset of play. Suits (1978) further defines these 'accepted non-normal rules' as often 'voluntarily overcoming unnecessary obstacles': to play a game players deliberately develop rules that would – in 'normal' life – be counterproductive (such as getting to the top of a Snakes and Ladders board through random movement, and deliberately stepping on snakes: whereas in 'normal' life we would get to our destination via the most direct route: up ladders and avoiding snakes). Accepting these new rules (i.e. stepping into Huizinger's 'magic circle') is what Suits describes as a *lusory* attitude: he argues that games are distinct from play in that they have *pre-lusory* goals (accepted before the game begins) and constitutive rules. Caillois (2001) makes a similar distinction: play is *paida* – unstructured play – whereas a game is *ludus* – structured and rule-bound. In reality, of course, the two terms – and definitions – are often blurred for particular activities (children often set up rules when they play together; visitors to a water park may be invited to play in a bounded space).

Do play and playfulness suggest fun? Advertising around family tabletop or computer games certainly suggests so; theme parks sell tickets to guarantee it: yet as many a never-ending game of Monopoly – or indeed arguing children during playtime – has proved, fun is not a guaranteed result of play. In an entertaining look at what game designers do to make games fun, designer Raph Koster fixes on one definition: 'the act of mastering a problem mentally' (Koster, 2004, p. 90), and goes on to say that 'real fun comes from challenges that are always at the margin of our ability' (p. 97). Koster, though, agrees with others such as Lazzaro (2005) and Leblanc (2004) who say that there are several *types* of fun. Lazzaro (2005) describes Koster's 'challenge accomplishment' as *hard fun*, and adds three other types: *easy fun* for the times we relax with friends, chill out, or show curiosity; *serious fun* for activities that are meaningful to us, or our interests; and *people fun*, which we gain from socialising or during effective teamwork. Perry (2012) linked fun within a museum context directly with learning: if a number of visitor learning motivations are met (such as curiosity, challenge and control) then visitors are more likely to have fun during their visit.

The notion of a magic circle separating play/game from non-play is a fascinating one for museum thresholds – which might be seen as a similar call to 'enter the circle': something we'll explore in more detail below. Blurring this boundary, though, is where some truly fascinating work has been taking place: games or experiences that test this *liminality* or break down the barrier between playing and non-playing; game-world and real-world. Both in the games industry (Montola et al., 2009) and in the museums sector (Moseley, 2011), the use of *pervasive, augmented* or *alternate reality* games has seen participants challenge their notion of when and how to play. They might, for example, meet a fictional character within the museum who tells them of a treasure buried in the real world; later that day, while back at work, they get a mysterious SMS message from the same character. When are they playing? What is real, and what isn't? And where, now, is the edge of that circle?

Working with the lobby using games: analysing the lobby as a game

Taking ideas of play into the museum is not novel, but the lobby seems to be an overlooked part of the museum in many aspects, and particularly with reference to games and playful performances. Games can be used just for fun or as a means to acquire knowledge in a specific domain by using the game as a format for the process (Laursen et al., 2016). Games can even be used as a framework for analysis. We aim to apply the process of gaming to the workings of the lobby. Understanding the lobby as a game leads to different views of 'lobby', as a game can be said to be built on a storyline, leading the players through a progression to the goal, hindered by challenges. As a design principle it is reasonable that we want a lobby game to have something to do with the activities of the lobby. The obvious players in the lobby are the visitors, the staff, or both. If the players are the visitors the goal could, in line with a basic understanding of the function of the lobby, be to reach the exhibition either as quickly or as prepared as possible. This tells us that the lobby is either a place to pass through or a place where you collect 'power-ups' in order to maximise your experience in the exhibition. The challenges may be all the things that could make it difficult: the staff, failure to find your way, detours to the cloakroom, delays caused by the queues. In contrast to this, the 'power-ups' are your helpers: friendly staff, short queues, refreshments such as coffee, and maps that assist wayfinding.

We might reverse the game and make the staff the principal players. This poses the interesting question: what is the goal of the lobby personnel? One such goal might be for the staff to help visitors. However, even while modern museums probably don't recognise the visitors as natural opponents, conflicts and challenges are still introduced into a lobby game by the visitors. Challenges for the museum staff could include visitors encountering problems, technical issues or long queues.

We may also arrange the lobby as a game where different roles are played depending on whether the players perform as visitors or staff. Our small experiment of understanding the lobby as a typical dice or role-playing game reveals common conceptions of the purpose and workings of the lobby. We may devise the building as a 2D board in a board game and the people as players pursuing different goals while overcoming obstacles and collecting power-ups. The game metaphor tells us where to aim our focus, if we want to enhance the lobby this way. A good game is characterised by its balance between challenges and rewards, while being fun to play. We may ask ourselves: is our lobby a good game to play?

Turning away from abstract thinking about the lobby as a game, we may direct our attention to a real lobby with real visitors and staff. What happens if the visitors accept the lobby as a magic circle that invites them to play? The perspective in our game changes from a god-like game where we manipulate game tokens on a board, to a game where we ourselves become the principal agents. The lobby and the museum may be designed in a way that invites the visitors to experience it as a game. It can be seen either as a kind of gamification of the lobby or merely as assigning a clear function to a space that is devoid of such. If the lobby is a game, in addition to the focus on game mechanics as already described, we also need to focus on fun in order to invite and enhance play. How can we make the lobby a fun place? We must examine the performance of visitors and staff with a view to making the elements fun. For example, standing in a queue is considered dull but this may be changed into a fun experience (Lazzaro's *easy fun*) by introducing things to do or watch: playful queue behaviour, patterns in the floor or ceiling. This is a method many amusement parks use to deal with long queueing times, such as tables with Lego every few metres in Legoland parks. The queue may be a part of the game where you accumulate more power-ups the longer you stand. Seeing the entrance into the lobby as a magic circle turns the lobby into a game board or playground. We must ensure that visitors become players either by inviting them into a formalised game or by inviting playful behaviour through the configuration of the lobby and the performance of the staff.

We may also use a game for analysing or designing existing or new lobbies. The traditional method of understanding a lobby is by conducting observation studies or interviews with visitors and staff. Another option we've explored is to make a game and then play through scenarios. Important insights are gathered through both designing and playing. For the Thresholds Festival (University of Leicester, 2014) we designed a 'lobby design game', or more precisely a meta-game: the goal of the game was to design a game. The object was to create a space for discussions regarding the lobby, which could be a replica of an existing lobby, a planned – but not built – lobby, or an imagined lobby. To create a space for discussion we needed to encourage the participants to work together and discuss the best solutions to meet the challenges. As a game, it was important to create an open, fun, and inviting game structure. This was obtained through a two-stage process: first the participants designed and created the game, then they played the game. The participants consisted of some 30 scholars and curators from museums and universities. This diverse group had different insights and goals, thus sometimes hindering optimal collaboration, but in general reaching productive insights about the lobbies of the museums that became the focus of each game.

The lobby design game

After a brief introduction, the participants were divided into groups of six to seven persons. Each group was provided with paper, scissors, and the game materials: sheets with cut-out figures representing visitors and staff. To make a role-playing game, each figure was accompanied by an information card, with spaces to note the age, likes and dislikes connected with the character. The first task was to agree on the kind of museum, and how the lobby should be constructed. Some groups chose to replicate an existing lobby, while others agreed on an imagined one. The lobby was constructed with scraps of cardboard, furnished with models of desks, doors, etc. Each participant chose five figures and filled out the information cards. This practical design and construction work led to playful collaboration both on practical issues (how do we glue this together?) and on design matters (where are audio guides handed out?). This was completed in 30 minutes. The remaining 30 minutes were used for playing the game. The rules were simple: the game takes place in real time; you may move your figures accordingly; when two figures meet, a conflict arises that must be dealt with immediately. This was done through discussion and sometimes a change to the design of the lobby was made. The subsequent evaluation revealed that the participants were surprised by the importance of the design phase. By designing the lobby themselves they held important discussions on how to create a welcoming atmosphere, focused on the necessary functions of the lobby, and they became a group of people working on the same project. This created a field for collaboration on enhancing and revealing the shortcomings of their lobby design in the ensuing game. In fact several groups admitted that the hour of playing had completely changed their understanding of their 'own' lobby, and that their design for a new lobby would have to be radically changed.

Enhancing the lobby

Based on earlier analysis of the communicative functions of the lobby (Rudloff et al., 2014) we may understand the lobby as a space that communicates values to the visitor. In this case we are interested in how it communicates a sense of play and we may examine each element for its playful potential. This is in line with what Fiona Wilkie called the *repertoire* of the site (Wilkie, 2002), when designing site-specific performances, as is also the case when designing a game that takes place in the lobby. The lobby is a space that usually is assigned a number of functions. Sometimes these functions have also made their impression on the architecture (built-in reception desks, cloakrooms, etc.), but they have probably never been specially designed for gaming or to maximise playful behaviour like a playground. We may thus consider the lobby a site that either works as a backdrop for playful activities or which we choose to integrate with gaming: that is, the game-performance becomes a palimpsest (Turner, 2004) where the original and necessary performances of the lobby are upheld and working, but are 'overlaid' with a game. The studies conducted by research group DREAM

Figure 9.1 The lobby design game

(Laursen et al., 2016) showed that the lobby can be said to support a number of functions. One significant observation is that although the lobby is normally viewed as an entrance hall, it is often also used to support slightly different functions (see Table 9.1). It is important to recognise that the lobby in many museums is also used for pauses during the visit as well as being the way out and thus leaving the final impression on the visitor.

Laursen et al. (2016) conducted a study on the lobby seen as a transformative (*liminoid*) space (Table 9.1). Four transformative functions were identified: separation, connection, support, and resolution with corresponding functions for entering and exiting. As we discussed earlier, we associate a game space with a *magic circle*, which we in turn regard as a *liminoid space*. We can therefore use the functions above to show where to direct focus when designing a game for the lobby. The game may target a single function (or part thereof) or comprise all functions. The functions stress the need for support during the transformation, thus the aim of the game would be to support the transition from entering the museum to entering the exhibition (a kind of prelude) or to support exiting the exhibition through the lobby and a transition back into the 'outside world'.

Table 9.1 and the suggestions above may help to identify areas where a game can support the transformative function of the museum threshold, either as discrete entities or by blurring the borders of the threshold (a 'fuzzy' edge to the magic circle). A game supporting a specific function of a lobby may be defined as a *game with a purpose* or a *serious game*, and we may devise games to address specific problems arising in the lobby, such as long queues, orientation problems, ticketing, and obtaining information. These are essential functions of the lobby that all museums have to address and which at the same time may be a hindrance to the good museum experience. Solving the problems by designing games may be a viable solution as

Table 9.1 Museum visitors' transformative foyer practices (Laursen et al., 2016)

Transformative functions	Entry phases	Exit phases
Separation	**Arrival** (entering the foyer)	**Departure** (leaving the space)
Connection	**Orientation** (deciding what to see and where to find it)	**Preparation** (visiting cloakroom, waiting for family, etc.)
Support	**Service** (ticketing, exhibition, technologies)	**Service** (e.g. interacting with foyer personnel)
Resolution	**Preparation** (visiting cloakroom, etc.)	**Evaluation** (e.g. discussing exhibitions)

it addresses the problems by adding a layer of familiar motivators, and the potential for play and fun.

On the basis of Table 9.1 we may derive a typology of various lobby games (summarised in Table 9.2) that are designed to address different transformative functions of the lobby. These games would be small casual games designed to address specific transformations. Larger games that address multiple problems of the lobby are discussed in the next section.

The typology identifies transformative functions and actions with respect to the main purpose of the lobby (arriving, exiting and – for some lobbies – pausing). The table suggests various game types that may be used to address specific problems in the lobby. As an example, let us take the transformative functions 'Resolution' and 'Departure'. Resolution is a phase where the visitor evaluates the exhibition before leaving the museum. Some museums provide questionnaires at this point. The object for a game is to support this transformation in a playful way. The table suggests that we use a 'rating game': this could be a game where the visitor rates the exhibition and compares the ratings with other visitors (in the style of *Top Trumps*). Or it could be a game where the visitor reviews the exhibition through a quiz-style game show. Another example from the table is 'Connection/Pause' which suggests a 'planning game'. When pausing in the lobby, but still connected to the museum, the visitors may be deciding what to see next. In this case,

Table 9.2 A typology of lobby games

Transformative functions	Arrival games	Pause games	Departure games
Separation	Presentation of museum (explorer game)	Cooling off (meditative game)	What are we going to do now? (explorer game) Finding your group (social game)
Connection	What to see (planning game) Finding your way (orientation game)	What to see next (planning game) Where to go next (orientation game)	Waiting for others (puzzle game)
Support	Ticketing (buying game) Queueing (puzzle game, social game)	Socialising, shopping (social game)	Remembering stuff (memory game) Where are we going? (orientation game)
Resolution	What to remember before entering exhibition (puzzle game, quiz game)	Reviewing exhibition (memory game, quiz game)	Evaluation (rating game, quiz game)

a planning game would be suitable. It could be a game where the museum presents several choices, leaving the visitor to find the optimal set of possibilities according to their interests. Another way of looking at the table is asking: in which transformations could 'orientation games' be used? In the 'Connection' row these games support spatial orientation, for example by providing plans and letting people find and learn routes to the exhibitions in question. Orientation games are also suggested in 'Support/Departure': visitors leaving the museum are often planning where to go next and figuring out how to get there. A playful app could support wayfinding to such onward locations.

In this section we have dealt with a systematic approach covering identification of the important functions of the lobby and which games may target these functions. This approach is summarised in Table 9.2 where common game genres are suggested. Using this as a basis may help address identified problems within the lobby using playful solutions.

Turning the lobby into a playground

The transformation of the lobby into a playful space is as much about mindsets within the museum as it is about the space design. Play, as defined at the opening of this chapter, requires a safe space: one removed from 'reality' where things can be tried, tested, pushed, and failed – without the fear of reprisal. Of course, just as games apply structures to play, so museums have certain structures that must be in place (including legal and moral requirements such as accessibility, the safety of staff, the safety of objects in collections, etc.) and some structures that they might want to be in place (visitor journeys, learning aims, missions and values). Many games succeed in applying their structures in an appropriate way to promote play and maintain engagement; and it is these methods that open the way for lobbies to become playful and yet practical.

Promoting play, or the invitation to play, is a notion the museum is familiar with. Many museums have objects or installations that invite investigation (touch, press, hold, play) although often inside the galleries, not in the lobby itself. Moving objects or installations into the lobby space can invite play as soon as visitors step inside the threshold, as many science or technology museums already experience.

In a project at Chatsworth House, Derbyshire, UK, we deliberately invited play at the edge of the threshold. We faced a particular problem with this large historic country house: the approach to the house is a large car park with small patches of lawn and multiple, dispersed and (as proved by existing visitor data) confusing entrances (Figure 9.2). In our initial planning phase, we looked at the way games approach orientation. In particular, we considered the way that players in massive multiplayer online games (such as *World of Warcraft*) have to orientate themselves in a large open space, where a number of options are open to them; in the game, clues are given using symbols, moving or flashing objects, or signs. This idea of 'suggesting'

Figure 9.2 Chatsworth House front view, Derbyshire, England

direction or guidance resonated with Huizinga and Caillois's definitions of play: 'free', 'distinct from the ordinary' and 'alea' play (where playfulness comes from a basis in chance or luck). These definitions apply favourably to a threshold where visitors may or may not actively seek guidance or orientation, but may be looking (consciously or subconsciously) for clues to guide and orientate their visit. We wanted to invite visitors to enter the magic circle: once entered, they might be more willing to participate in a playful experience, with the tangible benefit of orientation as a reward.

Our eventual solution was three different and playful takes on standard signage:

1 a simple but colourful opaque sign;
2 a transparent panel with black lines tracing the roofline of one of the entrances – inviting viewers to line up the lines with the roof and see other features revealed;
3 a lenticular hologram in which we placed 'ghosts' of movement which the visitor would see as they passed by.

An initial pilot installation told us little more than that people are generally unwilling to enter a magic circle when it's wet and a cold wind is blowing;

Games in the lobby 185

but we did find that a few visitors – even in those conditions – were willing to engage. A second pilot in better weather was more successful, with half of the visitors interacting in some way with the signage, and around 10 per cent stopping and interacting closely with one or more of the signs (the lenticular being the one most visitors remembered in subsequent interviews). Even a few small signs designed with playfulness in mind therefore had an effect on the visitors' threshold experience.

The lobby is usually one of the more static parts of the museum, and as such an unexpected change, such as the new signage at Chatsworth, might provide an opportunity for a playful experience. Museums have started to experiment with changing the lobby, making it more playful at certain times: Culture24's *Museums at Night* (2015) initiative invites museums in the UK, twice a year, to open their doors after hours so that visitors enter the museum in the dark, or under different illumination – and often interact in ways that are different from daytime visits. Other museums offer sleepovers or adult-only 'lates' in the lobby space at regular times in the year. The lobby might therefore not always be playful, but might become more playful at certain times and for certain audiences.

When playfulness extends seamlessly between the threshold and the museum itself, the magic circle doesn't need to break (or becomes *liminoid*): as is the case in the Experimentarium in Copenhagen, Denmark where visitors are asked to get their phones out in the lobby; they are then led into a secret underground mission throughout the museum (*EGO-TRAP*, Kahr-Højland, 2010); or in the Museum of Natural History and Archaeology in

Figure 9.3 Playful signage at Chatsworth House

Trondheim, Norway, where a smartphone app turns the whole museum into a game board, the visitors and artefacts representing pawns and treasures (Rokne, 2011).

This extension/blurring of a magic circle beyond the lobby resonates with the design of alternate reality games, of which EGO-TRAP is one example. Other implementations in museum contexts have extended beyond the museum itself, mixing the real world (including the museum) and fiction together. *Ghosts of a Chance* and *Pheon*, at the LUCE Foundation Centre for American Art at the Smithsonian Museum, Washington, USA, engaged visitors (in the museum, outside the museum, or sitting at home on the other side of the world) in a series of connected tasks including the creation of real-world objects that then made their way into the museum gallery via a series of clues: and saw the 'players' converge on the museum for live scavenger hunts (Moseley, 2011). In many ways these activities extend the museum 'lobby' out into the real world: for different participants the entrance to the museum might be the physical entrance, or might be a blog post, or an SMS message. Augmented reality applications move/multiply/distribute the 'lobby' in a similar way: the Museum of London's *Street Museum* app, for example, provides users with pop-up entrances to a museum visit: viewing historic photographs overlaid on modern streets wherever the user happens to be at that moment.

Conclusion: gamification of the lobby

In our exploration of play, and the museum's attitude towards it, it has become apparent that playfulness is not a state: not there for a season, or accompanying a redesign. Instead, playfulness is an attitude: one that museums can adopt on a temporary or longer-term basis – and one that, where the lobby is concerned, has often been in this temporary form. 'Museums at night', sleepovers, 'lates' and other events are an *invitation to play*, extended by the museum to the willing (lusory) visitor.

Part of the difficulty in making the lobby space playful on a more permanent (or more widespread) basis is the inherent formality of many museum thresholds: the airlock into the deep, serious collection beyond. Turning the spaces from formal to informal is the first step in inviting play: learning from the 'special events' and creating a playful setting at all times. And by starting with a playful experience, the visit into the museum beyond (or even extending the visit beyond the museum) may become more playful too: blurring the edges of the 'magic circle'.

The projects and examples we've covered during the development of this chapter have suggested two things: first, very little work has been done in this area to date; and second, where examples of playful lobbies exist they exemplify the potential for using these often large, open and undeveloped spaces for fun, engaging activities.

We have found usefulness in adopting a playful approach to lobby design; both in a playful attitude to design, and in the results of the design itself. In Table 9.2, we have suggested a typology of playful experiences that could match to the transformative functions of the lobby, and hope that this – and the examples of existing practice highlighted – will be of help in changing the mindset of other museums: inculcating a sense of play where the threshold and subsequent onward journeys are concerned.

References

Beale, K. (Ed.) (2011). *Museums at Play: Games, Interaction and Learning*. Boston, MA: MuseumsEtc.
Caillois, R. (2001). *Man, Play and Games*. Urbana & Chicago: University of Illinois Press.
Carse, J. (1987). *Finite and Infinite Games*. New York: Ballantine Books.
Culture24 (2015). *Museums at Night to Become a Biannual Festival; Connect Competition Announced*. Blog post, 19/1/2015. Available: https://museumsatnight.wordpress.com/2015/01/19/museums-at-night-to-become-a-biannual-festival-connect-competition-announced/. Accessed: 28/1/2015.
Erickson, R.J. (1985). 'Play Contributes to the Full Emotional Development of the Child'. *Education*, 1985:105, pp. 261–263.
Gurian, E.H. (2005). 'Threshold Fear'. In S. MacLeod (Ed.) *Reshaping Museum Space: Architecture, Design, Exhibitions*. Abingdon, UK: Routledge, pp. 203–214.
Huizinga, J. (1949). *Homo Ludens: A Study of the Play-Element in Culture*. London: Routledge & Kegan Paul.
Kahr-Højland, A. (2010). 'EGO-TRAP: A Mobile Augmented Reality Tool for Science Learning in a Semi-formal Setting'. *Curator*, 53:4, pp. 501–509.
Koster, R. (2004). *A Theory of Fun for Game Design*. Scottsdale, AZ: Paraglyph Press.
Laursen, D., Kristiansen, E. and Drotner, K. (2016). 'The Museum Foyer as a Transformative Space of Communication'. *Nordisk Museologi*, 2016:1, pp. 69–88.
Lazzaro (2005). *The Four Keys to Fun*. Available: www.nicolelazzaro.com/the4-keys-to-fun/. Accessed: 28/1/2015.
Leblanc, M. (2004). 'Mechanics, Dynamics, Aesthetics: A Formal Approach to Game Design'. *Lecture at Northwestern University*, April 2004. Available: http://algorithmancy.8kindsoffun.com/MDAnwu.ppt. Accessed: 28/1/2015.
Montola, M., Stenros, J. and Waern, A. (Eds). (2009). *Pervasive Games: Theory and Design*. Burlington, MA: Morgan Kaufmann.
Moseley, A. (2011). 'Immersive Games: An Alternate Reality for Museums'. In K. Beale (Ed.) *Museums At Play: Games, Interaction and Learning*. Boston, MA: MuseumsEtc., pp. 230–245.
Pellegrini, A.D. and Smith, P.K. (1998). 'The Development of Play During Childhood: Forms and Possible Functions'. *Child Psychol Psychiatry Rev.*, 1998:3, pp. 51–57.
Perry, D.L. (2012). *What Makes Learning Fun? Principles for the Design of Intrinsically Motivating Museum Exhibits*. Lanham, MD: AltaMira Press.
Rokne, A.S. (2011). 'Smartphone Interaction: The Museum as a Gaming Board'. In K. Beale (Ed.) *Museums At Play: Games, Interaction and Learning*. Boston, MA: MuseumsEtc., pp. 274–285.

Rudloff, M., Hviid Mortensen, C. and Vestergaard, V. (2014). 'Communicative Functions of the Museum Lobby'. *Curator*, 57:3, pp. 329–346.

Suits, B. (1978). *The Grasshopper: Games, Life and Utopia*. Peterborough, Canada: Broadview Press.

Turner, C. (2004). 'Palimpsest or Potential Space? Finding a Vocabulary for Site-Specific Performance'. *New Theatre Quarterly*, 20:4, pp. 373–390. doi:10.1017/s0266464x04000259.

Wilkie, F. (2002). 'Mapping the Terrain: A Survey of Site-Specific Performance in Britain'. *New Theatre Quarterly*, 18, pp. 140–160. doi:10.1017/S0266464X02000234.

Conversation 3
The British Postal Museum and Archive

Alex Moseley [AM] interviews Hannah Gledhill [HG], Project Manager at the British Postal Museum and Archive.

AM: *I'm here in a rather strange underground setting to talk with Hannah Gledhill, Project Manager at the British Postal Museum and Archive. So Hannah, where are we?*

HG: We are currently sat in the former maintenance depot of the Post Office Underground Railway, more widely known now as Mail Rail. This area here, this space, is going to form part of our capital project. The first half of the project is the Postal Museum that we're building across the road. But in parallel to that, we're opening up this space as an exhibition and events area and actually a train ride through part of the former Post Office railway network.

AM: *That sounds exciting! Can you tell us about your institution?*

HG: The British Postal Museum and Archive has been in operation for just over ten years now. But we're as close as we ever have been, really, to building a home for our five centuries' worth of collections that the public can visit in one place. We currently have an archive based at Mount Pleasant in London, but we also have a large museum collection stored in a warehouse in Essex. And that houses a lot of our vehicles, our pillar boxes, and we also have a lot of our collection currently on tour around the country in touring exhibitions. So the idea and the dream has always been to bring all these objects together and make them a lot more accessible for the general public.

AM: *On that front, what are your current visitors like, and what are you looking to move towards?*

HG: Currently, we have around 2,500 to 3,000 visitors a year. They are predominantly researchers, academic visitors who want to access our archive. The aim when we open the Postal Museum and Mail Rail is to increase that to 186,000 visitors a year. The intention is not to abandon those researchers and the academic visitors, but to open up to a much broader audience. Our target audience will be families with young children ages 7 to 11 and independent adults. So that's really one of the biggest challenges that we have, completely changing our target audience and who accesses our collection.

AM: *What would you like your threshold to be like?*

HG: What we really want is for the welcome space and the threshold to reflect the kind of visitors that we're trying to attract. So we want it to be family-friendly; we want it to have a sense of community; we want it to reflect our brand, which is changing quite considerably over the next year or so. It needs to reflect the organization we're going to become, not the organization we are now.

AM: *And what are the complexities of trying to fit that into a new build, into perhaps pre-existing designs that may have been drawn up before you thought about the threshold?*

HG: It's complex in the sense that we can't change the building envelope. The space is what it is. But we were fortunate in that our designs weren't so far along that we couldn't make changes to them.

AM: *Having consulted with other museum practitioners, designers and academics, what techniques have you brought back to the museum to look at in terms of your threshold?*

HG: What has really stood out for us was the technique of using gaming (see Chapter 9). We shared our existing architectural plan with external experts to play with it and pull it apart – which was a bit distressing at some points. But it was really good to then get feedback from experts, retail experts, museum experts, on the best layout for that space. And we took the feedback from that session to our architect.

But we also played the game here at the British Postal Museum and Archive with all staff. In an all-staff meeting, we got everyone to take part in it. This was good, because I think it was the first time everyone had been given the opportunity to feed into the designs. And we had such a variety of people working on them at that point, different points of views, that we came out of that with much better ideas of how to lay out that space.

AM: *Had the staff engaged in anything like that before?*

HG: No. We generally have a design team at the museum, and then those select few are responsible for feeding into the design. So this is really the first time that absolutely everyone had the opportunity to feed into it. And it was good, because it was very interactive: everyone took part. No one sat there and didn't take part.

AM: *Looking to the future when the museum is realized, what will the threshold look like, and what sort of job will it do?*

HG: It's very much been designed as a community space: we want it to be part of the community. We want it to be welcoming. We want people to just be able to visit the cafe should they wish or pop into the shop if they wish and not feel forced, if you like, to purchase an exhibition ticket and go around the exhibition, although that's obviously the main intention of the space. But we want it to be family-friendly, to reflect our brand, which is all about community and storytelling. That's the key, really, to make it reflect our brand. Because if that's not balanced, we're really not offering the full, rounded experience to the visitor.

In summer 2017, the new Postal Museum and Mail Rail opened to the public, selling out advance tickets for the first few months within hours.

10 Retail perspectives on the threshold

Tracy Harwood

Retailers have long taken the view that customer experience itself begins before entering the store, terming the retail environment as a 'servicescape', encompassing every aspect of the experience from the pre-marketing, to the car park, to the instore experience, to any follow-up interactions with the store brand. Thus the servicescape includes online channels of communication used through which offers and services may be promoted and the physical store visit experience may be augmented. Viewing the servicescape as a 'customer journey', the experience of the store can begin with online search behaviour and may culminate in a visit to a store, for browsing and/or purchasing products, or even returning unwanted or faulty items. The journey therefore includes the physical process of getting to a store and access prior to entering the store environment, say entry into a local service car park and shopping centre, as well as the more immediate approach to and entry into the store itself, over the threshold. The journey through the servicescape underpins the experience of the store environment, and is linked through the customer's motivation to visit to buy or consume a 'happening', say a time-limited event such as a seasonal sale, launch presentation of a new range or store card member-only activity. Taking this view, the threshold as a point of entry has multiple perspectives that retailers consider in different ways in relation to their online virtual and offline physical space.

The main focus of this chapter is how the retail approach to the customer's experience of the physical (offline) space can be applied to museum entrances. This can include how lighting, contrast and colour, browsing and scanning behaviour, navigational aids, flow and transitional mind/mood states, can all affect customer behaviour as customers enter stores, as well as how previously learned behaviour about the store can inform future visits. Following presentation of the core concepts, related to both stores and museums, the chapter discusses how thresholds can be thought of in relation to a 'customer journey' or 'experience environment' and how this can be linked to the 'corporate' strategy and identity of a particular organization through a 'servicescape'.

The servicescape as a physical space

The museum space and retail space are increasingly converging through personal, social and physical dimensions as servicescapes. In retail, the physical space comprises the store and its environs (all outside and inside areas through which consumers pass) yet the process of sense-making and familiarity with the experience of the store is reduced to a pattern of consumption that has been normalized by a near-standard design of the shopping environment in stores, retail parks and shopping centres (malls). At a store level, this is characterized by an entrance, immediate presentation of merchandise in a floor plan that determines access to all products, a customer servicing area and exit usually through the entrance, sometimes experienced over multiple floors. Whilst a few stores differ in their presentation of this experience (contrast the physical 'catalogue' experiences of the likes of the UK's homewares stores Argos and Sweden's IKEA to the browse/shop experience of many other retail brands), all use similar design cues to communicate with their customers. Where brands own multiple stores, the brand-specific design cues used are often replicated across the various locations in which the stores are found. For example, consider a store brand with which you are familiar, and then reflect on how similar that store is in all its locations that you have visited, including in different countries (for example, the British clothing and food retail brand Marks and Spencer or Spain's clothing retail brand Zara), in terms of its layout of goods and services, appearance and 'feel'. The familiarity established through this kind of design-related activity exists to facilitate a shopping experience by supporting and reinforcing browsing behaviour and providing resources that enable customers to make purchase decisions quickly and efficiently. In contrast, the museum has generally been considered to be a space for leisure-time experiences that fulfil an educational remit, albeit increasingly viewed as a hedonistic environment where visitors can enjoy socially interactive experiences (Gurian, 2005; Lehman and Leighton, 2010; Buckley, 2014). Thus, there is also homogeneity in the experience, resulting in a generic pattern of consumption related to a visit.

Increasingly, however, retail environments have become as much tourist destinations as spaces that fulfil utilitarian needs (see for example McIntyre, 2012); for example, various concept stores and well-known brands (for example, UK luxury goods store Harrods or New York's Bloomingdale's, and German sports shoe brand Nike, etc.) are now 'must sees' during a visit to a city centre. Whilst larger retailers often seek to homogenize the customer experience through tried and tested methods that have evolved to reinforce their brands, some have now adopted the 'concept' approach typically associated with the smaller independent stores, and have consequently become increasingly creative in their use of design features which are in turn attractive in their own right, for a variety of reasons. For example, across the sector, much marketing imagery pays special attention to the design ethos adopted by the store: the use of wood and recycled materials may be used to communicate sustainability; a minimalist presentation of products may communicate style; images that promote the types of customers who frequent the environment may draw in other similar customers, etc. This retail approach draws on the experience of an environment that is often used in the communication of a museum, where the uniqueness of the physical space of a museum is a key part of its attraction for visitors.

Despite the differences in the application of the approaches to managing the physical space, both make use of architecture, objects, atmosphere, sights and sounds to arouse curiosity and a sense of uniqueness and fun, with staff who welcome and facilitate the experience, in order to involve and immerse the customer. Yet, few museum environments are as easily configurable as contemporary retail store environments. For example, a new installation often takes weeks to prepare, effectively closing off a significant area to its public in the process. In a retail context, the ease with which the space can be adapted for new content is of paramount importance – without customers there are no sales and the brand will fail as customers quickly move to other store environments in order to satisfy their sensory desires and needs, whether based on utilitarian or hedonistic motivations. This seems to be of little importance to museums, a consequence of the different funding models they use. From the retail perspective, the use of configurable components, such as movable lighting rigs and merchandise display units that may be quickly adapted so as to enhance new store features and offers, the inclusion of space for events such as fashion shows, seating arrangements that enable customers to pause and hold social gatherings, pop-up in-store coffee shops, and so on, all facilitate the customers' ongoing (repeat visit) experience. An important aspect of this is the growing emphasis on the store as a social environment.

The growing trend for retail spaces to be seen as socially interactive spaces for leisure-time activity is more analogous to a museum visit, emphasizing a need for physical space that facilitates interactions among and between customers, encouraging them to linger and engage with products. Within the museum context, as Falk and Dierking (1998) suggest, 'a large part of [visitors'] attention in museums is devoted to the people with whom they arrive' (1998, p. 41). Social interactions have the impact of increasing customers' visit duration, which ultimately impacts on browsing and shopping behaviour. These ideas draw on theories of flow, where the consumer becomes so immersed in the experience that they lose their sense of time (for example, Csikszentmihalyi and Rochberg-Halton, 1981) and hedonism, related to the consumption of the experience for its own pleasurable sake, rather than to realize some utilitarian need (for example, Holbrook and Hirschman, 1982; McIntryre, 2012). Thus, the types of experiences that consumers come to expect from physical spaces include both shopping and social elements, communicated through promotional strategies that often incorporate the unique features and characteristics of the store design components.

The physical space also contributes to sense-making about the brand. Store layout promotes learning and reinforces the 'pattern of consumption' from which customers build mental models, or schemas, about the brand. This applies equally well to museums, many of which use similar models of customer engagement, such that the experience of entertainment/education (or edutainment) through the visit experience is similar across different branded environments. What remains unique to each museum (brand) is, however, the specific collection, which requires time to learn about and engage with, thus schemas relating to physical experience may be both macro-level, related to the generic experience of visiting museums, or micro-level, relating to a particular museum. Over time and through regular visits, retail store customers learn the location of their preferred products, in effect enabling them to shortcut and focus their attention, albeit that this may reduce their sensory visit experience to a previously determined focal area of interest, rather than them responding to any design cues in the store. Observations of visitor experiences in a museum context identify that orientation is a major part of the initial behaviour, with visitors sometimes taking up to ten minutes to make a decision on which direction to move. Hayward and Brydon-Miller (1984) suggest that this is a seminal moment in a museum visit experience that is rarely a straightforward process, particularly for a first-time visitor. This pattern of sense-making is observed less in visitors who have more experience of the specific environment, who attempt to eliminate what they perceive to be the most inefficient aspects of the experience by instead focusing on their main sensory experience. Clearly, the behaviour exhibited by customers depends on their motivations for visiting, and in turn this will influence the depth of learning about the environment.

Similar patterns of interaction with the space are also observed in retail and museum environments where design features of layout influence the 'traffic flow' of customers. In both environments, a majority of customers may be observed to navigate a right-handed pathway around the space. In the museum space, Melton (in Falk and Dierking, 1998), suggested that positioning of exhibits influences flow and up to 75 per cent of visitors follow a right-handed pathway through a museum on entry. In creating store layouts, designers will consider these processes of customer engagement and their experience or journey as they travel through the environment – this acknowledges that consumers tend to perceive such servicescapes holistically (Bitner, 1990; Mattila and Wirtz, 2001; Spence et al., 2014). For example, designers may attempt to optimize the visibility of merchandise by controlling speed of traffic flow through floor pattern, positioning of navigational materials, setting the width of aisles and the density of products on display. Such techniques may have the effect of slowing down the footfall of the visitor and, in so doing, increasing the potential for browsing products, which may ultimately impact on purchase behaviour. This is discussed further later in this chapter, where the view from the threshold becomes an important consideration communicating how the environment should be navigated. The next section, however, discusses the threshold itself.

Role of the threshold

Research into retail environments identifies the role of the threshold as being a transitional space in the built environment between store exterior and interior (see, for example, Kent and Kirby, 2009). Its role is to provide a presentational means to reflect the store's content, where features such as layout and navigational cues are communicated alongside products, displays, services and marketing materials (Turley and Milliman, 2000). Yet, depending on familiarity with and experience of the specific store environment, it is a space in which consumers often do not 'see' merchandise but instead attempt to orientate themselves to the store's inner construction (Ebster and Garaus, 2011). This suggests that the threshold is not a good place for the store to present its signature range of products. Similarly, museum visitors are often overwhelmed with environmental information that attempts to communicate the upcoming experience, such as maps, exhibits and location of helpers, as well as using other visitors in the space to draw conclusions about expectations of their own behaviour during the visit (see Barker and Wright, 1955).

In other respects a store threshold experience is momentary, unlike that of the museum experience, which tends to be more deliberate in communicating the sense of an experience beyond. Indeed, museums often seek to delay the flow of passage into the main experience environment, albeit so as to ensure visitors pay or acquire an appropriate demeanour, learned from others in the vicinity of the foyer. The store threshold, however, is entirely teasing in its presentation, aiming to draw consumers through the space and into the main shopping area as efficiently as possible. For this, the actual offer of the store tends to extend across the entire store frontage and visible exterior, through window displays. Much attention is given to the visual appearance of the 'shop window' or storefront. It is a component of the threshold that is aimed primarily at increasing attention and enhancing consumer perceptions of the store environment, with a view to generating visits. Importantly, the storefront is considered to be an antecedent of the competitive positioning of a store (for example, Pessemier, 1980; Kotler, 2006; Cornelius et al., 2009) which impacts on consumers' decisions to enter (Sen et al., 2002) and provides a cost effective means of generating a positive association between the exterior image and interior anticipated experience (Cornelius et al., 2009). Thus the threshold is not just the environs of immediate access and a means to control of flow of consumers.

From an architectural and design perspective, the positioning of the threshold plays an important role in communicating a general stylistic ethos that assists in differentiating one store from another, such as through the use of sound, light and colour as well as products that are uniquely associated with the brand name. Yet the physical position of the entrance, say, centrally or to one side of the shop frontage, may create an effect that influences how consumers navigate the store. For example, positioned to one side of the store, then consumers are likely to follow a pathway from that side rather than navigate across the entire store frontage to begin at another point. The threshold therefore has an important role to play in generating visitors and stimulating their experience. From a commercial perspective, the speed at which the browsing and shopping experience may begin are clearly an important design decision, thus thresholds tend to be short and perfunctory rather than expansive, as is often the case in museums.

The influence of sensory design cues

Ebster and Garaus (2011) highlight numerous store layouts where customer flow is controlled by the positioning of fixtures such as gondolas and store furniture (such as forced-path, grid, boutique and combined layouts, see Figure 10.1). These layouts influence the initial visual sight lines that draw attention through the store to fixed points that will ultimately attract customers beyond the threshold (Mesher, 2010).

Thus, the design of the threshold has a role in facilitating the view across the inner store environment that in turn indicates how consumers may begin their experience of the environment (see Figure 10.2). This

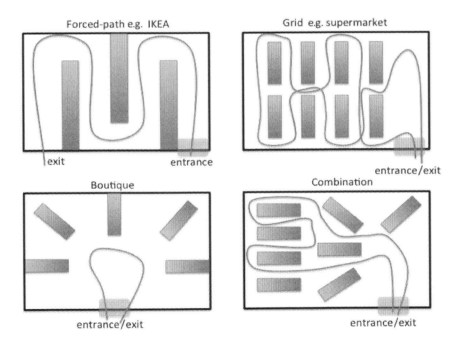

Figure 10.1 Typical store layouts

Figure 10.2 Aspects of the store environment

may be challenging to achieve in many museum environments, where the threshold is expansive and not necessarily related to the experience within, in turn 'breaking' the connection from the point of entry to the beginning of an interaction with the museum content. Indeed, much emphasis within a museum context is placed upon how the visitor is 'prepared' for the visit as they transit the threshold space.

Visual cues are however just one of a number of atmospheric considerations; others relate to auditory, tactile and olfactory stimuli, all of which begin in the immediate environs of the threshold, impacting cognitive and affective responses (Spence et al., 2014). Each of these cues is now discussed.

Visual stimuli

Visual stimuli include design-related aspects such as colour, brightness, size and shape (Kotler, 1974) that can positively influence a retail consumer's mood (Evans, 2002). Lighting in particular is used to attract attention in stores (Areni and Kim, 1994; Summers and Herbert, 2001), whilst different shades of lighting are considered to impact affective state by enhancing the ambient environment. For example, blue lighting may encourage increased browsing behaviour compared to red (Belizzi and Hite, 1992). Its positional use may also stimulate different types of behaviour; for example, brighter areas may be frequented more than darker areas in store environments (Ebster and Garaus, 2011). Visual stimuli also include the presence of other social actors in the space, with facial expressions that match the consumer's having been found to have a positive influence on behaviour (Puccinelli et al., 2013). These aspects are particularly challenging to operationalize as part of a brand-building strategy given the variability possible throughout the course of even a single day – consider, for example, the influence of natural lighting at different times of day and range of social activity that might fluctuate in any given store or museum threshold.

Sight lines are an important feature for facilitating the transitional moment between the external and internal store experience, acting as an atmospheric cue that influences the senses and enhances perception, and serving both functional and aesthetic needs. In the examples highlighted in Figure 10.3, at a simplistic level and assuming a small-scale environment, it is evident that the boutique-store style layout optimizes customer view of

Retail perspectives on the threshold 199

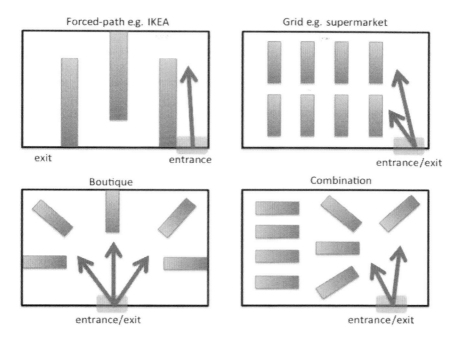

Figure 10.3 Sight lines across store layouts

the proposition from the threshold, whereas other layouts are most likely to obscure the customer view of aspects of the store.

Sight lines are an explicit component of store design that may enhance store merchandise security by providing increased visibility to products and consumers; aesthetically, sight lines support the organization's aims and objectives for consumption activities within the space that underpin the creation of store ambience (Cohen, 1998). Previous research (Harwood and Jones, 2014) has identified patterns of visual attention (using eye-tracking technology) that can be related to both vertical and horizontal sight lines. Visual behaviour at horizontal sight lines has been observed to invoke longer periods of time viewing before moving into the space. Visual behaviour is ultimately stimulated when the consumer fixates on feature-lit objects across the scene. In contrast, vertical sight lines tend to invoke directional flow. Thereby sight lines facilitate directional decision-making but this is also influenced by highly salient product presentation evident in the scene view.

Saliency (prominence) is highlighted as a dominant aspect that impacts on consumer attentional priorities. Previous studies have suggested that saliency using contrast and colour is associated with product and brand recall (Alba and Chattopadhyay, 1986; Lynch and Srull, 1982) and may also be a dominant visual cue in the environment used by customers to navigate stores. Saliency is therefore the degree to which something stands out in the visual scene (or contrasts), a consequence of its colour, finish, shape or highlighting. Colour blocking is also both an extrinsic and intrinsic motivational cue – salient within a scene but relevant to the consumer in some way. For example, there is evidence that colour preference is used in consumers' search patterns evoking empathy with the scene in some way (Klonk, 2005; Clynes, 1977). Colour has a long association with designed environments (Fortune, 1930), influencing customer behaviour by enhancing ambience (Nayar, 2008) and influencing mood states in stores (Martineau, 1958; Bellizzi et al., 1983). These aspects may be under-explored in museum environments, where often the emphasis is on functionality of the space, such as showing the exhibits to their best, rather than creating an ambient environment that is congruent with customer expectations of the brand. Nonetheless, these aspects highlight the importance of lighting as a key design component through which an engaging servicescape may be created. In turn, these visual stimuli collectively support traffic flow through the space.

It is important to realize, however, that irrespective of how well the view has been designed into the architectural fabric of the environment, it may well be 'blocked' by other customers or the inadvertent or even temporary positioning of service points and staff, which in effect act as barriers to entry. That said, in some environments the presence of social actors such as store staff around the threshold area may be particularly useful in dissuading inappropriate behaviour such as shoplifting. Conversely, staff in the museum threshold space might be seen in a less obstructive way, supporting the transition from outside to inside.

Social stimuli

Social considerations extend beyond the interactions between consumers and staff and include the whole environment. The author's previous research identified social consumption, where browsing and shopping in stores often takes place in a group of friends or family members, or is merely informed by the presence of other like-minded consumers in the environs. These social experiences are central to the ambience of the store and have been intentionally incorporated into the design of the space. Store staff are actively engaged in many areas across the store, are easily approachable and drawn into both browsing and purchasing behaviour, some of which is viewable from the threshold space. Within a museum environment, there may be mixed messages about the social dimensions of the space. The threshold may invoke certain kinds of interactive behaviours such as informal greeting, chatter and smalltalk, encouraged by the presence of staff and a 'welcome desk' but the interior beyond may attempt to dissuade that behaviour, for example by controlling numbers of people in areas, limiting opportunities for social exchanges and increasing formalities through the presentation of curated artefacts in stilted environments such as darkened rooms. The positioning of security staff, the uniforms they wear and presence of notices about key behaviours (such as no photography), may also now contrast with common social interactive behaviours such as taking selfies and snapshots for immediate upload to social media.

Crilly (2011) suggests there is a tension between informing and persuading through the design process that may imply 'persuasive intention', intimating that once in the store or museum the social interactions are intended to be part of the consumption experience. Thus social opportunities may be appealing to customers, giving them an indication of how to browse, relax and enjoy the physical and visual stimulation provided by the environment (Crilly, 2011). This is consistent with research into hedonic consumption (for example, Holbrook and Hirschman, 1982) but also highlights a brand's intentions in creating experiences through its designed layout and merchandise or artefact presentation.

Auditory stimuli

Auditory stimuli relate to the soundscape in an environment – these can be piped sound (such as music, or recorded birdsong) or general ambient noise (white noise) such as echo, social exchanges and sound that leaches into the space from neighbouring areas. Audio 'branding' (for example, Morrison and Beverland, 2003; Spence et al., 2014) is becoming a common technique used by stores to communicate or reinforce their distinctive 'look and feel'. Within retail, the soundscape often begins in the proximate area of the threshold, becoming clearer as consumers pass from the streetscape environment into the store. Research suggests that a background soundscape can be influential in generating a positive emotional response from consumers (Konecni, 2008), in turn enhancing experience of the environment (Grewal et al., 2003; Garlin and Owen, 2006). In museums, this may also be useful in impacting on perception of waiting times, for example, where flow and throughput may be impeded or decision-making slows down consumers, such as in the threshold area (Park and Young, 1986; Spence et al., 2014). Flow and throughput may also be influenced by the tempo of music, with research suggesting that increased beats per minute may increase walking and browsing speed and vice versa, impacting on the overall consumption experience (Milliman, 1982; Garlin and Owen, 2006). Volume of the soundscape has also been found to influence behaviour, with certain tones and volumes acting as a deterrent to entry into a retail environment (Forsyth and Cloonan, 2008).

It has been suggested that in order to enhance appropriate customer behaviour, soundscape needs to incorporate the 'right kind of sounds' relative to the environment. For example, North et al. (1997, 1999) found playing French music led to increased supermarket purchases of French wine.

Spence et al. (2014) hypothesize that auditory stimuli may be particularly useful where consumers have less understanding and familiarity with the specific product or environment because it provides an extrinsic cue they may relate to more directly. This is particularly interesting, given the findings from the installation of a soundscape for the Arts and Humanities Research Council project on Transforming Thresholds (Principal Investigator, Page) (see Mortensen and Deuchars, Chapter 11, this volume, and Page, Chapter 12, this volume). Installed in the threshold space (a set of stairs) at the Petrie Museum of Egyptian Archaeology, a soundscape was designed that incorporated music and sounds that might have originated from an Egyptian archeological dig a hundred years or so ago (including sounds of scraping and digging, and workers chanting). Whilst the aim was to evoke the sense of discovery and influence perceptions of the museum experience of Egyptian artefacts, instead some visitors related the soundscape to their experience of having navigated to the museum through an area of building works immediately outside the museum in the street. Although no workmen were present at the time of data collection in the museum, it is nonetheless anecdotally fascinating that visitors associated the noises with the other environmental factors that were more familiar from their immediate (and everyday) experience. This example points to the ways in which people attempt to match the soundscape, experience and environment in the threshold environment.

Tactile stimuli

Spence et al. (2014) and Kotler (1974) propose that tactile stimuli are sensory-discriminative, including aspects such as softness, smoothness and temperature that can also have positive affective associations (Gallace and Spence, 2014). It is for this reason that some retailers choose to have products accessible for consumers to feel as they pass by. On the other hand, there can be negative associations with contamination by others, implying that whilst consumers may like to touch, they do not like to purchase products that have been touched (Ellison and White, 2000). Opportunities to touch products at the threshold are, however, often limited; instead the main tactile stimulus at this point in the servicescape is likely to be temperature. Hadi et al. (2013) have reported that, for example, colder store environments may be more influential in the purchase of hedonic consumption items and warmer store environments more influential in the purchase of utilitarian items. Importantly, tactile stimuli need to be congruent with expectations of comfort and physical interaction, so may be determined by their apparent fit with the brand. For example, in a retail context, international cosmetics store Body Shop's use of a 'beauty salon' area that is clearly visible on entry to the boutique-style store encourages customers to test and experience products as they browse, whether or not they then seek a staff-facilitated test experience at the 'salon'. Once customers have tested a product in such an environment, they are more likely to purchase it, which is of course the store's intention.

A challenge of this type of experience in the museum context is, however, the visitor perception of appropriateness of touching precious artefacts, which is often precluded. Even when these may be replicas specifically designed to facilitate direct interaction, consumers may have difficulty in overcoming their belief that the item is precious and for viewing only. This may be despite the fact that touching may be considered to be an optimum way for visitors to gain insight into the object (see Weisenberger, 2015). Conversely the use of everyday objects as artefacts that, through their incorporation into an 'unfamiliar' space or environment, become 'precious' may be confusing. Recent examples of this are the Lego sculpture of a Zootopia character positioned in a contemporary gallery that was destroyed by a child who mistook it for a signal to play and a crossword exhibit in an art gallery completed as it hung on the wall by an elderly visitor (see, respectively, Tan, 2016 and Huggler, 2016). Thus the context and messaging around the display of items for tactile interaction needs to be both clearly communicated and considered appropriate from the consumer's perspective in order for this strategy to be successful at engaging customers in a positive experience.

Olfactory stimuli

Fragrance (scent) is another stimulus that is increasingly used by retailers to support differential branding and influence positive consumer associations (Mandler, 1975; Li et al., 2007; Yeshurun and Sobel, 2010). As Spence et al. (2014) state, however, beyond intensity and pleasantness, it is difficult to manipulate this particular sensory cue across an environment (Pacelle, 1992). That said, research suggests that environments scented with, say, floral, fruity or spicy scent, can influence browsing (Spangenberg et al., 2006), creating an enhanced experience (Gulas and Bloch, 1995) and can even draw people into an environment (Knasko, 1995). Other research has associated types of scent with use of colour schemes to stimulate an ambient mood state. For example, Fetterman and O'Donnell (2006) highlight a combination of vanilla scent and mandarin orange used to create a signature theme in Sony Style stores. Despite the challenges with designing and operationalizing a consistent scent, using and managing olfactory stimuli, research suggests that of all the sensory cues smell may resonate the most strongly and linger the longest in memory (Goldman and Seamon, 1992). This in turn may influence recall of memories (Krishna et al., 2010) or indeed influence the ways in which customers experience an environment. Thus, as with other stimuli discussion, it is important for there to be congruence between the fragrance, customer experience and expectations and the environment. When positioned at the threshold, this is subtly useful in attracting and retaining consumer attention that, within a retail environment, may be relatively straightforward to achieve.

Within a museum context, one of the key challenges may be developing an appropriate scent that 'brands' the link between the curated artefacts, the visitors and the environment. It may be, for example, that certain visitors are attracted to the scent of oil and machinery in a transport museum or cordite in a military museum, but it is difficult to imagine the scent of dust and sweat being attractive despite their reminiscence of Egyptian archaeological practice that might be considered congruent with the collections at the UK-based Petrie Museum of Egyptian Archaeology. That said, the use of scents by museums such as the UK's Yorvik Viking Museum's scent of horse urine in a streetscape to provide an 'authentic experience' of life during the Viking ages, has been found to evoke the sense of immersion ('being there'). Furthermore, there are now aroma development firms that work with stores and museums alike. One such firm has recently recreated the scent of Tyrannosaurus Rex – a long-extinct animal – using scents that invoke the smell of a mix of open wounds on its imagined skin and rotting prey animal flesh caught between its teeth, although such was its potency that the museum subsequently opted for a lighter, 'swamp-like' smell instead (see Hudson, 2004). This suggests that whilst there is scope for creative use of scent to build links between the artefacts and the customer experience, this can be overpowering to the extent that it may potentially negatively influence the customer's behaviour, leading to perhaps physical revulsion and nausea. The use of scent may therefore potentially also interrupt immersion and engagement with an experience environment.

Transferable practice

As highlighted in this chapter, retail practices, particularly through the process of design of spaces considering sensory stimuli, offer potential for rethinking the threshold space in museums. By breaking down what Gurian (2005) refers to as 'threshold fear' into its constituent cognitive and affective components, and by drawing on the research literature in retail studies about the potential for cognitive and affective engagement to be affected by visual, social, auditory, tactile and olfactory cues, it may be possible to create an inviting space that overcomes at least the perceptions related to physical barriers that inhibit visitors' transition through the museum threshold. These include the architectural design features as well as 'entrance sequences' related to sight lines (layout and wayfinding), acceptable social behaviours, the actions of staff, and the transference of meaning using multisensory cues such as sight, sound and smell. In turn, these may communicate a sense of comfort that extend beyond spatial configuration and functionality to enable visitors to focus on more programmatic aspects, say related to buying tickets, acquiring relevant information about the experience and transiting into the inner environment.

In retail contexts, interior designers seek to create an immersive 'theatre' (see for example Davis, 1991) such that architecture becomes advertising

(Cairns, 2010). The resultant store atmosphere influences the emotional state of the consumer, and this influences arousal levels that, if positive, may increase time spent in the store and likelihood of purchase (Mehrabian and Russell, 1974; Donovan and Rossiter, 1982; Bitner, 1992; Rook, 1987; Bagozzi and Dholakia, 1999). This is analogous to what Morris (2012) alludes to as imagination and storytelling through the curation of the museum space, although she does not go so far as to describe the threshold as prologue. This notion is, however, consistent with the desire to immerse consumers in the environment and experience. The aim is to achieve a sense of presence and immersion (or 'flow'), concepts developed by Csikszentmihalyi (1990) that are now commonly used to describe deep emotional involvement in a setting such that the customer/visitor becomes lost in the sensation of the experience. In retail store environments, this is achieved through the range of stimuli that create atmosphere and ambience, and these begin at the threshold as highlighted. Previous research by the author suggests that active consumption of the store environment is achieved through the dynamic interplay between the various sensory stimuli that generate a 'drama' of the store experience, influencing consumers to socialize and inducing flow (Harwood and Jones, 2014). In generating this, the sense of space stimulates consumer senses using the range of cues – visual, social, auditory, tactile and olfactory. Aesthetic surroundings influence perceptions and attitudes, product presentation influences customer reactions, social surroundings influence consumption patterns (such as conformity), and complexity, that is, number of components within the environment, influences arousal leading to preference (Markin et al., 1976; Belk, 1974; Nasar, 1987; Uhrich and Benkenstein, 2010). Thus, using imagination as a tool to enhance experience necessitates a multidimensional approach beyond a narrative framework to conceptualize the progression through space. As Morris states, 'visitors move through museums ready to use their empathy, creativity and understanding in order to reach a state of emotional and imaginative openness. It's a journey that requires museums [to offer back] to the visitors atmosphere and opportunities to feel' (2012, p. 10). This can really only be achieved by reflecting the multisensory desires and needs of visitors.

Summary

This chapter has examined a range of factors that are commonly used in retail store design and the evaluation of customer behaviour. The totality of a customer experience related to a store's servicescape, including both online and the physical visit, is the 'experience environment'. With an emphasis on physical experience within the vicinity of the store, the chapter has identified that the threshold space is a transitional area between outside and inside the store – both of which are important components of the servicescape. It is the role of the threshold to facilitate the transition between the two main areas on which, typically, much design emphasis is placed (for example, the website, the car parking and the product presentation) with a view to optimizing the customer's visit by increasing browsing time. In turn, the greater the browsing time the more likely it is that customers will purchase some product within the store. Yet it is most likely that the sensory cues make the experience memorable, leading to repeat visits in future.

Thus, the initial presentation of merchandise is achieved by highlighting products through window displays that the customer sees as they approach the threshold. As they cross a store threshold, consumers use visual cues such as layout and sight lines to make sense of the space – stores emphasize these natural behaviours through their design considerations, aiming to draw customers into the space quickly and efficiently. This is increasingly being supplemented with multisensory cues such as sounds, scents and tactile stimuli that are intended to enhance positive perception of the environment. This works best when there is congruence between the stimuli, customer expectations of the experience and the design of the physical environment, leading to customer/visitor comfort. Desirably, a store seeks to achieve deep levels of immersion ('flow') in a visit experience, such that they may lose track of time and remain in the environment browsing at least long enough to purchase an item. A museum needs to do likewise to achieve repeat visits, and in so doing justify its raison d'être. A mismatch, from the customer's or visitor's perspective, is likely to be confusing and distracting, leading to an interruption in through-flow beyond the threshold.

The retail context provides potentially useful considerations for developing the threshold experience in a museum context. Within museum literature, the primary perspective of a visitor experience is from the museum's perception of their role of educating or entertaining visitors. Thus, by taking a more retail-orientated approach to providing cues that stimulate and/or regulate comfort levels in visitors through consideration of design-related sensory cues, such as used in retail, it may well be possible to enhance the visitors' perceptions of the museum servicescape beyond the threshold to the curated experience.

References

Alba, J. and Chattopadhyay, A. (1986) 'Salience effects in brand recall', *Journal of Marketing Research*, 23 (Nov.), pp. 363–369.
Areni, C. S. and Kim, D. (1994) 'The influence of in-store lighting on consumers' examination of merchandise in a wine store', *International Journal of Research in Marketing*, 11, pp. 117–125.
Bagozzi, R. P. and Dholakia, U. (1999) 'Goal setting and goal striving in consumer behaviour', *Journal of Marketing*, 63, pp. 19–32.
Barker, R. G. and Wright, H. F. (1955) *Midwest and Its Children*. New York: Harper and Row.
Belk, R. (1974) 'An exploratory assessment of situational effects in buyer behaviour', *Journal of Marketing Research*, 11 (May), p. 160.

Bellizzi, J. A. and Hite, R. E. (1992) 'Environmental color, consumer feelings, and purchase likelihood', *Psychology and Marketing*, 9, pp. 347–363.

Bellizzi, J. A., Crowley, A. E. and Hasty, R .W. (1983) 'The effects of color in store design', *Journal of Retailing*, 59(1), pp. 21–45.

Bitner, M. J. (1990) 'Evaluating service encounters: the effects of physical surroundings and employee response', *Journal of Marketing*, 54, pp. 69–82.

Bitner, M. J. (1992) 'Servicescapes: the impact of physical surroundings on customers and employees', *Journal of Marketing*, 56, pp. 57–71.

Buckley, L. (2014) 'A hedonistic night at the museum', *Science Museum* (blog post). Available at https://blog.sciencemuseum.org.uk/a-hedonistic-night-at-the-museum/. Accessed 18 October 2016.

Cairns, G. (2010) *Deciphering Advertising, Art and Architecture: Communicating with the Sophisticated Consumer*. London: Libri Publishing.

Clynes, M. (1977) *Sentics: the Touch of Emotions*. Garden City, NY: Anchor Press.

Cohen, E. (1998) 'Trussardi alla Scala', *Interior Design*, New York, 69(5), pp. 178–185.

Cornelius, B., Natter, M. and Faure, C. (2009) 'How storefront displays influence retail store image', *Journal of Retailing and Consumer Services*, 17(2), pp. 143–151.

Crilly, N. (2011) 'Do users know what designers are up to? Product experience and the inference of persuasive intentions', *International Journal of Design*, 5(3), pp. 1–15.

Csikszentmihalyi, M. (1990) *Flow: the Psychology of Optimal Experience*. New York: Harper and Row.

Csikszentmihalyi, M. and Rochberg-Halton, E. (1981) *The Meaning of Things*. Cambridge: Cambridge University Press.

Davis, T. C. (1991) 'Theatrical antecedents and the mall that ate downtown', *Journal of Popular Culture*, 24(4), pp. 1–15.

Donovan, R. and Rossiter, J. (1982) 'Store atmosphere: an environmental psychology approach', *Journal of Retailing*, 58, pp. 34–57.

Ebster, C. and Garaus, M. (2011) *Store Design and Visual Merchandising: Creating Store Space that Encourages Buying*. New York: Business Expert Press.

Ellison, S. and White, E. (2000) '"Sensory" marketers say the way to reach shoppers is the nose', *Wall Street Journal*, 24 November.

Evans, D. (2002) *Emotion: the Science of Sentiment*. Oxford: Oxford University Press.

Falk, J. H. and Dierking, L. D. (1998) 'Free-choice learning: an alternative term to informal learning?' *Informal Learning Environments Research*, 2(2).

Fetterman, J. and O'Donnell, J. (2006) 'Just browsing the mall? That's what you think', *USA Today*, 1 September. Available at http://usatoday30.usatoday.com/money/industries/retail/2006-09-01-retail-coverusat_x.htm. Accessed: 15 October 2016.

Forsyth, A. J. M. and Cloonan, M. (2008) 'Alco-pop? The use of popular music in Glasgow pubs', *Popular Music and Society*, 31, pp. 57–78.

Fortune (1930) Color in Industry, February, 85–94.

Gallace, A. and Spence, C. (2014) *In Touch with the Future: The Sense of Touch from Cognitive Neuroscience to Virtual Reality*. Oxford: Oxford University Press.

Garlin, F. V. and Owen, K. (2006) 'Setting the tone with the tune: a meta-analytic review of the effects of background music in retail settings', *Journal of Business Research*, 59, pp. 755–764.

Goldman, W. P. and Seamon, J.G. (1992) 'Very long-term memory for odors: retention of odor-name associations', *American Journal of Psychology*, 105, pp. 549–563.

Grewal, D., Baker, J., Levy, M. and Voss, G. B. (2003) 'The effects of wait expectations and store atmosphere evaluations on patronage intentions in service-intensive retail stores', *Journal of Retailing*, 79, pp. 259–268.

Gulas, C. S. and Bloch, P. H. (1995) 'Right under our noses: ambient scent and consumer responses', *Journal of Business and Psychology*, 10, pp. 87–98.

Hadi, R., Block, L. and King, D. (2013) 'The impact of temperature on consumer decision-making: a mental thermoregulation framework'. *Paper presented at Said Business School Seminar*, Oxford University, 10 October.

Harwood, T. and Jones, M. (2014) 'Mobile eye-tracking in retail research', in Horsley, M. (ed.) *Current Trends in Eye Tracking Research*. London: Springer, pp. 183–200.

Hayward, D. G. and Brydon-Miller, M. (1984) 'Spatial and conceptual aspects of orientation: visitor experiences at an outdoor history museum', *Journal of Environmental Systems*, 13, pp. 317–332.

Gurian, E. H. (2005) 'Threshold fear', in MacLeod, S. (ed.) *Reshaping Museum Space: Architecture, Design, Exhibitions*. London: Routledge, pp. 203–214.

Holbrook, M. B. and Hirschman, E. C. (1982) 'The experiential aspects of consumption: consumer fantasies, feelings and fun', *Journal of Consumer Research*, 9, pp. 132–140.

Hudson, A. (2004) Firm kicks up a big stink for Tyrannosaurus rex, *Fairfax Digital (Sydney Morning Herald)*. Available at http://www.smh.com.au/articles/2004/07/09/1089000357350.html. Accessed: 18 October 2016.

Huggler, J. (2016) 91-year-old woman fills in crossword at museum – only to discover it was a £60,000 artwork, *The Telegraph*. Available at http://www.telegraph.co.uk/news/2016/07/14/91-year-old-woman-fills-in-crossword-at-museum---only-to-discove/. Accessed: 18 October 2016.

Kent, A. and Kirby, A.E. (2009) 'The design of the store environment and its implications for retail image', *The International Review of Retail, Distribution and Consumer Research*, 19(4), pp. 457–468.

Klonk, C. (2005) 'Patterns of attention: from shop windows to gallery rooms in early twentieth-century Berlin', *Art History* 28(4,) pp. 468–496.

Knasko, S. C. (1995) 'Pleasant odors and congruency: effects on approach behaviour', *Chemical Senses*, 20, pp. 479–487.

Konecni, V. J. (2008) 'Does music induce emotion? A theoretical and methodological analysis', *Psychology of Aesthetics, Creativity, and the Arts*, 2, pp. 115–129.

Kotler, P. (1974) 'Atmospherics as a marketing tool', *Journal of Retailing*, 49(4), pp. 48–64.

Kotler, P. (2006) *Marketing Management: Analysing, Planning, Implementation and Control*. Englewood Cliffs, NJ: Prentice-Hall.

Krishna, A., Lwin, M. O. and Morrin, M. (2010) 'Product scent and memory', *Journal of Consumer Research*, 37, pp. 57–67.

Lehman, K. and Leighton, D. (2010) 'The development of a hedonistic experience brand: Australia's MONA', *Proceedings of the Academy of Marketing Annual Conference*, Coventry University, 6–10 July.

Li, W., Moallem, I., Paller, K. A. and Gottfried, J. A. (2007) 'Subliminal smells can guide social preferences', *Psychological Science*, 18, pp. 1044–1049.

Lynch, J. and Srull, T. (1982) 'Memory and attentional factors in consumer choice: concepts and research methods', *Journal of Consumer Research*, 9 (June), pp. 18–37.

Mandler, G. (1975) 'Consciousness: respectable, useful and probably necessary', in Solso, R. (ed.) *Information Processing and Cognition: The Loyola Symposium*. Hillsdale, NJ: Erlbaum, pp. 229–254.

Markin, R., Lillis, C. and Narayana, C. (1976) 'Social-psychological significance of store space', *Journal of Retailing*, 52, pp. 43–54.

Martineau, P. (1958) 'The personality of the retail store', *Harvard Business Review* 36(1), pp. 47–55.

Mattila, A. S. and Wirtz, J. (2001) 'Congruency of scent and music as a driver of in-store evaluations and behaviour', *Journal of Retailing*, 77, pp. 273–289.

McIntyre, C. (2012) *Tourism and Retail: The Psychogeography of Liminal Consumption*. New York: Routledge.

Mehrabian A. and Russell, J. A. (1974) *An Approach to Environmental Psychology*. Cambridge, MA: MIT Press.

Mesher, L. (2010) *Retail Design*. Lausanne: AVA Publishing SA.

Milliman, R. E. (1982) 'Using background music to affect the behaviour of supermarket shoppers', *Journal of Marketing*, 46, pp. 86–91.

Morris, R. (2012) 'Imaginery museums', in MacLeod, S., Hourston Hanks, L. and Hale, J. (eds.) *Museum Making*. London: Routledge, pp. 5–11.

Morrison, M. and Beverland, M. (2003) 'In search of the right in-store music', *Business Horizons*, 46, pp. 77–82.

Nasar, J. L. (1987) 'Effect of sign complexity and coherence on the perceived quality of retail scenes', *Journal of the American Planning Association*, 53(4), pp. 499–509.

Nayar, J. (2008) 'Light and leisure', *Contract (San Francisco, CA 2000)*, 50(11), pp. 52–56.

North, A. C., Hargreaves, D. J. and McKendrick, J. (1997) 'Instore music affects product choice', *Nature*, 390, p. 132.

North, A. C., Hargreaves, D. J. and McKendrick, J. (1999) 'The influence of in-store music on wine selections', *Journal of Applied Psychology*, 84, pp. 271–276.

Pacelle, M. (1992) 'Many people refuse to check in if a hotel has odors in the lobby', 28 July, *Wall Street Journal*, B1.

Park, C. W. and Young, S. M. (1986) 'Consumer response to television commercials: the impact of involvement and background music on brand attitude formation', *Journal of Marketing Research*, 23, pp. 11–24.

Pessemier, E. A. (1980) 'Store image and positioning', *Journal of Retailing*, 56, pp. 94–106.

Puccinelli, N. M., Chandrashekaran, R., Grewal, D. and Suri, R. (2013) 'Are men seduced by red? The effect of red versus black prices on price perceptions', *Journal of Retailing*, 89, pp. 115–125.

Rook, D. W. (1987) 'The buying impulse', *The Journal of Consumer Research*, 2(14), pp. 189–199.

Sen, S., Block, L. G. and Chandran, S. (2002) 'Window displays and consumer shopping decisions', *Journal of Retailing and Consumer Services*, 9, pp. 277–290.

Spangenberg, E. R., Sprott, D. E., Grohmann, B. and Tracy, D. L. (2006) 'Gender-congruent ambient scent influences on approach and avoidance behaviours in a retail store', *Journal of Business Research*, 59, pp. 1281–1287.

Spence, C., Puccinelli, N. M., Grewal, D. and Roggeveen, A. L. (2014) 'Store atmospherics: a multisensory perspective', *Psychology and Marketing*, 31(7), pp. 472–488.

Summers, T. A. and Hebert, P. R. (2001) 'Shedding some light on store atmospherics: influence of illumination on consumer behaviour', *Journal of Business Research*, 54, pp. 145–150.

Tan, A. (2016) Kid destroys $15,000 LEGO sculpture an hour after new exhibit opens, *Mashable UK*. Available at http://mashable.com/2016/06/01/lego-sculpture-destroyed-china/#Nmiu2YLDr8qF. Accessed: 18 October 2016.

Turley, L. W. and Milliman, R. E. (2000) 'Atmospheric effects on shopping behaviour: a review of the experimental evidence', *Journal of Business Research*, 49, pp. 193–211.

Uhrich, S. and Benkenstein, M. (2010) 'Sport stadium atmosphere: formative and reflective indicators for operationalizing the construct', *Journal of Sport Management*, 24, pp. 211–237.

Weisenberger, C. (2015) 'Please touch the objects: tactile models and alternative approaches to curation', *O Say Can You See?* (Blog post, Smithsonian). Available at http://americanhistory.si.edu/blog/please-touch-objects-tactile-models-and-alternative-approaches-curation. Accessed: 18 October 2016.

Yeshurun, Y. and Sobel, N. (2010) 'An odor is not worth a thousand words: from multidimensional odors to uni-dimensional odor objects', *Annual Review of Psychology*, 61, pp. 219–241.

11 Setting the tone for the visit
Soundscape design

Christian Hviid Mortensen and Angus Deuchars

Museums have traditionally been viewed as places of silence (Bubaris, 2014). Already in the *Museographica* from 1727, considered the very first museological work, Caspar Neikelius writes in regard to the threshold between the museum and the surrounding society: 'at the entrance to the museum should sit terrible lions or tigers to symbolize the silence necessary for study' (Pearce, 1992, p. 99). The culture of silence in museums is not the absence of sounds, however. The presence of human activity is always accompanied by sounds as the frequently encountered sounds of echoing footsteps and creaking floorboards in museums testify. Rather it is a normative regulation of sound that differs between museums as sound is often more acceptable in institutions that do not aspire to an aura of high culture, as observed by Nathalie Angier: 'the differential acoustics tell the story. Zoos and museums of science and natural history are loud and bouncy and notably enriched by the upper registers of the audio scale. Theaters and art museums murmur in a courteous baritone' (Conn, 2010, p. 138).

Recently museums have begun to embrace the audio dimension, actively deploying sounds as part of the museum experience – most notably in the use of audio guides. Thus, sound is no longer considered a problem for museums by default, but increasingly seen as an opportunity (Bubaris, 2014; Angliss, 2005). In his studies of sound in film Michel Chion has introduced the notion of added value: 'Added value works reciprocally. Sound shows us the image differently than what the image shows alone, and the image likewise makes us hear sound differently than if the sound were ringing out in the dark' (1994, p. 21). A similar reciprocal relationship exists between sound and the museum environment. Sound influences our experience of the museum environment and in turn the museum environment influences the way we listen. This chapter addresses the issue of deliberately using soundscapes in a threshold context to prime the visitors for the impending museum experience thus setting the tone for the museum visit. We build on the experiences from a design intervention at the Petrie Museum of Egyptian Archaeology in London conducted in 2013.

A soundscape can consist of a collection of sounds that work in unison or a singular sound. Any acoustic environment is considered a soundscape and can be isolated as a field of study and description, but it is also a field open for manipulation and interventions via design (Schafer, 1994). The most obvious example of manipulating the acoustic environment is the personal soundscape that many of us bring with us everywhere with earphones connected to our portable music player devices whereby the acoustic environment is sounded out in favour of our chosen musical environment (Bull, 2014). Truax (2001, p. 12) considers listening to be the interface between the individual and the environment through the mediating relation of sound and has developed an abstract communicational model, later modified by Wrightson (2000), illustrating such an acoustic ecology (see Figure 11.1). As a field of study the focus of acoustic ecology is primarily on environmental soundscapes of either an urban or natural nature, but the model also applies to built interior environments such as museums.

All the relationships in the model are bidirectional, in contrast to a transmission model of communication. The individual listens and ascribes meaning to the sounds heard, maybe emits sounds of their own. These meanings influence the perception of the environment (colouration), and the environment in turn influences both what is heard (acoustic architecture) and the meaning (context). The individual can manipulate the environment for example by opening a window thereby directly affecting what is heard. Listed below each entity are the main variables: for example the thoughts, feelings and memory of the individual visitor.

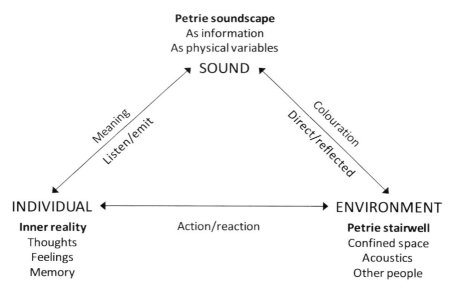

Figure 11.1 The mediating relationship between individual and environment through sound at the Petrie Museum

Source: Adapted from Truax (2001) and Wrightson (2000)

Sound is often hailed for its effectiveness as an emotional trigger (Barrett et al., 2010; Böhme, 2000; Keightley and Pickering, 2006a, p. 155; 2006b, p. 935; 2012, p. 116; Truax, 2001, p. 29; Wildschut, Sedikides, and Arndt, 2006; Wrightson, 2000). A summer's day beach soundscape would probably elicit positive emotions in most people, while a funeral soundscape would give rise to more negative emotions such as sadness and fear. The meanings ascribed to sounds are often bifurcated in good (I like) vs bad (I don't like) (Truax, 2001). The human hearing mechanism is largely responsible for whether we have a positive or negative reaction to a given sound. We are most receptive to sounds at the same pitch as human speech and most sensitive around the frequencies where babies cry. Outside this range our hearing decreases rapidly. One of the reasons people find loud high-pitched sounds uncomfortable is because they coincide with the most sensitive range of human hearing. Therefore, each individual part of the model is equally important, as personal aspects such as psychological makeup and historic experiences are co-constitutive of the cognitive response to a soundscape.

However, sound is only one aspect and form of sensual stimuli we receive when moving through multidimensional space and thus all museum visits are by their nature multisensual; however, the multimodal experiences of such visits can be both unintended or the product of deliberate design process (Levent and Pascual-Leone, 2014). Gernot Böhme suggests that atmospheres are the in-between between the qualities of the environment and our human sensibilities (Böhme, 2000, p. 14). Atmospheres are constituted by different sensory variables (visual, aural, olfactory, tactile) and establish a certain mood for the environment. According to Böhme, atmospheres are best experienced in contrast or 'via the change which occurs when one enters them from the inside of another atmosphere' (Böhme, 2000, p. 15). Thus, the threshold is where atmospheres are most prominent and therefore is also a particularly promising site for a soundscape design intervention. Within the retail sector atmospherics is the study of how to produce specific emotional effects in customers to stimulate their inclination for purchase (Kotler, 1974; see also Harwood, Chapter 10 of this volume). Atmospherics is the applied version of Böhme's notion of atmosphere, and applying it to the *experiencescape* (O'Dell, 2005) of the museum environment requires a broadening of the intended scope of atmospherics from stimulating customer purchases into facilitating more complex emotional responses such as inspiration and learning.

From a design standpoint the different variables constituting atmospheres can be orchestrated as a series of mood cues eliciting the moods intended. Soundscape design in public places takes many forms, from the soothing sounds of a waterfall to attention-grabbing sound art. Soundscapes and sound art are both the result of a creative process, but they differ in purpose as the soundscape tends to be a facet of the environment, whereas sound art is intended as an experience in itself. Orchestrating atmospheric mood cues is not a simple case of 'the whole is greater than the sum of its parts', however. Mood cues can be both complimentary, thus reinforcing each other, or counteracting, and it can be difficult to manipulate atmospheric variables in isolation (Forrest, 2013). Multisensory perception is complex and the added value of another sense modus alters our perception in ways that are not necessarily cumulative (Shams and Kim, 2010; Spence, 2010). The unidirectional stimulus–response causality often implied in atmospherics is only achievable under controlled environmental conditions and such conditions are not achievable in the complex experiencescape of a museum (Rounds, 2012). This is especially the case in the threshold area as museum lobbies can be bewildering environments that have to serve many diverse functions at once (Mortensen, Rudloff and Vestergaard, 2014).

While we might be able to inter-subjectively agree on the mood of the present environment, there can be significant difference between the intended and the perceived atmosphere. Therefore, it is essential to include the user perspective, as a person-in-environment, in the analysis of a soundscape intervention.

The role of the sound designer

Sound designers frequently find themselves working alongside other design disciplines and while it is important to carve out a meaningful contribution, it is equally important to strike a balance with the other design disciplines. That is to say, where balance between the disciplines is required they need to work together and be complimentary to achieve a holistic outcome.

The contribution of a soundscape for the Petrie Museum, as described in the following case study, was developed through multidisciplinary design workshops, where all of the design stakeholders provided input across the proposal for a stairwell intervention. This collaborative approach brought the design team together and allowed individual contributions to be explored, overall themes to be examined and contributor roles to be determined.

The primary contribution of the soundscape design for the Petrie Museum was to complement the visual intervention and to establish an aural theme as a link to the exhibits within the museum. A secondary contribution was to provide a temporal dimension providing a sense of transition and movement between the thresholds, i.e. upon entry and exit.

With a clear brief that the soundscape was acting in a contributing capacity to the visuals, this clarity provided clear direction transitioning into the design phase.

Several proposals were developed for the soundscape component of the intervention to allow varying characteristics, such as speech playing a primary compared to a tertiary role, to be evaluated by the team. This allowed the final soundscape to be shaped by the designers and Petrie Museum.

Speech in the final soundscape played a tertiary role because it would be muddled due to the acoustics of the stairwell. The primary elements of

Setting the tone for the visit 215

the soundscape were sounds of an archaeological dig and music with a low cadence to suit the acoustics and to prevent visitors feeling rushed.

Case study: transforming the threshold at the Petrie Museum

The Petrie Museum is a university museum celebrating the work and career of renowned Egyptologist and archaeologist William Flinders Petrie (1853–1942). The museum is part of University College London (UCL) and situated on their Bloomsbury campus. The museum has an academic focus as a teaching resource for the Department of Egyptian Archaeology and Philology, but serves a mixture of researchers and the general public.

The museum premises are located along a narrow cobbled Georgian street in an old predominantly brick building. The entrance to the building is at street level and the museum concessions desk is located at the other end of a stairwell that comprises three flights of stairs. The space between doors at either end of the stairwell forms the foyer or threshold area of the Petrie Museum and would be the setting for the design intervention.

On the street the Petrie Museum is advertised with a UCL sign mounted above eye level perpendicular to the wall with the museum name. Below the sign and to the left of the black double door are a glass framed notice board with the museum opening times and other practical information. Mounted inside a glass pane on the door is a red sign stating 'The museum is open. Please push the door.'

The walls of the stairwell are painted white with several visible pipes and electrical fittings. On the landings for each of the two flights of stairs the visitor encounters a quote painted on the wall in a white font on a red background. Just before arriving at the door to the museum the visitor encounters a large 'Petrie' logo in black on the wall and a smaller sign below with 'Museum of Egyptian Archaeology'.

Despite the quotes and signage in the stairwell, museum staff felt that it lacked a sense of arrival and did not portray a clear image of the museum (see Page, Chapter 12 in this volume for a fuller discussion of this). Thus it provides a poor threshold to the museum as visitors do not connect with the museum before they arrive at the concessions desk on the second floor. The entrance is similar to the other university buildings within the courtyard and it is easy to be unsure if you have entered the correct building.

Methodology

The case study presented here involves a design intervention with a soundscape at the Petrie Museum and as such the project can be considered as a form of action research (AR). The soundscape was a response to the challenges posed by the threshold area at the Petrie Museum as part of the overall Transforming Thresholds project (see also Chapter 12 of this volume). Action research consists of a five-phased cycle: diagnosing, action planning, action taking, evaluating and specifying learning (Susman and Evered 1978, p. 588). The learning outcome from the AR cycle can form the basis for another cycle, but we went through the cycle only once in this case. The following is an outline of the AR phases as they applied to our case study:

> **Diagnosing:** The diagnostic phase involved a visual inspection of the threshold area at the Petrie Museum in order to assess the spatial confines in regard to installation and understand the visitor journey from the street outside to within the museum as well as the context of the location.
>
> **Action planning:** Based on the preliminary diagnosis a design brief was formulated stating the objectives of the intervention. Also, in the action planning phase a series of sound tests were conducted in a similar environment to ascertain what kinds of sound would be suitable for this location. These tests resulted in the development of a prototype soundscape.
>
> **Action taking:** The prototype was refined into the final soundscape based on insights from the testing. The soundscape was then installed in the threshold to the Petrie Museum.
>
> **Evaluating:** A visitor study was conducted on site in order to assess the impact of the design intervention. The study consisted of a survey administered before and after the intervention.
>
> **Specifying learning:** The results of the visitor study were analysed and the primary findings are presented in this chapter.

One of the authors, Angus, was the sound designer responsible for producing and installing the soundscape and he participated throughout the project. While the other author, Christian, only joined the project in the final phase for analysing results and situating the case study within a wider scholarly discourse on sound and museums. The visitor study was conducted by a team of researchers from the University of Leicester, the University of Westminster and De Montfort University (Transforming Thresholds Research Network, 2012).

The visitor study consisted of two surveys conducted before and after the design intervention. The pre-intervention survey was used to establish a baseline from which to ascertain the impact of the design intervention. The questionnaire consisted of eight closed questions, some of them answered via a five-point Likert-type scale ranging from 'very well' (1) to 'not at all' (5), and one open-ended question asking the visitor to describe the threshold area in one sentence. The questionnaire for the post-intervention survey added a closed question if the visitor noticed the sounds at all and five open-ended questions asking the visitor to elaborate on different aspects of the design intervention. The pre-intervention survey had 41 participants, while the post-intervention survey had 46. The composition of the two groups of respondents is similar (see Table 11.1) so the results of the two surveys are comparable both in regard to sample size and composition. A majority of visitors were first-timers and between 30 and 59 years old. Both sexes were roughly equally represented.

In the action planning phase, it was decided that the design intervention at the Petrie Museum would have both a visual and an aural component. The intervention should uphold the academic rigour of the museum and not be too avant-garde or experimental. The visual component consisted of adding more images to the stairwell showing artefacts from the collection and of Petrie himself (see Page, Chapter 12 of this volume). The aural component consisted of installing a soundscape in the stairwell. This chapter primarily concerns itself with the aural component of the design intervention.

The stairwell at the Petrie Museum of Egyptian Archaeology has a challenging acoustic. Sounds within the space resonate for a long time and it only takes the presence of a few visitors for the space to become saturated

Table 11.1 Sample size and composition of participants in the pre- and post-intervention survey

	Pre-intervention	Post-intervention Total	Post-intervention Sound
Participants			
Total	41 (100%)	46* (100%)	25 (100%)
Male	15 (37%)	23 (50%)	12 (48%)
Female	26 (63%)	22 (49%)	12 (48%)
Age			
18–29	12 (29%)	12 (26%)	8 (32%)
30–59	19 (46%)	24 (52%)	13 (52%)
60+	10 (24%)	9 (20%)	3 (12%)
Visit			
First time	33 (80%)	38 (83%)	22 (88%)
Repeat visit	8 (20%)	8 (17%)	3 (12%)
Knowledge			
Very knowledgeable	9 (22%)	1 (2%)	0 (0%)
Knowledgeable	4 (10%)	14 (30%)	10 (40%)
Average	9 (22%)	14 (30%)	6 (24%)
Not knowledgeable	10 (24%)	14 (30%)	7 (28%)
Not at all knowledgeable	9 (22%)	3 (7%)	2 (8%)
Sound			
Noticed	N/A	25 (54%)	25 (100%)

* One participant did not disclose their gender and age.

with sound and become noisy. The stairwell also imposes constraints on the installation possibilities as the loudspeakers and cabling infrastructure would need to be installed at a high level so they do not pose safety (trip) hazards.

The soundscape designer performed an aural assessment of the threshold area to determine what types of sound would complement the architectural acoustics. The diagnostic also involved visiting the museum exhibitions to understand the context and location as well as discussions with museum staff about their visions for the threshold in relation to the exhibitions of the museum, how this could be reflected through sound and the visitor profile of the museum.

Based on the initial diagnostic the objectives for the soundscape were defined as follows:

- Uphold the academic rigour of the museum, while appealing to all visitor types.
- Create intrigue, while aurally projecting the image of the artefacts held by the museum.
- Establish a better connection with visitors earlier in their journey over the threshold before they arrive at the concessions desk.

During the action planning phase it was quickly decided by the design team and stakeholders that Egyptian music would be an ideal mood cue for the soundscape, but the soundscape should also reflect the extreme challenges and hard work associated with obtaining the artefacts on display at the Petrie Museum. Therefore, the team carried out a rapid prototyping experiment off site with different kinds of music, recordings of speech and digging sounds that might be suitable for the soundscape. To replicate the acoustic conditions of the stairwell at the Petrie Museum, the experiment was carried out in a stairwell at the University of Birmingham. This allowed the compatibility of various sounds within the acoustics of a similar space to be determined. It also allowed the stakeholders to be involved in the sound selection process.

We listened to a variety of sounds during the experiment to allow team members and stakeholders to understand the positive and negative interactions of different sounds within the acoustics of a stairwell environment. We listened to different kinds of Egyptian and Arabic music and noticed that the tempo was frequently fast. Not only could this make visitors feel rushed, but the acoustics of the stairwell suited a slower cadence. Also, it became evident that a soundscape focused on speech should be avoided, as speech was only intelligible close to the loudspeakers, while quickly reduced to noise when further away.

It was decided that in addition to the music, digging sounds would be used to evoke images of Petrie being on an archaeological dig and excavating the objects on display at the museum. Because the stairwell is easily saturated with sound, the music and digging sounds would be played at different locations, thus providing a temporal aspect to the soundscape as the visitor ascends the stairs creating different blends of music and digging while moving between the two entrances.

The budget for the design intervention was limited, so there were no funds for purchasing music or to have something especially recorded. Both music and sounds of digging were taken from licence-free online resources. The archaeological digging composition was created using music sequencing software. It comprised a mixture of discrete digging sounds, a few sequences of sounds and conversational snippets. The conversational snippets were used to evoke communication between the imaginary archaeologists but were set to the background of the soundscape to prevent the known complications with speech intelligibility. The tempo of the digging sounds was set to provide the context of people digging. The digging component was made to the same length as the music but was not aligned to the transitions within the music. This allowed the soundscape to be mastered to a single stereo digital file that could be played from a standard consumer media player. A stereo recording has two channels that can be used for separate content. One channel would play the music, while the other would play the archaeological composition. The mixing of the sounds would occur on-site in the stairwell. A temporary sound reinforcement system was installed. This included high-quality consumer components and cabling to achieve the highest fidelity on a budget. The playback device was located in the administrative offices just off the lobby. The volume of the soundscape was set at a modest level, which felt appropriate for a museum environment and to subtly complement the threshold space.

Findings

The pre-intervention visitor study should establish a baseline from which to ascertain the impact of the design intervention, at the threshold to the Petrie Museum.

Figure 11.2 shows the results of the quantitative element of the questionnaire. The responses have been grouped as either positive (1–2) or negative (4–5) in regard to signage and images respectively and then converted to percentages. The neutral middle position (3) answers were left out in this count. The figure shows the overall distribution of responses and the distribution with regard to the different variables of knowledge, age, sex and visit in the sample population.

Overall, just over 50 per cent of respondents did not think that the signage and images in the stairwell prepared them for the visit. Looking at the self-reported level of knowledge about the subject matter of the museum, the knowledgeable visitors seem more positively inclined towards the pre-intervention signage and images in the stairwell, indicating that these match their level of knowledge in a way that enables them to decode and

220 *Christian Hviid Mortensen and Angus Deuchars*

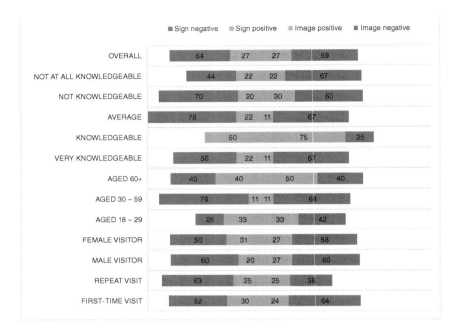

Figure 11.2 Positive vs negative ratings of how the stairwell prepared the visitor before the intervention. When reading the numbers, the size of the different sub-groups should be taken into account. Consult Table 11.1 above

be inspired by them. However, it must be taken into account that the group of knowledgeable respondents included only four individuals. With regard to the age variable the middle-aged group were markedly more dissatisfied by the signage and images. There is no difference in how the two sexes perceive the threshold. Also, repeat visitors show no significant difference in their valuation of the stairwell.

The qualitative descriptions of the stairwell have been coded through a single round of open coding resulting in the grouping of the most common descriptors as shown in Table 11.2. The groups are non-exclusive so a given response can figure in more than one group.

By far the most common descriptors are those that describe the threshold area as functional, unexciting and bland. These pointed to the fact that this was a plain stairwell in an office building. For some visitors the threshold left a decidedly negative impression when they described it as dark, depressing or forbidding. A minority ascribed positive descriptors to the threshold, one even finding it beautiful. A few also found the threshold intriguing thus stoking the anticipation for the visit.

Table 11.2 Grouping of descriptors in the qualitative comments on the stairwell at the Petrie Museum before the intervention

Descriptors				
Cold	Adequate	Comfortable	Beautiful	Inviting
Dark	Basic	Intimate		Intriguing
Narrow	Ordinary	Safe		Anticipation
Uninviting	Functional			
Depressing	Utilitarian			
Forbidding	Plain			
Dingy	Unexciting			
Inaccessible	Bland			
Unwelcoming	Bleak			
Small	Clinical			
	Sparse			
	White			
	OK			
Total instances in data 9	24	3	1	3

The post-intervention visitor study similarly asked the respondents to rate how the threshold prepared them for the visit on a five-point scale. This time they should not distinguish between the signage and images. The variables were the same with the addition of one: whether they had noticed the sounds. Figure 11.3 shows the distribution of responses in the post-intervention visitor study. In addition to the rating, the questionnaire asked the respondents how the stairwell prepared them for their visit. In relation to the sounds the respondents were also asked to describe them, how they made them feel and what they made them think of.

After the design intervention respondents overall are less negatively and more positively inclined towards the preparatory attributes of the threshold compared with before. Significantly, for the focus on this chapter, whether respondents noticed the sounds does not seem to influence whether they felt positively prepared by the threshold. With regard to the variable of knowledge the two outlier groups of 'not at all knowledgeable' and 'very knowledgeable' seem to be all positively inclined, but this is probably just a function of the very small size of the groups with one and three respondents respectively. With regard to age, again the middle-aged group was the least positive and most negative. Females seem much more positively disposed towards the threshold than their male counterparts. First-time visitors felt more prepared by the threshold than repeat visitors, even if several repeat visitors in their comments describe the design intervention as an improvement: 'it was better than usual' (Female, 30–59 years) and 'there was more info. The visitor has more idea what to expect (Male, 30–59 years).

Now we focus on the impact of the sound aspect of the intervention. Only 25 out of the 46 respondents noticed the sounds in the stairwell and

222 Christian Hviid Mortensen and Angus Deuchars

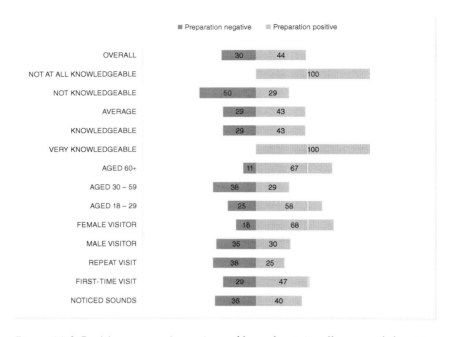

Figure 11.3 Positive vs negative ratings of how the stairwell prepared the visitor after the design intervention. When reading the numbers, the size of the different sub-groups should be taken into account. Consult Table 11.1 above

only 10 of those felt positively prepared by the threshold, reflecting the overall appreciation of the stairwell. This points to the challenges of using sound in an enclosed space not suitable for this purpose. For example, the environmental acoustics could counteract the soundscape, such as the noise created when several visitors ascended the stairs at the same time.

Again, the qualitative responses about the sounds have been coded via an open coding process resulting in the grouping shown in Table 11.3.

Respondents found that the sounds created an atmosphere in the stairwell and helped evoke a fitting mood for their visit. Several respondents also found the sounds to be relaxing, calm and peaceful.

Thus, they felt welcome and that they were in the right place. Entering a markedly different atmosphere also signalled the transition from outside into the world of the museum. In the words of one respondent: 'it created a difference, showed I was entering a distinct space . . . made a transition from outside to inside. Coming into a different area, welcoming, considered as visitors' (Female, 60+ years). According to Böhme, atmospheres are most perceptible when they change and establish a contrast. Here the sounds

Table 11.3 Grouping of descriptors from the qualitative comments on the sound aspect of the design intervention

Descriptors	Atmosphere Ambient	Relaxing Calming Peaceful	Welcomed Inviting In the right place	Mood	Egypt	Digs Archaeology	Transition	Intrigue Exploration Adventure Curious
Total in data	8	7	8	4	8	8	9	4

clearly distinguished the threshold of the Petrie Museum from a stairwell in an ordinary office building. The atmosphere established that you were entering the threshold to a museum, not an office, and therefore there was the potential to feel welcomed in your role as visitor, not an intruder.

The soundscape also signified important aspects of the subject matter and content of the museum, namely that of Egyptian archaeology, situating the visitor spatially in the Middle East and thematically at an archaeological dig. Apparently the sounds of digging evoked a sense of anticipation and exploration associated with archaeology in some visitors: 'there was a sense of exploration/adventure, it was good not to be too prescriptive, discovering museum in ones [sic] own, sounds were discreet' (Female, 30–59 years) and 'made me feel curious, made you feel like you were going to discover something, made you prepared to absorb some information' (Male, 18–29 years).

Atmosphere is a subjective experience and not all respondents felt that the sounds were appropriate: '[the sounds] didn't seem relevant, wondered why that music was playing in particular' (Male, 60+ years). Another commented: 'No – used to museums playing "noise" that is what this felt like' (Male, 30–59 years). For these visitors, the sound of music clashed with their expectation of the museum visit, probably formed by previous experiences of the culture of silence at museums.

Discussion

Applying the conceptual model to the findings above we can see how the three entities interact. The individuals influence the environment when present in the stairwell, because the noise they create drowns out the soundscape, resulting in only half the respondents noticing the sounds. The environmental variables of the confined space, poor acoustics and other people proved paramount, preventing many visitors from experiencing the soundscape and thus for the soundscape to have any effect. However, for the visitors who noticed the soundscape it apparently established a contrasting atmosphere to the one outside. The meaning visitors ascribed to the soundscape gave a colouration of the stairwell environment, distinguishing it from an ordinary office stairwell and thus making them feel welcomed and 'in the right place'.

Unfortunately, an opportunity to describe the stairwell was left out of the post-intervention questionnaire, so we do not know if the soundscape was able to offset visitors' perception of the stairwell as being functional, ordinary and bland. The environmental and architectural properties are still the same, so visitors probably still see the stairwell in this way, but the soundscape provides another level of meaning to the environment whereby the ordinary properties of the stairwell are pushed into the background. While a soundscape cannot overcome the constraints of the built environment and transform an ordinary stairwell into a fantastic, stimulating and exciting threshold environment, it can add meaningfulness to the environment that helps situate the visitor and help them on their journey into the world of the museum.

Memory is an important variable of the individual and sound, especially music, is an effective trigger of memories and feelings such as nostalgia (Barrett et al., 2010). Memories were not present at all in the comments of the respondents, however. This indicates that while they correctly identified the connotations of Egypt and archaeology in the soundscape, these themes did not resonate with their previous experiences. The atmosphere can thus seem foreign to many visitors, evoking curiosity and intrigue in some, possibly also alienating others.

Now we will revisit the three objectives of the design intervention in light of the findings for the purpose of evaluation. The first objective concerned striking a balance between the academic rigour of the museum and appealing to all kinds of visitors. None of the respondents complained that the soundscape undermined or clashed with the academic rigour of the museum. One respondent just found the music irrelevant and another assumed the digging sounds stemmed from the construction work going on outside. After the intervention, the threshold appealed to 44 per cent of respondents as preparation for the museum visit compared to 27 per cent before. It seems to appeal equally to all visitor types, slightly more to females than males, but with no significant differences in positive or negative evaluations with regard to the other variables of knowledge, age and visit. Thus, while there is still room for improvement in the overall appreciation of the threshold, the intervention achieved the first objective.

The second objective involved creating intrigue and aurally projecting an image of the artefacts on display at the museum. The quotes above indicate that the soundscape established a feeling of intrigue and anticipation. However, there are only four mentions of intrigue and related feelings in the data from the post-intervention study, which is equal to the three mentions in the pre-installation study. So, it seems that the soundscape did not generate more intrigue than the silent stairwell. The soundscape was more successful in conveying the themes of Egypt and archaeology as '[the sounds] were Middle-Eastern and put you in mind that you would see material from that region' (Female, 30–59 years). This visitor clearly felt that the images of the artefacts were projected into the stairwell by the soundscape.

The aim of the third objective was to establish a better connection with visitors earlier in their journey over the threshold. The level of satisfaction with the preparatory work of the threshold has risen after the intervention, so the connection with the visitors has been guided in the right direction. But as fewer than half of respondents are positively disposed towards the threshold there is still room for improvement.

Concluding remarks

Throughout its history, as with most traditional museums, the focus of the Petrie Museum has been foremost on the collection. With the advent of the 'new museology' (Vergo, 1989) the focus of museums shifted slowly towards their visitors. This change in focus resulted in developing more engaging exhibitions and activities within museums. Just recently we have begun to conceive of the museum visit as a journey, a small part of the visitor's life journey, that begins long before arriving at the museum and will continue long after leaving the museum (Falk and Dierking, 2013). And it is just now, with this volume, that we begin to address the threshold of the museum as a significant part of this journey.

Therefore, it is unsurprising that the design of the threshold of the Petrie Museum is less than optimal. After all, the important contribution of the museum prioritises the artefacts on display in the exhibition area. But the exhibition cannot be viewed in isolation, it is only one part of the total museum experience and the visitor's journey.

The design intervention, with the soundscape installation at the threshold to the Petrie Museum, showed promise for soundscape design in museum threshold areas. While the soundscape was not able to completely offset the blandness of the stairwell, it was able to make visitors feel more welcome and that they were in the right place. Also, it was able to convey the central themes of the museum.

The visitor study was conducted before the visitors left the museum, so we only have data on how the visitors perceived the threshold as they entered the museum and not on the threshold as exit point. It is possible that more visitors would notice the soundscape on their way out as they would be less focused on what lies at the end of the stairs and perhaps they would also be more attuned to the themes of Egypt and archaeology after having visited the exhibition. Therefore, the soundscape might be even more significant as the last impression of the Petrie Museum that will linger on long after the visitor has left the building. Studies show that visitors form long-term memories of visits to museums (Falk and Dierking, 2013); however, there have been no studies of the influence of sound on such memories. But correlated with other studies into the connections between sound, especially music, and memory, it seems plausible that sound will play a significant role in forming and later recalling these memories.

Thus, soundscape design has potential for enriching the visitor's passing between the surrounding society and the world of the museum. We can only imagine the wonderful threshold experiences that await when soundscape design and acoustics become integral to the design of new museum buildings and not as an add-on with the difficult task of remedying existing counter-productive architecture.

References

Angliss, S. (2005). 'Sound and Vision', *Museums Journal* 105, pp. 26–9.

Barrett, F.S., Grimm, K.J., Robins, R.W., Wilschut, T. and Sedikides, K. (2010). 'Music-Evoked Nostalgia: Affect, Memory, and Personality', *Emotion* 10, pp. 390–403.

Böhme, G. (2000). 'Acoustic Atmospheres: A Contribution to the Study of Ecological Aesthetics', *Soundscape* 1, pp. 14–18.

Bubaris, N. (2014). 'Sound in Museums – Museums in Sound', *Museum Management and Curatorship* 29(4), pp. 391–402.

Bull, M. (2014). *Sounding Out the City: Personal Stereos and the Management of Everyday Life*. Oxford: Berg Publishers.

Chion, M. (1994). *Audio-Vision: Sound on Screen*. Translated by Claudia Gorbman. New York: Colombia University Press.

Conn, S. (2010). *Do Museums Still Need Objects?* Philadelphia: University of Pennsylvania Press.

Falk, J.H., and Dierking, L.D. (2013). *The Museum Experience Revisited*. Walnut Creek, CA: Left Coast Press.

Forrest, R. (2013). 'Museum Atmospherics: The Role of the Exhibition Environment in the Visitor Experience', *Visitor Studies* 16, pp. 201–16.

Keightley, E. and Pickering, M. (2006a). 'For the Record: Popular Music and Photography as Technologies of Memory', *European Journal of Cultural Studies* 9, pp. 149–65.

Keightley, E. and Pickering, M. (2006b). 'The Modalities of Nostalgia', *Current Sociology* 54, pp. 919–41.

Keightley, E. and Pickering, M. (2012). *The Mnemonic Imagination: Remembering as Creative Practice*. Palgrave Macmillan Memory Studies. Basingstoke, UK: Palgrave Macmillan.

Kotler, P. (1974). 'Atmospherics as a Marketing Tool', *Journal of Retailing* 49, pp. 48–64.

Levent, N. and Pascual-Leone, A. (2014). 'Introduction', in *The Multisensory Museum: Cross-disciplinary Perspectives on Touch, Sound, Smell, Memory, and Space*, ed. Levent, N. and Pascual-Leone, A., pp. xiii–xxvi. Lanham, MD: Rowman & Littlefield.

Mortensen, C.H., Rudloff, M. and Vestergaard, V. (2014). 'Communicative Functions of the Museum Lobby', *Curator: The Museum Journal* 57(3), pp. 329–46.

O'Dell, T. (2005). 'Experiencescapes', in *Experiencescapes: Tourism, Culture and Economy*, ed. O'Dell, T. and Billing, P., pp. 15–35. Copenhagen: Copenhagen Business School Press.

Pearce, S.M. (1992). *Museums, Objects and Collections: A Cultural Study*. Leicester, UK: Leicester University Press.

Rounds, J. (2012). 'The Museum and Its Relationships as a Loose Coupled System', *Curator: The Museum Journal* 55(4), pp. 413–34.
Schafer, R.M. (1994). *The Soundscape: Our Sonic Environment and the Tuning of the World*. 2nd ed. Rochester, VT: Destiny Books.
Shams, L. and Kim, R. (2010). 'Crossmodal Influences on Visual Perception', *Physics of Life Reviews* 7, pp. 269–84.
Spence, C. (2010). 'Multisensory Integration – Solving the Crossmodal Binding Problem: Comment on "Crossmodal Influences on Visual Perception" by Shams & Kim', *Physics of Life Reviews* 7, pp. 285–6.
Susman, G.I. and Evered, R.D. (1978). 'An Assessment of the Scientific Merits of Action Research', *Administrative Science Quarterly* 23, pp. 582–603.
Transforming Thresholds Research Network (2012). *Transforming Thresholds* http://transformingthresholds.weebly.com/ (Accessed 1 October 2016).
Truax, B. (2001). *Acoustic Communication*. 2nd ed. Westport, CT and London: Ablex Publishing.
Vergo, P. (1989). *The New Museology*. London: Reaktion Books.
Wildschut, T., Sedikides, K. and Arndt, J. (2006). 'Nostalgia: Content, Triggers, Functions', *Journal of Personality and Social Psychology* 91, pp. 975–93.
Wrightson, K. (2000). 'An Introduction to Acoustic Ecology', *Soundscape* 1, p. 13.

Conversation 4
The Royal Shakespeare Company

Ruth Page [RP] interviews James Kitto [JK], Theatre Manager at the Royal Shakespeare Company.

In this last of four conversations presented throughout the book, we discuss the Royal Shakespeare Company's (RSC) multiple and complex thresholds in Stratford-Upon-Avon, and how the RSC are changing their thinking around them based on a playful approach to design.

JK: Here we are at the Royal Shakespeare Theatre, home of the RSC in Stratford; we create the finest experience of Shakespeare in performance. We have two theatres in Stratford: the Royal Shakespeare Theatre, which seats about 1,000 people; and the Swan Theatre, which holds around about 450 people. We have about 330 performances in both theatres over 12 months, and we also welcome visitors to walk around our building and foyers. In total, we have about a million visitors every year.

RP: *Can you tell us about the people who come here to the Royal Shakespeare Theatre? Do you have a typical visitor?*

JK: We do have typical visitors. If you were to come on a weekday matinee performance, you would see a very typical audience. Equally, if you came on a Saturday night performance, you'd see a very typical audience for that as well. But generally speaking, we have 92 per cent of visitors from the UK; 50 per cent of those are from the West Midlands region. And then we have a large contingent of visitors from abroad, the USA providing most of that those at just under 4 per cent.

RP: *Can you tell us a little bit about the Royal Shakespeare Theatre?*

JK: It's a very complicated building. There are essentially three parts to it: the Swan Theatre that was built in the late nineteenth century, the RST that was built in 1932, and then the foyers or thresholds that link those spaces, which were part of the redevelopment that we went through in Stratford in 2010. So there are three centuries' worth of buildings. And that brings with it an incredibly complex variety of thresholds, with multiple entrances across the site.

We have great challenges in how we welcome those visitors. There isn't a single place where we have a main entrance: visitors can enter through one of many entrances. The spaces we have, have to function as theatre foyers, which have very distinct purposes for a very short amount of time. So perhaps half an hour before a performance begins, 20 minutes during the interval, and maybe 20 to 30 minutes after performances, our spaces are predominantly theatre foyers. They handle the incoming audience to that performance.

However, the building is open outside of performance time as well. So for the majority of time they're public spaces. And in Stratford, we attract a huge number of visitors who just want to come in and have a look at our spaces. We have exhibition spaces, cafés, and restaurants. We have a shop. So there is a huge draw on people just to visit and wander around the building as well.

The challenge we have is how we balance the design and use of those spaces. Where a bar is particularly a theatre bar, how do we make that a public space that the public can interact with and have a meaningful experience of during their visit? That's quite a difficult thing to achieve.

RP: *So what's the split between the number of visitors who come here to see a play and the number of visitors who just come to experience the public spaces of this theatre?*

JK: We have around 440,000 visitors coming to see a performance. And we estimate that about 580,000 visitors a year are here to just see the building. We've done further research, and we think around 50,000 people come in just to visit the restaurant. About 20,000 people come in to take part in a theatre tour, and very few of these people actually then go on and see a performance. So there's a large number who come into the building just to experience the building, rather than see a show.

RP: *Tell us about the staff who work in these very complex threshold spaces.*

JK: We are a theatre company, first and foremost, so theatre takes the priority. The purpose of the theatre foyer therefore takes the lead. However, there are challenges where we would like to identify how we could maximize the use of the public space, incorporating the limitations put on that space through its use as a theatre foyer.

There are a huge number of people who work at the RSC who will each have a stake in how we use our thresholds, from the artistic director of the RSC, through to our commercial team, who want to make money out of our space, through our cafés, through our shops, through our bars, through to our events and exhibitions team who want to interpret the spaces as best as they can, through to the front-of-house assistants who are here on the floor interpreting the space and interacting with the customers. They're at the coalface, and they will see what works and doesn't work. So there is forever a balance in being a theatre and being a public space.

We have The Other Place, a studio space which is being brought back into life over the next 12 months. So that's a living project, and within that we've been able to use a couple of tools that we got from the festival. We used the foyer game by Erik Kristiansen [see Chapter 9], for example. We already had a model describing how the staffing of The Other Place might work. But we were able to say, OK, let's play a game and test it. So we made a plan of the foyer, and we got some play people, and we moved the play people around. We were able to see that actually, how we thought we might like to operate that space, it wouldn't work. So it really helped us put our thinking caps back on, and I think it also visualized it for those staff who are involved in those decisions, who perhaps aren't operational people, who can't see these things as quickly as those of us who work in operations can: I think it really enabled those people to understand the challenges of operating and working in that space.

RP: *Looking to the future then, what are your future plans for the threshold spaces of the Royal Shakespeare Theatre and The Other Place?*

JK: Within this building there's been some work carried out over the last few years where we're looking at just redefining some of the spaces, redefining some of thresholds, and making them 'less open', I think: more intimate, so we're actually able to have more private spaces within the building. We're looking at our exhibitions as a revolving programme of exhibitions. And we're looking at how we can animate the building, drawing on ideas from the Festival, particularly how people experience the tower; so that's an ongoing project.

12 The visitor as evaluator

Using appraisal theory to understand 'threshold fear'

Ruth Page

In her field-shaping exploration of 'threshold fear', Gurian (2005) provoked museums to lower their barriers to access and become more inclusive. As a powerful metaphor, threshold fear associates three-dimensional space and emotion. In this chapter, I use the appraisal framework developed in applied linguistics (Martin and White, 2005) to analyse the experiences of visitors in two contrasting museum thresholds. The analysis gives empirical substance to the metaphor of threshold fear and brings to light its multiple dimensions. The use of appraisal is important for it helps build a theory about the affective nature of three-dimensional space and its organisation. Specifically, I develop Stenglin's (2008, 2009, 2016) work on binding, in which she argues that the architectural design of space can generate responses such as security or insecurity. Borrowing from pedagogic research (Wood et al., 1976), I propose that spaces such as those found in the museum threshold are not just bound or unbound, but also more or less 'scaffolded'. There are three aspects to scaffolding that relate to threshold fear: physical orientation (wayfinding, locating an object or place), cognitive orientation (engaging attention) and emotional orientation (relating to atmosphere). The appraisal framework has much to offer museum studies, for it provides a robust set of categories for discussing affective responses, not only in the threshold but in relation to the visitors' experience of the museum more generally.

Introducing the appraisal framework

Evaluation is a central concept in visitor studies and in applied linguistics. However, in these two fields of research, the term is used in different ways and associated with different methods. In visitor studies, evaluation is thought of as a measuring process by which an institution (such as a museum) determines the outcomes of a particular programme or offer. In applied linguistics, evaluation relates to the verbal choices that speakers make to show their attitude or stance towards a particular object, person, event or outcome. In this chapter, I will show what appraisal as a recent model for evaluative language can offer museum studies as a method to categorise how visitors talk about their experiences.

It is perhaps surprising that applied linguistics has had so little impact within the recent history of visitor studies, since both share similar interests in how people evaluate experiences, especially as this evaluation is documented through spoken or written interactions. Typically, within applied linguistics, these interactions are considered as forms of discourse; that is, examples of language that are larger than a sentence (Brown and Yule, 1983) and function as a form of language-in-action (Blommaert, 2005, p.2). Yet the cross-fertilisation between discourse analysis and visitor studies with a particular focus on museums has thus far been relatively scarce and has tended to focus on the discussion of non-linguistic concepts of large-scale 'Discourse' (that is, macro-social patterns of thinking, belief or social organisation). For example, scholars have begun to interpret the ways in which the communication between visitors and museums constructs particular, ideologically loaded and often contested histories for particular groups and individuals (see scholarship from Katriel, 1997, 2001; Noy, 2016; Thumim, 2010). However, there is much more that discourse analysis might offer to visitor studies at the micro-level of the language that visitors use when documenting their experiences, especially in relation to as yet under-scrutinised areas of the museum such as its threshold spaces.

The need for a method that can categorise the evaluative language used by visitors when they talk about their experiences is all the more pressing given the increasing interest in the affective nature of visiting museums and other heritage or cultural sites of interest (Harris, 2016). The affective nature of the visitors' experience has begun to be documented in research that has used of a number of tools to gather audience responses to spaces, objects and events in museum and other informal learning contexts. Within qualitative research, semi-structured surveys, focus groups interviews (Rajka, 2015) and think-aloud protocols (Achiam, et al., 2014) have been used to elicit feedback, whilst other studies have observed forms of feedback provided without researcher intervention, such as contributions to comment books (Noy, 2008; Rami and Budtryte-Ausiejiene, 2015) or on forms of social media (Gronemann et al., 2015). The data gathered through these tools has built rich pictures of visitors' physical, cognitive and emotional responses to a museum visit. However, to date, most of this research has focused on evaluation of in-gallery experiences, such as exhibitions and interactives, or reflected on the museum site as a whole. There has been little empirical data gathered about visitors' experiences in spaces of the museum outside the galleries, such as the entrance foyer or lobby. The few studies that have begun to scrutinise the museum threshold have used observational methods to document visitor behaviour in these spaces. For example, Goulding's (2000a) assessment of the entrance at Birmingham Museum and Art Gallery used a 'setting based' approach where the museum environment and its visitors were observed over time. Tröndle et al. (2014) used tracking techniques to gather physiological data about visitors' attention to artworks, including an artwork temporarily repositioned in a foyer. Mortensen et al. (2014)

used ethnographic observation of visitor practices in Danish museums as the basis for understanding the lobby as a communicative space. In their study, Mortensen and colleagues compiled a 'thick' observational dataset, including interviews with museum staff, but did not interview visitors. As yet, we know little about how visitors articulate and so make sense of their experience in the threshold spaces of museums and art galleries. This gap in knowledge is important, given the emotional and cognitive aspects of the visitor experience that might be at risk in the threshold, captured by Gurian's (2005) metaphor of 'threshold fear'. We need to know more about the experiences of visitors in these spaces if we are to find ways to mitigate negative affective outcomes such as 'threshold fear' to which Gurian gestured.

Appraisal theory is useful as a way of enhancing the qualitative methods used in visitor studies to analyse the data gathered through the various aforementioned eliciting tools. Typically, the methods used in visitor studies to analyse *what* participants have said (for example, in an interview or focus group) have used forms of content analysis that interpret recurring themes or categories of experience within a particular dataset. In this approach, the analyst works from the responses in the data using open coding practices similar to grounded theory (Goulding, 2000b) which do not predetermine the kinds of themes that the research might interpret. This is well suited to the qualitative research that emphasises the situated nature of the audience experience (Schrøder, 2013) and the necessarily subjective nature of an individual visitor's experience of a particular space (Falk and Dierking, 2012, p.65). The need to account for individual variation in experience is especially relevant when categorising vague and rather intractable notions such as aesthetic experience and emotion (Markovic, 2012), which may well be incorporated in the evaluations of spaces within a museum or art gallery. However, inevitably, the kinds of themes that emerge in a content-based approach to categorising visitors' responses will reflect the specific nature of the data in which these themes occur. This can be a problem if we wish to make comparisons of visitor experiences across different contexts. Given that emotional responses are generated by many types of spaces (of which the threshold is one), and that thresholds in different museums may vary considerably, a transferable framework is needed that can be used to categorise the affective nature of visitors' experiences both in the threshold and beyond.

One solution is to harness the existing models of evaluative language that have developed in applied linguistics. Studies of evaluative language are well established in applied linguistics, including taxonomies developed within narrative analysis (Labov, 1972), within the broader field of stance (Hyland, 2005), as derived from large-scale corpora (Hunston and Thompson, 2000) or with a focus on emotion (Bednarek, 2008). The range of frameworks reflects the ubiquitous nature of evaluative language. The variety of frameworks also points to the difficulties that occur when trying to establish a single set of categories that can account for the evaluation that occurs across different contexts of use, such as different modes and genres of communication. As Millar and Hunston (2015) argue, the most fully refined account of evaluative language that accounts for different modes, genres and contexts has been developed by Martin (2000) and Martin and White (2005) in their appraisal theory.

Appraisal theory was developed within Systemic Functional Linguistics, a field in which language is not treated as an abstract, decontextualised system but rather as a means of understanding how people construe their experience within particular social and cultural contexts (see Eggins, 2004 for an introduction). As its name implies, Systemic Functional Linguistics attempts to model the systematic organisation of the interrelated choices that people make when they talk about their experiences. Martin and White's model of appraisal sets out three main categories that emphasise different types of attitude or opinion, which they call attitudinal appraisal. These three categories distinguish between linguistic expressions of evaluation, which are reflected in the lexical choices. This includes:

Affect – types of emotional response

I thoroughly enjoyed my visit

I was disappointed by the exhibit;

Judgement – ethical assessments of a person's appropriate behaviour relative to social norms

The lady at the reception was helpful and friendly

Visitors must not take photographs in the galleries;

Appreciation – aesthetic opinions of an entity

The sounds worked well with the pictures

The space is confusing.

In line with a systemic approach, each category of attitudinal appraisal contains further options which can distinguish between the more fine-grained types of evaluation. There are specific subtypes of affect (happiness, security and satisfaction), judgement (normality, tenacity, capacity, veracity and propriety), and appreciation (impact, quality, composition and value). Each subtype of appraisal can be expressed in positive or negative terms, as suggested by the illustrative examples above. Like the content analysis found in the scholarship of visitor studies, the analysis of appraisal is empirical and categorises the words used by the visitors as different kinds of appraisal. However, in contrast to the open coding of grounded theory or content analysis, appraisal incorporates a top-down approach in its macro-categories that allows the analyst to trace points of connection between seemingly disparate sets of responses. In taking this comparative approach, appraisal should not be taken as a mechanistic tool that uniformly interprets every instance of a particular word as always construing the same meaning.

Rather, the evaluative norms that are interpreted from the language are understood relative to particular contextual constraints, such as the genre of the interaction and the wider cultural context in which the interaction takes place. The flexibility within the framework is important, as it allows researchers to apply appraisal to the affective responses prompted by a wide range of multimodal phenomena, in different cultural contexts.

Appraisal was originally developed to account for the evaluation of written texts, but has been developed in order to account for other kinds of objects and experiences. Stenglin (2007, 2008, 2016) particularly focused on the subtype of affect that relates to evaluation of security or insecurity within three-dimensional space, which she described in relation to the theoretical concept of binding. Like Gurian's 'threshold fear', Stenglin argues that the affective dimension of security can prohibit a person's ability to experience further positive affective outcomes, and thus is crucial for understanding how visitors might experience museum spaces and entrance spaces in particular. Stenglin (2008, p.426) suggests that in relation to three-dimensional spaces, feelings of (in)security are related primarily to architectural design, though other multisensory factors such as climate, lighting and texture might also contribute to an extent to how 'firmly the space encloses a person'. With the caveat that spaces are experienced in culturally specific and potentially idiosyncratic fashion, the central claim Stenglin made in relation to binding is that there is an optimum point at which the boundaries of a space can be constructed. According to her, a space must not be perceived as too bound, for this might provoke feelings akin to claustrophobia, whilst being too unbound can leave a person feeling vulnerable and unprotected.

From binding to scaffolding: affect and three-dimensional space

The theory of binding is intuitively attractive and borne out by interview data that Stenglin draws upon from her work with architects and their clients. However, there is more work to be done to test and refine the ways in which three-dimensional spaces are experienced affectively. The analysis presented in the present chapter takes the theory of binding forward in two ways. First, Stenglin did not consider threshold spaces, which are distinctive areas through which visitors pass to reach a subsequent point of destination, rather than a space in which they are encouraged to dwell. We do not know how binding applies to liminal spaces, such as those found at the entrances and exits to the museum. Second, I question binding's emphasis on insecurity as a particular aspect of the visitors' experience and ask what other kinds of appraisal may be important when people talk about their experience of spaces in a museum.

In what follows, I propose that (in)security is only one dimension of the affective responses that are generated at the museum threshold. Binding is not the only factor that contributes to threshold fear. Three-dimensional space is experienced affectively as bound and unbound, and also as more or less scaffolded. Intellectual scaffolding is a concept that emerged in education and relates to the resources that can be provided to help learners solve problems and generate new knowledge in informal learning contexts. Within a museum context, scaffolding has been explored in relation to the visitors' engagement with the interpretation of objects (Achiam et al., 2014), interactives (Kahr-Højland, 2011) and with the museum personnel (Stenglin, 2016). These examples suggest that when scaffolding is employed effectively, then the visitors' cognitive and affective responses to the collections within the museum can be enhanced. However, scaffolding is not just required to help visitors engage with particular objects or exhibitions. It is also required in order to structure and support their experiences that precede entry into the galleries.

Like binding, scaffolding explains the affective relationship between emotion and three-dimensional spaces. Also like binding, scaffolding is a scalar concept, where a visitor's experience of a space may be more or less scaffolded, and the degree and kind of scaffolding that is required may vary according to the individual context of the space in question. However, scaffolding is distinct from binding, for scaffolding can operate independently of the architecture and can be provided by the less permanent resources like furnishings, fabric, décor and human interventions (e.g. the presence and activity of other people such as museum personnel or other visitors). Empirically, the emotional responses that relate to scaffolding relate to different aspects of the appraisal framework, thereby illuminating the complex and multilayered nature of threshold fear. I will illustrate the ways in which binding and scaffolding relate to appraisal by drawing on data gathered in relation to two museum thresholds: one at the Petrie Museum of Egyptian Archaeology in London and one at New Walk Museum and Art Gallery in Leicester.

Data and procedures

Setting

In order to explore how visitors evaluated their experience in threshold spaces, semi-structured surveys were carried out with visitors at two museums in the United Kingdom. As a preliminary study, the data does not attempt to account for all museum entrances, which can vary according to style and complexity. The museums were selected on the basis that the thresholds were relatively simple, in that each had only one point of entrance that led to a single building, and which also functioned as the point of exit for visitors. Given that the evaluation of space may vary according to cultural context, it should be noted that the results and discussion reported here are situated in British traditions of architecture. However, the two museums at which the evaluation took place are quite different in style,

The visitor as evaluator 237

the nature of their collections and the extent to which the architecture of the entrance was open or enclosed.

The first is New Walk Museum and Art Gallery in Leicester. This is a local-government-funded museum with a wide-ranging collection, thematically

Figure 12.1 New Walk Museum and Art Gallery approach to the entrance

238 *Ruth Page*

organised in a series of galleries situated over two floors. The museum has around 180,000 visitors each year. On average, three quarters of the visitors are returning, rather than first-time, visitors. Most visit the museum for recreation, often using the café as a social meeting place or to attend specific events. The museum's building was designed and constructed in the mid-nineteenth century. The entrance is reached from a pedestrian walkway, via a small courtyard and a portico flanked by four double-storey columns (see Figure 12.1). The double doors of the entrance open onto a square foyer (or lobby), from which all other areas of the museum can be reached. The foyer contains a reception desk, stairs leading to the first floor galleries, a bench and donations box. A brightly lit shop and café lie behind a second set of glass doors which face the visitor directly as they enter the foyer from the main portico (see Figure 12.2). In terms of architectural enclosure, the foyer is relatively unbound, with high ceilings and glass doors, which create sight lines into further spaces within the museum.

The second museum is the Petrie Museum of Egyptian Archaeology. This is a university-owned museum. The collection was originally developed in the later Victorian period as a teaching resource for the Department of Egyptian Archaeology at University College London. The extensive collection of Egyptian and Sudanese antiquities is associated with Flinders Petrie, after whom the museum is now named. The museum has around 13,000 visitors each year, the majority of whom are visiting the museum for first time. Although many visit the museum as a leisure activity (often as tourists), the

Figure 12.2 New Walk Museum and Art Gallery view from the door into the foyer

The visitor as evaluator 239

museum also serves scholars wishing to use the collections and archives for professional purposes. The museum is located on the campus of University College London amongst other university buildings (see Figure 12.3). Visitors enter the museum through a door from the main university thoroughfare and must then proceed up a flight of stairs in order to reach the galleries on the first floor of the building (see Figure 12.4). In terms of its built environment, the 'threshold' constituting the stairwell and its landings is relatively enclosed within a narrow space, albeit lit by high-placed windows on each landing.

Figure 12.3 Petrie Museum of Egyptian Archaeology approach to the entrance
Source: Juan Luis Sanchez

Figure 12.4 Petrie Museum of Egyptian Archaeology view to the entrance door from the stairs
Source: Juan Luis Sanchez

The responses from visitors discussed in this chapter were collected in two phases.[1] In both cases, the initial data collection took place when the museum entrances were functioning without any kind of experimental intervention. The décor, signs and activities were those regularly in place at each museum. In the second phase of data collection, a temporary intervention was made to the resources provided at the entrance. At New Walk Museum and Art Gallery, the content of the digital screen in the foyer was altered to contain social media content about the exhibits in galleries. At the Petrie Museum, a series of images and a soundscape were displayed in the stairwell alongside existing visual signage. Only the latter of these is discussed in detail in this chapter.

Participants

The visitors who participated in the surveys constituted a non-probability sample. All the participants were over 18 years of age and native English speakers. A total of 86 visitors were interviewed at the Petrie Museum and 149 visitors were interviewed at New Walk Museum and Art Gallery. The sample accounts for 32 per cent of the population of Petrie Museum visitors and 4 per cent of the possible population for New Walk in the respective time periods of data collection. Given the relatively small numbers of visitors interviewed and the non-probabilistic nature of the sample, the analysis does not attempt to be quantitative or claim to be generalisable but instead is qualitative in nature. The surveys were collected alongside other observational data, which included hand-drawn route diagrams that mapped where visitors moved through the foyer of New Walk Museum and Art Gallery. It was not possible to gather this observational data at the Petrie Museum given the structural restrictions of the stairwell. The focus of this chapter is on the verbal analysis of the survey responses collected in both museums.

Procedure

The survey was designed to collect information about the demographic of the respondents (such as their age and gender), the regularity of their visit to the museum and the purpose of their visit. The visitors were then asked an open-ended question to elicit their impressions of the entrances to the respective museums: 'What do you remember of the museum's entrance?' In both museums, the visitors were then asked to recall what they remembered seeing in the entrance spaces in relation to a closed list of possible objects or images. In the Petrie museum, during the second phase of data collection, additional questions were also included which asked the visitors to describe their responses to the sounds in the stairwell. The results of the survey were then transcribed and manually coded for all instances of appraisal. Where it was possible for more than one type of appraisal to occur in the response, double coding was used in order to capture as fully as possible the range of affective responses that were reported in relation to these spaces.

Results and discussion

The visitors provided a variety of responses to the question, 'What do you remember of the entrance to the museum?' In New Walk Museum and Art

Gallery, 23 per cent of the participants said that they could not remember anything and that they had come straight through to the other spaces of the museum, such as the shop, café or a gallery. Similarly, in the Petrie Museum, 36 per cent of the survey participants did not report any recollections of the entry to the building. Of the remaining responses, 47 per cent of the participants (N=92) made statements that included evaluative language in the form of at least one instance of appraisal, whereas the remaining participants gave descriptions that listed objects or people without any evaluative language. The difference in these types of responses is illustrated in the following examples:

> Response with no appraisal
>
> *I remember the donation box and the desk on the right.*
>
> Response with appraisal
>
> *It was very grey, quite anonymous, not very friendly, wasn't really a lot there.*

The number of responses containing appraisal is perhaps surprising given that the question prompt in the survey did not explicitly invite an aesthetic or affective evaluation of the entrance spaces. The survey did not ask the visitors how they felt, what they liked or disliked, which might have primed the affective descriptions that emerged from the visitors. This suggests that the threshold spaces are like other museum spaces that can prompt strong cognitive and emotional response, that are 'the hardest to verbalize but the easiest to recall' (Falk and Dierking, 1992, p.31).

The nuanced forms of 'threshold fear' can best be examined by a more fine-grained analysis of the types of appraisal that the visitors used in their answers. If the primary response to the threshold space is expected to be anxiety (as a form of 'fear'), then the analysis of the appraisal in the survey responses is remarkable in that of the 92 responses which contained evaluative language, only two participants made a comment including the subtype of appraisal that directly construes 'fear' as affect: (in)security. The two responses were a description of their experiences, where the visitors explained, 'We were concerned whether we had found the right place,' and, 'I was not sure I was even going the right way.' However, this should not be taken to imply that all experiences of the entrance spaces were evaluated in language that was positive or free from emotion. Amongst the responses, there were occasions where visitors used inscribed (that is, explicitly stated) instances of affect. This included responses such as:

> *I was surprised by what came after it*
>
> *It made me curious*
>
> *I was drawn in*

More importantly, the visitors' responses included a wealth of appreciation, the type of appraisal that concerns the aesthetic evaluation of entities. This pattern is not surprising given that the respondents to the survey were asked to recall what they remembered of the entrance, which might be more likely to elicit an evaluation of the environment or an object rather than explicit statement of emotion. However, within appraisal theory, appreciation is understood to overlap with affect (see Martin and White, 2005, p.57) such that the emotional experience or stance of the speaker is inferred as a secondary aspect of the speaker's evaluation of an object. The affective response interpreted in relation to appreciation is often evoked from the data. For example, a statement like 'It was dingy and uninviting' would be coded as appreciation, but also carried emotional valence of unhappiness. Similarly, 'it was beautiful' would be coded as appreciation, but carried the emotional valence of happiness.

Martin and White (2005, pp. 56–58) subdivide appreciation into four further categories, each of which can be thought of as an axis expressed along a positive-negative polarity.

- Impact – the item's ability to engage its audience

    The gift shop is striking

    Not very stimulating, though there were some pictures, they were not attention-grabbing

- Quality – the characteristics which appealed to the speaker

    It has an attractive layout

    It was depressing, unwelcoming

- Composition: balance – the coherence and integrity of the item

    Combinations of images of dig and quotes prepared me for exhibits

    Like the backstairs, with no relation to anything

- Composition: complexity – is the item hard or easy to follow?

    Good pictures of people discovering stuff. Let you know that you were coming into a museum about Egypt

    There is too much information, confusing

The subcategories of appreciation are useful, for they point to the different aspects of the physical environment that prompted positive and negative affective responses from the visitors that show how binding and scaffolding operate in threshold spaces.

Binding as construed through the appraisal type: quality

The appraisal subcategory of quality was often expressed in the evaluative adjectives that visitors used in their appreciation of the foyer. Given the subjectivity of visitor experience, it is not surprising to find both positive and negative appraisal of the threshold's qualities in their responses. The adjectives used for appreciation of the threshold are summarised in Table 12.1.

The attributes included in this list confirmed the ongoing importance of Stenglin's concept of binding, even for liminal three-dimensional spaces like the threshold. The extent to which a space was perceived as enclosed or open was associated with the categories of appreciation. For example, the quality of the foyer at New Walk was described as *open* and *spacious*, and hence unbound, whilst the stairway at the Petrie Museum was described as *small* and *short*, and hence bound. Other similar interpretations of binding are found in the visitors' evaluative use of light to evoke positive appreciation (*airy, bright, light*) whereas the antonyms of these terms (*dark, dingy*) were used for the opposite effect. Notably, the appreciation of space as light/dark is not dependent on the physical architecture of the threshold. Respondents from both museums described the entrances as *dark*, despite the differences in the actual lighting of the spaces, and visitors to the New Walk Museum and Art Gallery described the same space as variously *light* and *dark* even on the same day and under the same conditions. In part, this reflects the metaphorical rather than literal senses in which these adjectives were used, but also reinforces the subjective nature of the affective evaluation of space.

The examples of appreciation in the surveys suggest that visitors' responses to the space did not just relate to the architecture. Beyond the qualities associated with how bound or unbound a space might be, other attributes suggested that the entrance could prompt positive appreciation, where the threshold was evaluated as *welcoming* and *inviting* or with negative appreciation as *unwelcoming, clinical, imposing* or *formal*. These attributes were applied to the environment, whether or not people were present (e.g. reception staff or greeters) in the museum threshold. These qualities suggest that it is not the perception of enclosure alone that causes a space to produce feelings of anxiety or confidence. Instead, these qualities relate to the aspects of atmosphere. This suggests that regardless of architectural design, one of the key aspects of 'threshold fear' relates to the extent to which the

Table 12.1 Appreciation of the threshold

Positive Appreciation	Negative Appreciation
Alluring, airy, attractive, beautiful, bright, comfortable, clean, colourful, friendly, intimate, inviting, light, open, nice, safe, spacious, shiny, striking, welcoming, well-organised	Anonymous, bland, bleak, busy, clinical, cold, cluttered, confusing, dark, depressing, dingy, empty, forbidding, formal, frustrating, functional, imposing, inaccessible, grey, grim, not calm, noisy, plain, short, small, sparse, plain, unexciting, uninspiring, uninviting, unwelcoming.

atmosphere as welcoming or unwelcoming. The affective preference for a welcoming atmosphere was found in many responses, as illustrated by this visitor to New Walk Museum and Art Gallery who elaborated, saying that the foyer 'needs to be welcoming and approachable. It should be the opposite of a church vestibule. The opposite of ostentatious, people should feel at home.' There is no evidence from this dataset that the sense of enclosure or the physical size of the foyer or entrance correlated with the perception of welcome, for example, where smaller spaces felt more welcoming than larger spaces or vice versa. Visitors to the same museum entrance space in the same conditions subjectively experienced the threshold as welcoming or unwelcoming. This raises further questions of what resources might support a welcoming atmosphere and how these might be provided in flexible enough forms to meet the subjective expectations of atmosphere held by individual visitors.

The resources that might scaffold the emotional orientation of a visitor are many and various, including the use of lighting, colour and texture used in the décor of the physical environment and the interpersonal style used by the museum personnel (which might be more or less formal). The intervention carried out at the Petrie Museum of Egyptian Archaeology suggested that sound could contribute effectively to supporting the affective atmosphere within the threshold. The soundscape installed in the Petrie Museum was composed of music and sounds that were associated with an archaeological dig (described in more detail by Mortensen and Deuchars, this volume). In their survey responses, the visitors evaluated the quality of the sounds with positive forms of appreciation. The sounds were described with evaluative adjectives, including:

> *Inviting, atmospheric, welcomed, relaxed, calming, unexpected, subtle, not overpowering, intriguing, peaceful, quite pleasant*

The appraisal suggests the appreciation overlapped with positive affect in terms of security (e.g. *calming, peaceful, relaxed, inviting, welcomed*). Further evidence for the potential of music to generate security is found in comments from other visitors who pointed out that the soundscape 'confirmed I was in correct place – an archaeology museum', and that the sounds 'were reassuring and signified that the museum was open'.

Scaffolding: the appraisal of composition

The analysis of the appraisal in the visitors' responses showed that there were further qualities of the threshold spaces that prompted an affective response, but did not fit so readily within the category of (in)security. These further forms of appreciation point to the second dimension of scaffolding that relates to 'threshold fear': the visitors' need for physical orientation. The need for this form of scaffolding was evident in the appreciation subcategory of composition that incorporates complexity, which Martin and White (2005, p. 56) gloss with the question, 'was it hard to follow?' The appraisal of the threshold in terms of its composition relates to the ways in which the design and architecture enable wayfinding for the visitors. Packer and Bond (2010, p. 425) point out that as an aspect of the physical environment, wayfinding is an important precursor that enables the restorative attributes of a museum visit to emerge. Threshold spaces pose particular challenges in terms of physical orientation for the visitors who may need reassurance that they have found the correct venue, and then, as a place where navigation decisions need to be made (Bitgood, 2013, p. 179), they must provide sufficient resources so that visitors may proceed with their visit. Without these resources, the visitors expressed negative emotions such as anxiety.

Deciding exactly how much wayfinding information to provide in the threshold, or the formats in which that information might be provided, is difficult to manage effectively. Given that thresholds are spaces where the visitor's attention may well be distracted, physical signs containing verbal information may be overlooked. Conversely, too much information may be difficult to process, especially if visitors are seeking orientation in line with a visit to a particular event or part of the museum. At New Walk Museum and Art Gallery, one visitor explained that they found the foyer contained 'too much information for children' and not enough to help them locate the temporary event they had arrived to attend. Likewise, at the Petrie Museum, one visitor commented that there was, 'a bit too much information as compared to a bold arresting image which would have been better'.

Scaffolding: impact and cognitive orientation

The analysis of the appraisal in the visitors' responses in the thresholds to the New Walk Museum and Art Gallery and to the Petrie Museum of Egyptian Archaeology suggests that it is not insecurity (for example, related to wayfinding) that is the primary affective response to the threshold. Instead, the most frequent type of appraisal found in the responses from the visitors to these museums was the appreciation subtype of impact reaction. Reaction is glossed by Martin and White (2005, p. 56) as 'did it grab me?' The appraisal categorised as impact suggests that threshold spaces need to provide more than security to promote a positive experience for visitors. They must also provide stimuli that help generate what Packer and Bond (2010 p. 422) describe as 'fascination' or 'being engaged without effort'. Another visitor to New Walk Museum expanded on this, explaining, 'You need something to feel excited, a focal piece from the museum'. In terms of scaffolding, activating attention is a necessary first step towards supporting the visitors' cognitive engagement with the museum.

Thresholds are particularly challenging spaces in which to engage visitors' attention, or in appraisal terms, to achieve positive impact. This is apparent in the visitors' responses, where they described their lack of attention to the threshold, in statements which used negative forms of impact, such as:

Functional, it didn't make any impression

Adequate, but I didn't take much note

Didn't really pay attention to it

In other cases, the evaluation of the threshold as an aesthetic space was sometimes downgraded, using the qualifier, *just* to preface the description, as in:

It's just an access point

It was just an ordinary stairwell

These descriptions reduced the threshold to its function as a space to pass through, rather than a place to dwell. Thresholds are, after all, by their very nature, spaces that usually precede entering other internal areas of the museum rather than necessarily constituting the desired end point to a museum visit. At New Walk Museum and Art Gallery, visitors repeatedly recalled only that they 'came straight through' the foyer on their way to another part of the museum such as the shop (located immediately next to the foyer) or on their way to a particular gallery or event. Specific affordances and constraints of certain entrances can underscore this functional aspect of threshold as a transition space. Visitors at the Petrie museum pointed out that the staircase was 'not a natural place to stop' or a 'place to linger' as it would not be safe or convenient to hinder the access to the museum for other visitors.

The challenges of engaging attention in the museum's threshold were further complicated by other factors in the visitors' experience. In the descriptions of the threshold spaces that were characterised by low levels of impact, visitors mentioned other aspects of their experience which hindered their attention in this space. For example, familiarity with the venue made is less likely for returning visitors to experience impact. One visitor responded, 'I'm used to it, so went straight in. I'm blinkered.' The flow of visitors in the threshold also reduced visitors' potential attention in this space. Other visitors said, 'I don't really remember the foyer, it was busy.' For visitors who adopted a particularly goal-oriented approach to their visit and came with a specific purpose in mind, their attention was focused on the spaces beyond the threshold, rather than on the threshold itself as a potential point to engage with the museum. As one visitor commented, 'I would have lingered if I hadn't come for a specific purpose – other visits might have been different', while another explained, 'I was focused on where I was going.'

The risks of failing to stimulate visitors' attention in the threshold spaces of a museum are particularly important, given the role that the entrance plays as a cognitive precursor to the other spaces within the museum. The relationship between the threshold and the other spaces of the museum was reflected in the visitors' appreciation of the threshold's structural organisation. The need for scaffolding as a form of cognitive orientation is also seen in the use of the appraisal subcategory of composition, which Martin and White (2005, p. 56) describe as 'balance' or the extent to which an object or entity 'hangs together'. When applied to three-dimensional space, balance is similar to the textual function of framing within two-dimensional spatial organisation (for example, of diagrams or pictures). Kress and Van Leeuwen (1996, p. 183) refer to framing as the strength of the (dis)connection between the elements in a visual composition. The compositional balance of a threshold might be considered as a particularly difficult design challenge, for thresholds are necessarily, in part at least, unbound and bound spaces which both connect and disconnect with the outside and inside of the museum. As liminal spaces they are often transitional and physically situated in between the outside world and the inner, gallery spaces of the museum that the visitor will subsequently encounter. The liminality of the foyer is reflected in what Mortensen et al. (2014) describe as the foyer's 'adaptive borders', where the content of the galleries may 'bleed' into the foyer, for example by including artworks or objects that may preface the theme of a particular exhibition. In other cases, the visual signage in the foyer may reproduce objects or artwork found in the galleries. For example, the banners displayed in the foyer of Birmingham Museum and Art Gallery include iconic images that reflect some of the well-known collections found in the galleries, such as the Staffordshire Hoard and the pre-Raphaelite collection (see Conversation 2). In other cases, the adaptive borders of the foyer may mean that the space can be temporarily subdivided so that the 'outside' and 'inside' of a performance or display are redrawn. An example of this is found in the screens that are used regularly to partition the entrance to the Royal Shakespeare Theatre (see Conversation 4).

The extent to which the threshold is coherently connected to or disconnected from the other spaces of the museum is clearly separable from binding, in that the balance of a space does not relate to how enclosed or not that space might be. However, the extent to which a space is experienced as more or less connected to other spaces within the complex of a museum building or estate can generate affective responses from the visitors who experience these spaces. The appraisal in the responses gathered from visitors to the New Walk Museum and Art Gallery and to the Petrie Museum suggests that a sense of disconnection between one area and the next can be problematic. For example, one visitor described the foyer of New Walk Museum and Art Gallery as, 'it's grey and grim, not reflective of the rest of the museum', whilst another described it as 'greyish, a sharp contrast with the shop'. At the Petrie Museum, the mismatch between entrance and exhibits was also observed; as one visitor commented, it is 'modern and professional. The collection is not in that style.'

The composition of the threshold also has the potential to set (or fail to set) the expectations about what the visitors would later see. This is similar to the kind of informational organisation described by Kress and Van Leeuwen where the content with which a reader or viewer is familiar precedes that which is unfamiliar. In three-dimensional spaces, the composition of 'familiar' information needs to be provided appropriately before progressing towards less familiar or new content. Where the threshold does not 'set the scene' by providing this initial, known content, negative affective responses can result. For example, at New Walk Museum and Art Gallery, some visitors commented that the foyer gave 'no sense of what the museum is about', so that 'you don't know what you are expecting'. At a more general level, the design and architecture of the foyer could provide cognitive cues that evoked certain schematic expectations, so that visitors commented that 'you know you are in a museum because of the high ceiling'. Of course, the subjective evaluation of these schemas (what being in a museum might mean for particular visitors), and whether the expectations in terms of style, identity and content were appropriate to the museum in question might vary considerably. However, it seems that the coherence of the threshold is at risk particularly when a museum is located in buildings not originally designed for the purpose of housing museum collections (see also Kruse, Chapter 8 in this volume). Such was the case at the Petrie Museum, where the entrance and stairwell to the museum are part of a university building and estate, and as such, architecturally constrained in terms of how far the stairwell might prepare the visitor for the museum collection itself. As one visitor put it, 'it feels like you are entering a university building, not a museum'.

To scaffold the visitors' cognitive orientation requires the museum to consider the composition of the threshold holistically, in relation to the other spaces and content of the museum, such as the galleries and shops. It is possible to provide resources that support cognitive orientation in many ways. The survey responses from the intervention carried out at the Petrie Museum suggest that visual resources in the form of images can be used to scaffold this aspect of the visitors' experience. The images that were used in the multimodal soundscape included photographs of Flinders Petrie and objects from the collection. Edwards and Lien (2014, p. 3) argue that photographs are an important element of the museum's visual strategy and can be used in many, interconnected practices. Photographs can be used to provide information about objects (for example, as part of a catalogue), as part of the contextual interpretation to illustrate objects or exhibitions, to signal the museum's identity or brand as part of their marketing strategy, and to create tone or atmosphere. In their ability to represent, symbolise and invoke, photographs (like other kinds of images) are apt visual resources that can generate knowledge and activate attention as a form of impact. As duplication of images found elsewhere, photographs can also contribute

250 *Ruth Page*

to the visitors' appreciation in terms of composition, for photographs can reproduce and so emphasise the visual content found in promotional materials used by the visitor prior to the visit (such as images used in leaflets or web pages), or foreshadow objects that might be seen in the galleries. The remediated nature of photographs suggests that these are items that can 'travel' through the adaptive borders of the threshold and are open to repurposing, where their original functions can be reshaped or augmented in their new location of the threshold.

In the responses from the visitors to the Petrie Museum, the positive appreciation of the photographs repeatedly suggested that the images generated impact, in the form of reaction.

> *The photographs were fascinating, and made me feel that the museum would be an interesting place*
>
> *The Petrie image turns your attention on*
>
> *The images made you feel you wanted to get in*
>
> *[They] alerted interest*

In this sense, the photographs increased the potential for coherence, where the content prepared the visitors for what would follow. Another visitor used positive composition to describe the scaffolding effect of the images:

> *Good pictures of people discovering stuff. Let you know that you were coming into a museum about Egypt.*

The potential for positive composition to overlap with positive impact is reflected in other responses. One visitor explained that having seen the images, they were 'prepared to be in a "museum" frame of mind', whilst another described the images as 'good appetizers', or as something that said 'this is coming'.

Conclusion

This chapter has demonstrated the value of using frameworks from applied linguistics, namely, appraisal theory, to understand more fully how visitors evaluate their museum experience. Specifically, it shows how appraisal theory can bring to light the multiple, affective dimensions of 'threshold fear' (Gurian, 2005). In this way, it not only shows us the value of using this methodological framework, but it also proposes an evidenced and robust way of articulating the complex range of emotional responses that can be bound up with the visitors' experience of the museum threshold. The results of the appraisal analysis suggest that we should not underestimate the importance of the threshold and the challenges that this space presents visitors.

The analysis confirms that three-dimensional spaces, including those found at the threshold of the museum (such as foyers, lobbies and staircases) are experienced in ways that generate affective responses, such as those proposed by Stenglin (2008, 2009, 2016) in her theory of binding. However, there are other forms of appraisal, especially those in the subcategory of appreciation, that suggest 'threshold fear' is more complex. The analysis of the appraisal in the responses from visitors categorised as quality, reaction, composition and complexity suggest that visitors do not just experience the threshold as bound or unbound. Instead, they also experience spaces as more or less scaffolded. This scaffolding has three dimensions: physical orientation (wayfinding, signalled through the appraisal subtypes of composition), cognitive orientation (stimulating attention and intellectual preparation, signalled through the appraisal subtypes of impact and complexity) and emotional orientation (signalled through the appraisal subtype of quality).

There are theoretical and practical implications for the further use of appraisal theory in visitor studies. First, the appraisal theory offers a method for categorising evaluative language that is transferable beyond this data and is useful for the qualitative analysis of any kind of visitor evaluation, both of thresholds to museums outside this data sample, to thresholds in other kinds of built environments (such as hotels, retail environments, theatres and so on), and indeed to visitors' experiences more generally. As this chapter has shown, identifying the dimensions of the visitors' experience using appraisal has the potential to build a clearer picture of the affective nature of three-dimensional spaces. Better understanding of the interpersonal challenges that particular spaces pose is the first step towards providing design solutions. Other thresholds and indeed other kinds of three-dimensional spaces may entail different forms of scaffolding to enhance the visitors' orientation. Second, the complex nature of the scaffolding needed to address the physical, cognitive and emotional aspects of the visitor experience in threshold spaces opens up interdisciplinary lines of inquiry for future research. Within applied linguistics, this research contributes to future theory building within geosemiotics and multimodal discourse analysis as a model of how semiotic resources are interpersonally experienced within physical spaces. Appraisal theory approaches the affective nature of visitor experience via the language that people use. However, there are other methods that extend beyond the analysis of verbal transcripts, such as those found in cognitive linguistics, which may have much to contribute to visitor studies by further refining the analysis of how the physical, emotional and cognitive aspects of scaffolding operate. The potential for scaffolding to transform visitor experience suggests that further explorations in this area will be beneficial, not only to researchers but also to museums and their visitors.

Note

1 Visitors at New Walk Museum and Art Gallery were interviewed over six days in October 2011. Visitors at the Petrie Museum of Egyptian Archaeology were interviewed over six days in July 2013. In both cases, the visitors were invited to participate in an interview midway through their visit to the museum, either conducted in the café at New Walk Museum and Art Gallery or after they had spent time in the first gallery of the Petrie Museum. This inevitably limits the responses gathered as evidence of the visitors' experience of the museum threshold as an entrance (rather than exit point).

References

Achiam, M., May, M. and Marandino, M. (2014) 'Affordances and distributed cognition in museum exhibitions', *Museum Management and Curatorship*, 29 (5), pp. 461–481.

Bednarek, M. (2008) *Emotion talk across corpora*. Basingstoke, UK: Palgrave Macmillan.

Bitgood, S. (2013) *Attention and value: keys to understanding museum visitors*. Walnut Creek, CA: Left Coast Press.

Blommaert, J. (2005) *Discourse: a critical introduction*. Cambridge: Cambridge University Press.

Brown, G. and Yule, G. (1983) *Discourse analysis*. Cambridge: Cambridge University Press.

Edwards, E. and Lien, S. (2014) *Uncertain images: museums and the work of photographs*. Farnham, UK and Burlington, VT: Ashgate.

Eggins, S. (2004) *An introduction to systemic functional linguistics*. London: Pinter.

Falk, J. and Dierking, L. (1992) *The museum experience*. Washington, DC: Whalesback Books.

Falk, J. and Dierking, L. (2012) *The museum experience revisited*. Oakland, CA: Left Coast Press.

Goulding, C. (2000a) 'The Museum environment and the visitor experience', *European Journal of Marketing*, 34 (3/4), pp. 261–278.

Goulding, C. (2000b) 'Grounded theory, methodology and consumer behaviour: procedures, practice and pitfalls', *Advances in Consumer Research*, 27, pp. 261–266.

Gronemann, S., Kristiansen E. and Drotner, K. (2015) 'Mediated co-construction of museums and audiences on Facebook', *Museum Management and Curatorship*, 30 (3), pp. 174–190.

Gurian, E. (2005) 'Threshold fear', in MacLeod, S. (ed.) *Reshaping museum space: architecture, design, exhibitions*. Abingdon, UK: Routledge, pp. 203–214.

Harris, J. (2016) 'Affect based exhibition', in Davis, A. and Smed, K. (eds.) *Visiting the visitor: an enquiry into the visitor business in museums*, Bielefeld, Germany: transcript Verlag, pp. 15–38.

Hunston, S. and Thompson, G. (2000) *Evaluation in text: authorial stance and the construction of discourse*. Oxford: Oxford University Press.

Hyland, K. (2005) 'Stance and engagement: a model of interaction in academic discourse', *Discourse Studies* 7 (2), pp. 173–192.

Kahr-Højland, A. (2011) 'Hands on, mobiles on. The use of a digital narrative as a scaffolding remedy in a classical science centre', *MedieKultur Journal of Media and Communication Research*, 50, pp. 66–83.

Katriel, T. (1997) *Performing the past: a study of Israeli settlement museums*. London and New York: Routledge.
Katriel, T. (2001) '"From Shore to Shore": the Holocaust, clandestine immigration and Israeli heritage museums', in Zelizer, B. (ed.) *The Holocaust and visual culture*. New Brunswick, NJ: Rutgers University Press, pp. 198–211.
Kress, G. and Van Leeuwen, T. (1996) *Reading images: the grammar of visual design*. London: Routledge.
Labov, W. (1972) *Language in the inner city*. Philadelphia: University of Pennsylvania Press.
Markovic, S. (2012) 'Components of aesthetic experience: aesthetic fascination, aesthetic appraisal and aesthetic emotion', *I-Perception*, 3, pp. 1–17.
Martin, J. (2000) 'Beyond exchange: APPRAISAL systems in English', in Hunston, S. and Thompson, G. (eds.) *Evaluation in text: authorial stance and the construction of discourse*. Oxford: Oxford University Press, pp. 142–175.
Martin, J. and White, P. R. (2005) *The language of evaluation: appraisal in English*. Basingstoke, UK: Palgrave Macmillan.
Millar, N. and Hunston, S. (2015) 'Adjectives, communities, and taxonomies of evaluative meaning', *Functions of Language*, 22 (3), pp. 297–331.
Mortensen, C. H., Rudloff, M. and Vestergaard, V. (2014) 'Communicative functions of the museum lobby', *Curator: The Museum Journal*, 57, pp. 329–346.
Noy, C. (2008) 'Mediation materialized: the semiotics of a visitor book at an Israel commemoration site', *Critical Studies in Media Communication*, 25 (2), pp. 175–195.
Noy, C. (2016) '"My Holocaust experience was great!" Entitlements for participation in museum media', *Discourse and Communication*, 10 (3), pp. 274–290.
Packer, J. and Bond, N. (2010) 'Museums as restorative environments', *Curator: The Museum Journal*, 5 (3), pp. 421–436.
Rajka, S. (2015) 'Art appreciation as a learned competence: a museum-based qualitative study of adult art specialist and non-specialist visitors', *Center for Educational Policy Studies Journal*, 5 (4), pp. 141–157.
Rami, K. I. and Budryte-Ausiejiene, L. (2015) 'Interpreting the emotions of visitors: a study of visitor comment books and the Grūtas Park Museum, Lithuania', *Scandinavian Journal of Hospitality and Tourism*, 15 (4), pp. 400–424.
Schrøder, K. (2013) 'From dogmatism to open-mindedness? Historical reflections on methods in audience reception research', *The Communication Review*, 16 (1–2), pp. 40–50.
Stenglin, M. (2008) 'Binding: a resource for exploring interpersonal meaning in three-dimensional space', *Social Semiotics*, 18 (4), pp. 425–447.
Stenglin, M. (2009) 'Space odyssey: towards a social semiotic model of three-dimensional space', *Visual Communication*, 8 (1), pp. 35–64.
Stenglin, M. (2016) 'Building bridges: design, emotion and museum learning', in Carvalho, L., Goodyear, P. and Maarten de Laat, M. (eds.) *Place-based spaces for networked learning*. London and New York: Routledge, pp. 131–143.
Thumim, N. (2010) 'Self-representation in museums: therapy or democracy?', *Critical Discourse Studies*, 7 (4), pp. 291–304.
Tröndle, M., Greenwood, S., Bitterli, K. and Van den Berg, K. (2014) 'The effects of curatorial arrangements', *Museum Management and Curatorship*, 29 (2), pp. 140–173.
Wood, D., Bruner, J. S. and Ross, G. (1976) 'The role of tutoring in problem solving', *Journal of Child Psychology and Psychiatry*, 17 (2), pp. 89–100.

Index

acoustic ecology 212
action research 215–216
'adaptive borders' 248
added value 211
admissions/reception desks 157, 162, 166
advertising 43, 44, 48, 204–205
aesthetic experience 233, 243
affective responses 231, 232, 234–236, 242–243, 246, 248–251; *see also* emotions
affordances 2–3, 8, 247
Aga Khan Museum 5, 91–95
Alliance Library System 128
alternate reality games (ARGs) 175, 177
AltSpaceVR 141
ambient media 111
Anderson, R. 2
Angier, Nathalie 211
anxiety 24–25, 26, 33, 49, 242, 244, 246; *see also* 'threshold fear'
applied linguistics 7, 231–232, 233–234, 251
appraisal analysis 6–7, 231–253
appreciation (as a type of appraisal) 234, 243, 244, 245, 251
apps 34, 59, 65, 137, 183, 186
architecture: artworks in relation to 92, 104; classical 2, 24; Ely Cathedral 163; modernist 92, 94; retail environments 204–205; use reconstituting 168–169; 3D visualisation 130, 131, 132
Argos 193
ARGs *see* alternate reality games
Arts and Humanities Research Council 202
artworks 5, 24, 81–106, 232, 248; Aga Khan Museum 91–95; Brooklyn Museum 96–99; concept of 81;

Msheireb Museum 83–86; Museum of London 99–103; Seattle Museum of History and Industry 88–91; Victoria & Albert Museum 86–88
assessment 148–149
atmosphere 213, 222–223, 231, 244–245, 249
atmospherics 213–214
attention 6; Attention-Value model 34, 37; cognitive orientation 231, 246–248, 251; olfactory stimuli 203; visual stimuli 199
audio guides 46, 147, 211
auditory stimuli 6, 201–202, 205, 206; *see also* sound
augmented reality 177, 186
'authentic experience' 82
AutoCAD 130
avatars 127, 131, 145, 146, 148
awareness 43

balance 243, 248
Ballantyne, Roy 35, 36
Barrett, Terry 83
Baudrillard, Jean 20
Beaux Arts 97–98
Bennett, Tony 13, 16, 17, 18
Bentham, Jeremy 16–17, 21
Bibliotheque Nationale 16
BIM *see* Building Information Modelling
Bin Jelmood House 83–85
binding 231, 235–236, 243–245, 251
Birmingham Library 132–141, 147, 149, 150
Birmingham Museum and Art Gallery 119–123, 232, 248
Bitgood, Stephen 34, 35, 37
Black, Graham 35, 37, 48
Bobbitt, P. 18, 26

Index 255

Body Shop 202–203
Boettger, T. 108–109
Böhme, Gernot 213, 222–223
Bonaventure Hotel 14, 15
Bond, N. 246
Boston Museum of Fine Art 18
boundary object, threshold as 8
brand 195, 200; audio branding 201; British Postal Museum and Archive 191; photographs 249; retail 193; Victoria & Albert Museum 86
British Museum 2, 15, 16, 20, 21–22, 24
British Postal Museum and Archive 189–191
Brittain, Paul 42, 45
Brooklyn Museum 19–20, 21, 96–99
Brown, T. 68, 69
Brydon-Miller, M. 195
Buchanan, R. 70–71
builders 130, 131, 132
Building Information Modelling (BIM) 131, 132, 142, 150
Burden, David 5, 124–152

Caillois, R. 176, 184
Camera Obscura and World of Illusions, Edinburgh 43, 44
Carse, J. 176
Chatsworth House 6, 183–185
Chau Chak Wing Museum 107, 112–115
Chihuly, Dale 86–87, 90, 94
Chion, Michel 211
Churchman, C.W. 71
civilisation 16, 18
classical architecture 2, 24
Clifford, James 3, 18
'co-evolutionary' design 72
cognitive orientation 7, 231, 246–250, 251
Cohen, June 35
collective memory 82
colour 199–200, 203
commercialism 20, 115–116
commitment 41–43, 44–45, 49, 52
communication 108, 109; discourse analysis 232; evaluative language 233–235; marketing 48; visualisation 73–74
community engagement 83, 99
complexity 70–71, 243, 245–246, 251
composition 243, 245–250, 251
concept stores 193

conceptual mapping 60, 110, 115
conceptual thresholds 108–110, 116, 117
Conklin, J. 71
Conn, S. 16, 24
'connected museum' 5, 107, 110–111, 116
connection 181–182, 183
constructivism 89
consumerism 20
'contact zone' 3, 18
content analysis 233, 234
contestation 153, 167, 168–169
cosmopolitanism 18
Coste, Didier 104n3
costs 39–40
courtyards: Aga Khan Museum 92–93; Museum of Archaeology and Anthropology 156, 157, 158–159, 167; New Walk Museum and Art Gallery 238
Cox, Roger 42, 45
creativity 82, 205
Crilly, N. 201
Crimp, D. 17
cross-disciplinary approach 59, 67, 68, 70, 73–74, 214; *see also* interdisciplinarity
Cross, N. 71
Csikszentmihalyi, M. 194, 205
Cullen, Gordon 108
cultural heritage 111, 112
'cultural package' 38
culture 108–109
Culture24 *Museums at Night* initiative 185
curators 81–82, 107, 112, 115, 161
curiosity 194, 224
customer experience journey map 62, 63–64
customer journey 192, 225
customer satisfaction 42–43, 103

Dalley, Rebecca 54–57
data collection: of affective responses 232, 252n1; design thinking 69; ethnographic research 61–62; Petrie Museum soundscape 216–217
Davis, B. 116
decision-making 34–36, 38, 43–46, 48, 49; Portsmouth Historic Dockyard 50, 51; retail buying process 41–42; shopping experience 193; visitor satisfaction 42–43

Deere, Lauren 119–123
democratisation: Instagram 116; of 3D visualisation techniques 127–130
Design Ethnography 62
design thinking 4–5, 58–77; design brief 60–61; empathy 69; exploratory phase 61–63; iterative design process 66–67, 70, 71–72, 74; multidisciplinary collaboration 70; prototyping 65, 66, 72–73, 74; storyboarding 64–65; as strategic asset 68, 74; threshold complexity 70–71; user experience framework 63–64; visualisation 73–74
design with intent 147
Deuchars, Angus 6, 211–227
Dierking, Lynn 34, 37, 39, 40, 44, 194, 242
digital media 1, 3, 33, 45, 58, 107, 116–117; Brooklyn Museum 99; Instagram images 111–116; Marriott hotel project 59, 61, 65; multidisciplinary collaboration 70; prototyping 73; threshold complexity 70–71; *see also* technology; 3D visualisation
disabled users 146
disciplinary atria 27, 28
disciplinary power 13, 16–17, 19, 22–23, 25, 28
disconnection 248–249
discourse analysis 232, 251
disorientation 24–25, 49, 149
displays 34, 45, 47; Museum of London 100; Portsmouth Historic Dockyard 51; retail 206; Virtual Library of Birmingham 138
diversity 13, 18
Dong, A. 69
Dorment, R. 86
Dorst, K. 71
DREAM 180–181
Drotner, K. 111
Duncan, C. 16, 17, 19, 21, 24, 26

Eaton Centre Shopping Mall 14
Ebster, C. 197
education 111, 193, 195
Edwards, E. 249
EGO-TRAP 185, 186
Elkins, James 83
Ely Cathedral 5, 153, 155, 159–163, 167
emails 43, 44
embedded thresholds 5, 153–171; Hunterian Museum 163–168; Museum of Archaeology and Anthropology 155–159; Stained Glass Museum 159–163
emotional orientation 7, 231, 251
emotions 205, 213, 233, 236, 243; *see also* affective responses
empathy 67, 68, 69, 205
encounter 108, 110
engagement: Aga Khan Museum 93, 94; artworks 89, 103, 104; Brooklyn Museum 96, 98, 99; cognitive orientation 246; community 83, 99; 'connected museum' 111; immersive environments 149; olfactory stimuli 204; playfulness 183; retail 195; scaffolding 236; sensory design cues 204; spatial sequences 108; Virtual Library of Birmingham 136–138
'engaging museum' 109
Epps, Tom 138
ethnographic research 61–62, 232–233
evaluation 181, 182, 231–232
evaluative language 231, 233–235, 242
Evans, Robin 108, 117
expectations 2, 13, 249; artworks 83, 86; brand 200; 'connected museum' 111; customer satisfaction 42–43; design thinking 69, 70; digital experiences 116; first impressions 49; pre-purchase activity 48; retail 196, 206; 'visitor offer' 37, 45
'experience environment' 192, 205
experiencescape 213, 214
Experimentarium 185

façades 2, 44
Facebook 110, 115
Falk, John 34, 37, 39, 40, 44, 194, 242
familiarity 193, 196, 247, 249
feedback 136, 148, 232
Fetterman, J. 203
first impressions 44, 49
Flickr 110
flow 194, 195, 197, 201, 205, 206
formality 186
Forney, A. 145
Foucault, Michel 13–14, 16–17, 19, 20, 21, 24–25, 28
fragrance 203–204
'frontier space' 3

frontispieces 2
fun 176–177, 178, 182, 194
'Future Hotel Experience' project 59–74

Gambles, Brian 141
game-engine based 3D visualisation 127, 130, 141, 147
games/gaming 6, 175–188; British Postal Museum and Archive 190; gamification 147, 178, 186–187; lobby design game 56, 179–180, 230; virtual worlds 127–130
Garaus, M. 197
Gaskell, I. 25
gaze 13, 17, 21
gender 55
gift-giving 96
Gilbert, R.L. 145
Gledhill, Hannah 189–191
Golding, Viv 3
Google Cardboard 149
Google Earth 142
Goulding, C. 232
Goulding, Christina 3
governmentality 17
Grade, John 88–91
Guggenheim 15
guidance 99, 103
guidebooks 33, 43, 44, 46
guides: audio 46, 147, 211; virtual 135, 145
Gurian, Elaine Heumann 3, 6–7, 176, 204, 231, 233

Hadi, R. 202
Harwood, Tracy 6, 192–210
hashtags 112–113, 115
Hayward, D.G. 195
hedonic consumption 201, 202
hedonism 194
Helsinki Design Lab 70
Hennes, Tom 35, 37
heritage assets 144
Hewson, Phil 138–141
history 94
Hook, D. 25–26
Hooper-Greenhill, Eilean 16, 34, 37
hotels 4, 59–74
Huizinga, J. 175, 176, 184
human-centred design 58, 74
Hunston, S. 234
Hunterian Museum 5, 153, 155, 163–168

hyper-crowds 15–16, 18, 19, 21, 24
hysterical atria 27, 28, 29–31
'hysteric's discourse' 14, 26–27

identity 108, 128–130
IKEA 193, 197
imagination 205
immersion 204, 205, 206
immersive environments 58, 141–149; see also virtual worlds
impact (as a category of appraisal) 243, 246–247, 250, 251
inclusion 13
information desks 98, 100
information overload 246
'information space' 58, 154
information systems 59, 60, 67
innovation 68, 69, 70, 73, 74
insecurity 231, 235, 242
Instagram 5, 107, 111–116, 117
institutional tensions 168–169
interactivity 96, 99, 103; virtual environments 144, 147, 148–149; Virtual Library of Birmingham 134–136; 3D visualisation 131
interdisciplinarity 4, 5, 7; see also cross-disciplinary approach
intermediary design deliverables 74
internet see social media; websites
interpretation 115
intrigue 218, 220–221, 224
investment 39–40
invisible performance 111
Islamic art 92–94

James, Henry 15, 16, 24
Jameson, Frederic 14–15, 16, 19, 24
Jones, Colin 84, 85
judgement 234

Kelly, L. 110
Khalid, Aisha 92, 93–94, 95
Kitto, James 228–230
Kluitenberg, E. 18
Kolb, Bonita M. 35, 38, 39–40, 43
Koolhaas, Rem 20–21, 24
Koster, Ralph 177
Kotler, P. 202
Kress, G. 248, 249
Kristiansen, Erik 6, 56, 111, 175–188, 230
Krug, Steve 35
Kruse, Steve 5, 153–171

258 Index

Lacan, J. 14, 25–26, 28
Lacanian psychoanalysis 14, 21, 25–26
language: discourse analysis 232; evaluative 231, 233–235, 242
Laursen, D. 181
layouts 49, 204, 206; digital artefacts 67; retail 195, 197, 198–199; 3D visualisation 135, 136, 138, 143, 147, 148, 150
Lazzaro, Nicole 177, 178
leaflets 33, 43, 44, 45
learning 176, 177, 213
Leblanc, M. 177
Lefebvre, H. 154
Lego 56, 203
liberatory culture 13, 14
libraries: Virtual Library of Birmingham 132–141, 147, 149, 150; virtual worlds 128
Lidar 142, 144, 150
Liedtka, J. 73
Lien, S. 249
'lifestyle curation' 114
light: appraisal analysis 244; artworks 93–94
lighting: feelings of (in)security 235; retail environments 198, 200; scaffolding 245; virtual environments 144–145
liminality 8, 58, 95, 109, 177; 'adaptive borders' 248; liminoid space 181, 185; virtual worlds 128–130
lobby design game 56, 179–180, 230
local communities 82, 99
Lockton, Dan 147
Louvre 16
LUCE Foundation Centre for American Art 186

Macdonald, S. 68
MacLeod, Suzanne 154–155
'magic circle' 6, 176, 177, 178–179, 181, 184–186
Maki, Fumihiko 92
maps 122
marginalized communities 82
marketing 4, 48, 193–194, 249
Marriott hotel project 59–74
Marsh, John 137, 138
Martin, J. 234, 243, 246, 248
Mason, Marco 4–5, 58–77

Massachusetts Institute of Technology (MIT) 59
meaning: artworks 92, 103–104; meaning making 83, 111, 114, 117, 167; shared entrances 154, 155, 167, 168, 169; soundscapes 223–224
memory 82, 203, 224, 225
mental models 195
metaphor 81–82, 85–86, 87–88, 94–95, 96, 104
Metropolitan Museum of Art 24
Millar, N. 234
Milrod, Linda 94
Mind Maze 100, 103
Mingwei, Lee 96–97, 99
mobile technologies 1, 110, 147; *see also* apps; smartphones
modernist architecture 92, 94
Moggridge, B. 69
MOHAI *see* Seattle Museum of History and Industry
mood cues 213–214, 218; *see also* sensory design cues
Morris, R. 205
Mortensen, Christian Hviid 6, 211–227, 232–233, 248
Moseley, Alex 1–9, 111, 175–188, 189–190
Mostafavi, M. 108
motivation 4, 36, 177, 192
The Moving Garden 96–97, 99
Msheireb Museum 5, 83–86
Mulberg, Colin 4, 33–53
Muller, L. 82
multi-touch screens 65, 67, 71
multidisciplinary collaboration 59, 67, 68, 70, 73–74, 214
multimedia environments 59
multisensory perception 214
Murray, Kyle 45
mu[see]um.net 19, 21
museology 1, 17; 'new' 225
'museum as platform' 1
Museum of Archaeology and Anthropology, University of Cambridge 5, 153, 155–159, 167
Museum of London 99–103, 186
Museum of Natural History and Archaeology, Trondheim 185–186
Museums at Night initiative 185
music 201, 202, 218–219, 223, 224, 225, 245
Muslim culture 92–95

Index 259

narrative 3, 154, 162, 185; artworks 81–82, 83, 94, 95, 104; Museum of Archaeology and Anthropology 157; shared entrances 168, 169; Stained Glass Museum 162
narthex 162, 163
National Football Museum, Manchester 38
National Museum of the Royal Navy 4, 51
navigation 195, 197; *see also* wayfinding
needs 69, 70
Neikelius, Caspar 211
neoclassicism 22, 163
neoliberalism 16
'new museology' 225
New Walk Museum and Art Gallery 7, 33, 143, 236, 237–238, 240–242, 244–249, 252n1
Nicholson Museum 107, 112–115, 117n3
North, A.C. 201

Oculus Rift 149
O'Donnell, J. 203
Ogilvie, T. 73
olfactory stimuli 6, 203–204, 205, 206
online user experiences design 35, 37, 40
open data 1
open spaces 92
openness 108, 164, 166, 167
OpenSim 141
orientation 3, 4, 49, 59, 195; artworks 99–100; Birmingham Museum and Art Gallery 122, 123; cognitive 7, 231, 246–250, 251; emotional 7, 231, 251; lobby games 181, 182, 183; physical 7, 231, 245–246, 251; playful signage 183–185; Virtual Library of Birmingham 136, 137; *see also* wayfinding
the Other 25–26, 28, 31
The Other Place 230

Packer, Jan 35, 246
Page, Ruth 1–9, 119–122, 228–230, 231–253
Palais de Tokyo 15
'Panopticon' 16–17, 21, 28
paratexts 83, 104
Parry, Ross 1–9, 54–56, 111

participation: barriers to 99; 'participatory museum' 109; public participation with artworks 96, 98–99
perceived value 39–40, 52
Perry, D.L. 177
Petrie Museum of Egyptian Archaeology 6–7, 202, 204, 211–212, 214–225, 236, 238–241, 244–250, 252n1
PHD *see* Portsmouth Historic Dockyard
photogrammetry 142, 144, 150
photographs 110, 201, 249–250; augmented reality apps 186; Instagram 5, 107, 111–116; virtual environments 144
physicality 168
Piano, Renzo 19
Pier, John 104n3
planning 47, 182–183
plans 3, 108, 117
play 175–188
playfulness 6, 13, 175–177, 179, 180, 182, 183–187, 228; playful artworks 24
playgrounds 24
'playing the lobby' 56, 175–176
plazas 98
Pompidou Centre 14, 15, 19
Pond, Philip 5, 107–118
popularity 113
porticos 97–98, 166, 238
Portsmouth Historic Dockyard (PHD) 49–51
postdigital 1, 3, 58
posters 33, 44, 45
postmodernism 17–18, 19, 24
poststructuralism 19
power: disciplinary 13, 16–17, 19, 22–23, 25, 28; of institutions with shared entrances 168
pre-purchase activity 41, 43, 48–49, 51
prices 39–40, 45–46
private space 85
probes 148
'problem space' 4, 71–72
promotional literature 48, 49; *see also* leaflets
protocols 2–3
prototyping 65, 66, 72–73, 74
psychoanalysis 14, 21, 25–26
public participation 96, 98–99
purchase decision 41–42, 193
Putnam, James 82

Qatar 83–86, 90
quality 243–245, 251
questions 35–36, 51–52
queues 178, 181, 182

RAMM *see* Royal Albert Memorial Museum
refurbishments 27
Renaissance 2
resolution 181–182
'responsive museum' 109
retail 6, 38, 192–210; atmospherics 213; buying process 41–43, 44–45, 48, 52; entrances 45; perceived value 39; role of the threshold 196–197; sensory design cues 197–204; servicescape as physical space 193–195; transferable practice 204–205
Ride, Peter 5, 81–106
Rittel, H.W. 71
rituals 3, 16
Rodin, Auguste 98, 99
Rogers, Richard 19
Royal Air Force Museum, London 54–57
Royal Albert Memorial Museum (RAMM) 27–31
Royal College of Surgeons 5, 153, 155, 163–168
Royal Marines Museum 36–37
Royal Shakespeare Company (RSC) 228–230, 248
rules (within game play) 176
Russo, Angelina 5, 107–118

Salazar, J.F. 110
saliency 199–200
scaffolding 7, 231, 236, 243, 245–250, 251
scent 203–204, 206
schemas 195, 249
Schrøder, K. 111
sculpture 86, 88–91, 98, 99, 162
Seattle Museum of History and Industry (MOHAI) 5, 88–91, 96
Second Life 127–130, 142; Oculus Rift 149; Virtual Library of Birmingham 133–141
Second Louvre Museum 128
security: appraisal analysis 231, 235; shared entrances 165, 166, 167, 168; soundscapes 245; staff 201
Sedgwick Museum of Earth Sciences 156

self: 'care of the' 20; 'practice of the' 22; self-development 19, 21; 'technologies of the' 13, 19; 3D visualisation 131
selfies 110, 201
semiotic resources 251
sense-making 193, 195
sensory design cues 6, 197–204, 205, 206; *see also* mood cues
Senyapili, B. 130
separation 181–182
sequentiality 154
'servicescape' 6, 192, 193–195, 200, 205, 206
Sfinteş, I.A. 109
shared entrances 5, 153–171; Hunterian Museum 163–168; Museum of Archaeology and Anthropology 155–159; Stained Glass Museum 159–163
Sherlock Holmes exhibition 100–103
'shop windows' 196
shopping 6, 20, 21; *see also* retail
sight lines 198–199, 204, 206, 238
signage 4, 33, 49, 246; augmented 111; Birmingham Museum and Art Gallery 122, 123; Brooklyn Museum 98; Petrie Museum of Egyptian Archaeology 215, 219–220; playful 183–185; Portsmouth Historic Dockyard 51; virtual environments 147; Virtual Library of Birmingham 138
silence 211, 223
Skellon, Katherine 4, 13–32
slave trade 82, 83, 84–86
smartphones 110, 147, 185–186; *see also* mobile technologies
Smith, C. 109
Smithsonian American Art Museum 186
social interaction 33, 61, 194, 200–201
social media 1, 34, 43, 44, 58, 110, 201; Brooklyn Museum 99; feedback on 232; Marriott hotel project 59; New Walk Museum and Art Gallery 241; pre-purchase activity 48; *see also* Instagram
social relationships 154–155, 168
social stimuli 6, 200–201, 205
Sony Style stores 203
sound 6, 206, 211–227; affective atmosphere 245; multimedia environments 59; Museum of London 100; Petrie Museum case

study 215–225; retail environments 201–202; role of the sound designer 214–215; virtual environments 144
soundscapes 201, 211–227, 241, 245
South Kensington 16
space 8, 20, 109, 117; artworks 82–83, 104; binding 235–236; digital experiences 116; liminoid 181, 185; retail 193–195; transitional 58, 59, 108, 109, 167, 247
Spence, C. 202, 203
staff: barriers to entry 200, 204; Birmingham Museum and Art Gallery 122; British Postal Museum and Archive 190; Hunterian Museum 165; lobby as a game 178; retail 194, 200; Royal Shakespeare Company 229–230; scaffolding 245; security 201; virtual 145; Virtual Library of Birmingham 138
Stained Glass Museum, Ely Cathedral 5, 153, 155, 159–163, 167
Starax 128, 129
Stein, Gertrude 81
Stenglin, M. 231, 235, 244, 251
store layouts 195, 197, 198–199
storefronts 196
storyboarding 64–65, 73
storytelling 64–65, 205
Strobel, P. 109
Stuedahl, D. 109, 111
'subjectivation' 14, 17, 21, 24, 26
subjectivity 25, 26
Suits, B. 176
support 181–182, 183
the 'symbolic' 14, 25–26
symbolic order 26, 29–30
symbolism 13, 16, 58, 163
symbols 70–71
Systemic Functional Linguistics 234

tactile stimuli 6, 202–203, 205, 206
tapestries 92, 93–94
Tate Modern 2, 15, 20, 24
'technologies of the self' 13, 19
technology: communication 109; mobile technologies 1, 110, 147; 3D visualisation 5, 124–152; see also apps; digital media; social media; websites
theatres 2, 228–230
3D visualisation 5, 124–152; architectural use of 130; assessment of user experience 148–149; creating the digital threshold environment 141–148; democratisation of 127–130; development of 124–127; Three Ring Model 130–132; Virtual Library of Birmingham 132–141
'threshold fear' 3; appraisal analysis 6–7, 231, 235–236, 242, 244–245, 250, 251; cognitive and affective components 204, 233; playful approach 176; see also anxiety
ticketing 4, 46, 49, 51, 181, 182
time 8, 109
touchpoints 64
tour guides 147; virtual 135, 145
tourist information 43, 44
transformative functions 181–183
Transforming Thresholds project 70, 215
transitional space 58, 59, 108, 109, 167, 247
TripAdvisor 55
Tröndle, M. 232
Truax, B. 212
Tunstall, Ben 4, 13–32
Turbine Hall, Tate Modern 2, 15, 24
Turing Test 145
Twickenham Stadium 4, 37
Twitter 110

Unity3D 127, 130, 141, 142
University College London (UCL) 215, 238, 239
'university discourse' 14, 27, 28
University of Cambridge 5, 153, 155–159, 167
University of Sydney 107, 112–115
Unreal 141
user experience: assessment of 148–149; Marriott hotel project 69; sequentiality 154; storyboarding 73; user experience framework 63–64, 67; UX design 35, 37, 38, 40; Virtual Library of Birmingham 134–136; 3D visualisation 131, 132, 146–149; see also visitor experience
user tracking 148

V&A see Victoria & Albert Museum
value, perceived 39–40, 52
Value Proposition 38, 39, 42
values 13, 87–88, 180
Van Leeuwen, T. 248, 249
Vavoula, G. 74
Verganti, R. 68

Index

Victoria & Albert (V&A) Museum 20, 21, 22–23, 86–88, 90, 94
Victorian era 17
video: Marriott hotel project 62; Msheireb Museum 85; virtual environments 144
Virtual Library of Birmingham 132–141, 147, 149, 150
virtual reality (VR) 149–150
Virtual Spaceflight Museum 128
Virtual Starry Night 128
virtual worlds 5, 127–130, 132, 149–150; assessment of user experience 148–149; creating the digital threshold environment 141–148; Virtual Library of Birmingham 132–141
visibility 159, 163
visitor experience 2–3, 4, 33–53; affective nature of 232; appraisal analysis 6–7, 235–251; artworks 82; Brooklyn Museum 96, 98; challenges for museums 47–49; commitment 41–43, 44–45, 49, 52; 'curated experience' 107; decision-making 34–36, 38, 41–42, 43–46, 48, 49; design thinking 68, 74; heterogeneity 109–110; Instagram images 111–116; integrated approach 49–51; investment 39–40; lobby as a game 177–178; Marriott hotel project 63–64, 67, 69; research 36–37, 38, 44, 49–51, 103, 216–217, 219–223, 232–233; retail perspective 194, 206; Royal Air Force Museum 57; scaffolding 236; shared entrances 168, 169; social role of the museum 109; sound 201, 216–217, 219–225; structure of a visit 46–47, 49, 50, 51; visitor insight 47–48; 'visitor offer' 4, 37–39, 45, 47, 49, 51, 52; visitors as cultural broadcasters 110–111; *see also* user experience
visitor numbers and demographics: Birmingham Museum and Art Gallery 119–120; British Postal Museum and Archive 189–190; New Walk Museum and Art Gallery 238; Petrie Museum of Egyptian Archaeology 238; Royal Air Force Museum 55; Royal Shakespeare Company 228, 229
visitor studies 33, 231–232, 233
visual media 144
visual stimuli 6, 198–200, 205, 206, 249–250
visualisation: design thinking 73–74; 3D 5, 124–152
VR *see* virtual reality
vTime 141

waiting times 201
Waldorf Astoria 15
Warhol, Andy 20
Wawona 88–91
wayfinding 204, 246; Birmingham Museum and Art Gallery 122; Museum of London 99–100; playful apps 183; scaffolding 231, 251; *see also* orientation
WebGL 141
websites 34, 43, 44; Birmingham Museum and Art Gallery 122; Marriott hotel project 59; online user experiences design 35, 37, 40; *see also* social media
welcoming atmosphere 13, 222–223, 225, 244–245
White, P.R. 234, 243, 246, 248
'wicked problems' 71
WiFi coverage 138–140
Wilkie, Fiona 180
Wilson, Fred 82
workload 35
World Rugby Museum 4, 37
Wrightson, K. 212

yoga 19–20, 21
Yorvik Viking Museum 204
YouTube 110

Žižek, Slavoj 18, 26–27
Zukin, S. 15–16, 18, 19, 20, 24